THE HISTORY OF AMERICA

AF084719

THE HISTORY OF AMERICA

FROM NEW WORLD COLONY TO GLOBAL SUPERPOWER

KIERON CONNOLLY

This revised paperback edition first published in 2023

First published in 2017

Copyright © 2023 Amber Books Ltd

All rights reserved. No part of this publication may be reproduced, stored in a retrieval system, or transmitted in any form or by any means, electronic, mechanical, photocopying, recording, or otherwise, without prior written permission of the copyright holder.

Published by
Amber Books Ltd
United House
North Road
London
N7 9DP
United Kingdom
www.amberbooks.co.uk
Facebook: amberbooks
Twitter: @amberbooks
Pinterest: amberbooksltd

Project Editor: Sarah Uttridge
Designer: Zoë Mellors
Picture Research: Terry Forshaw

ISBN: 978-1-83886-272-5

Printed in United Kingdom

CONTENTS

Introduction — 6

Chapter 1: **A New World** — 10

Chapter 2: **The American Revolution** — 36

Chapter 3: **Going West** — 52

Chapter 4: **The Civil War** — 70

Chapter 5: **Freedom and Closing the Frontier** — 88

Chapter 6: **The New Age** — 106

Chapter 7: **World War II** — 124

Chapter 8: **The Early Cold War** — 142

Chapter 9: **The Civil Rights Movement** — 156

Chapter 10: **The 1960s** — 172

Chapter 11: **Discontent and Revival** — 190

Chapter 12: **The Sole Superpower** — 204

Bibliography — 220
Index — 221

INTRODUCTION

Today the United States is the size of a continent and still the most powerful country in the world. Yet 250 years ago it didn't even exist. The Declaration of Independence in 1776 may have proclaimed the ideals of 'life, liberty and the pursuit of happiness', but America's rise has been coloured by wars, rebellions and racial conflict.

That the United States rose to dominance partly through wars and conflict may not be a surprise. But when you reflect on American history – bloody or otherwise – you might not automatically picture US troops occupying Mexico City in 1847, or the British, long defeated in the Revolutionary War, coming back in 1814 to set Washington on fire. And it might well be surprising to learn that Founding Father John Adams, having won American independence from Britain, then became the US ambassador in London.

Nor might you imagine that Robert E. Lee, before he became commander of the Confederate Army in the Civil War, had just turned down another job offer – that of commander of the Union Army. Or that in its desperate, final days, the Confederate Army, fighting to defend the institution of slavery and the subjugation of black people, accepted blacks into its ranks as soldiers. These, too, all happened.

OPPOSITE: The valour of the armed forces. On 23 February 1945, six US Marines raise the Stars and Stripes on Mount Suribachi during the Battle of Iwo Jima in World War II. Three of the Marines died in battle in the following days.

But it is such ironies, and the paradoxes that both George Washington and Thomas Jefferson, while proclaiming the equal rights of man, were slave owners, that make the fabric of American history so rich. On which side, you may wonder, did Native Americans fight in the Revolutionary War and in the Civil War? The answer was that they fought on both sides in both wars. And some of them kept slaves, too.

This book traces the story of the United States from the first contact between Europeans and Native Americans in the late fifteenth century through to its continued involvement in Iraq and Afghanistan, and to America's debate about gun laws today. However, it is not solely an account of America's conflicts at home and abroad. It is also the story of the gradual expansion of the country from the original 13 states to reach across the continent, of the ill treatment of Native Americans, of slavery, segregation and the Civil Rights Movement. It is the narrative of religious hysteria as expressed in the Salem Witch Trials in the seventeenth century, as well as suicidal cults in the twentieth century. And it is about how the values of the Founding Fathers laid down in the Bill of Rights, such as freedom of speech, the free exercise of religion and the division between states' rights and those of the federal government, have continued to shape America.

> 'America is a young country – yet it has the oldest written constitution.'

Each nation follows its own peculiar course through history. America is a young country, yet it has the oldest written constitution in the world. Its first European settlers went west to seek a new world: some to look for gold, others in search of new opportunities, and, in the case of the separatist Pilgrim Fathers on the *Mayflower*, to establish their religion in a promised land free from persecution. For them, as with so many who followed, America would represent liberty.

Today's United States is four times the size of the country that first gained independence from Britain in 1783. It has been built not only on successive waves of immigration but on internal emigration, too; of people abandoning their houses and farms in the east in the hope of seeking a better life further west. At first, they went as far as the Mississippi River, then to the Rocky Mountains, and ultimately all the way to the Pacific Ocean. And in that pioneering world, battling the elements, starvation and hostility, life could certainly be brutal.

BELOW: The removal of the Cherokee to land west of the Mississippi River in 1838. The liberty and equality declared by the Founding Fathers was not extended to Native Americans, who were repeatedly forced from lands the United States had allocated to them.

Way out west

To a degree, America celebrates its own bloody history. What is more American than a cowboy? In reality, the life of cow herders in the Old West was not particularly heroic and not one that was often troubled by gunfights. But once the Old West passed into history at the end of the nineteenth century, Americans – and, in time, the rest of the world – began to enjoy through fiction and paintings, then movies and television, chivalric

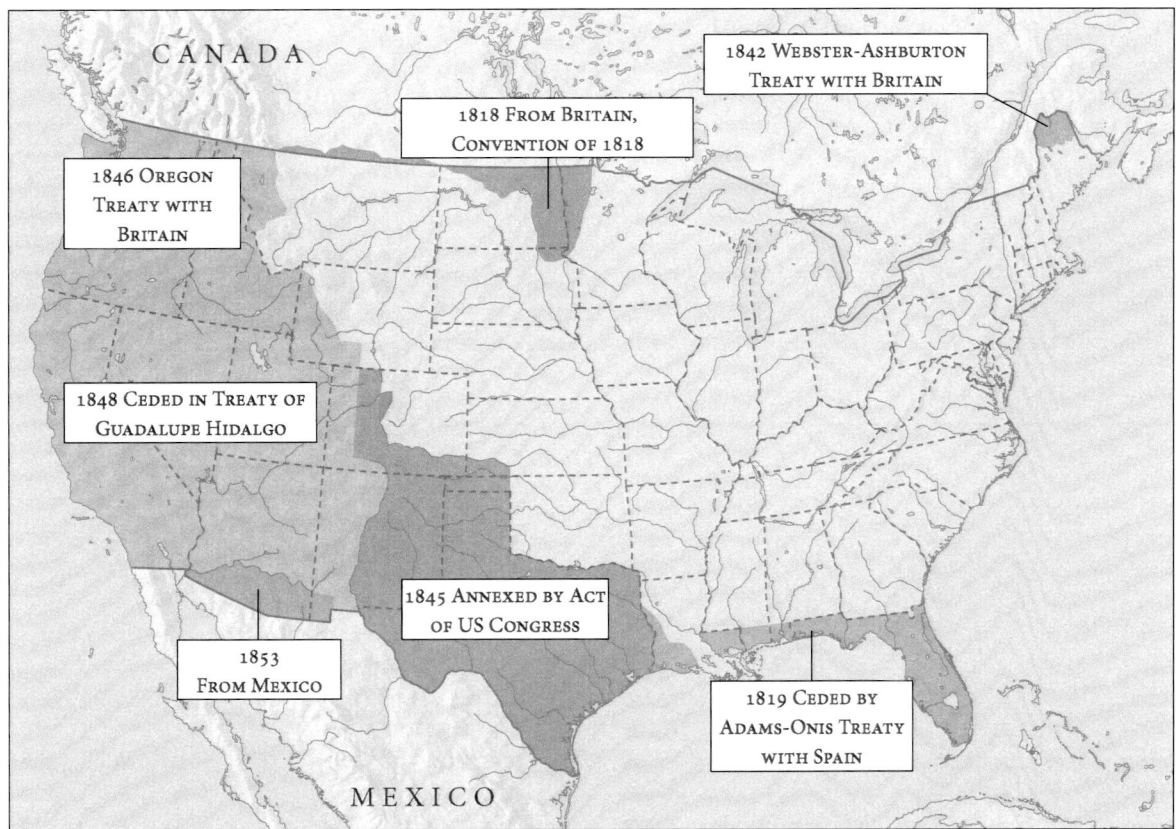

myths of noble gunslingers and imperilled homesteaders. It's no accident that presidents Ronald Reagan and George W. Bush were photographed wearing Stetsons on their ranches. One an actor and the other a businessman before they entered politics, they were tapping into that American folk memory of the rugged, honest life of the frontier. And, as the United States is such a young country, that wasn't so long ago.

America's mobsters, such as Al Capone, its bank robbers, such as John Dillinger, and its thieves, such as Bonnie and Clyde, have also been elevated to folk heroes, not least in American movies. Hollywood still leads global film-making action, and that action – in police stories, gangster sagas and war movies – is often excitingly bloody. Many of us enjoy it.

The Stars and Stripes

The history of America has certainly been bloody, but so has the history of every large country. Violence is common to all countries, great and small. And, brutal though war is, it can also be an engine of social and technical change. Not only did the Civil War bring slavery to an end, but the two world wars helped push away lasting segregation against African-Americans and Native Americans.

This book traces the tragedies and the victories, the massacres, mistakes and the heroism, in the story of the United States. Whether they were victorious or defeated, whether their actions were just or unjust, the fallen victims, scarred civilians and brave veterans of these riots and rebellions, battles and wars, are the people who helped make America.

ABOVE: 'Go west, young man, and grow up with the country,' became a popular saying for pioneers in the mid-nineteenth century. Firstly, though, it was through wars, treaties and land purchases that the United States was able to expand across the continent, and reach 'from sea to shining sea'.

A NEW WORLD

1

Between 1492 and the 1760s, America was transformed from a hitherto isolated continent to one which, for free Europeans, represented liberty and opportunity. For its native peoples, convicts and African slaves, however, it meant disease, displacement and servitude. The New World would have a bloody birth.

IT IS NOW most commonly accepted that the first Americans were people from northeast Asia, who lived between 12,000 and 10,000BC, and who walked from Asia into America. Where today 89km (55 miles) of water separates Siberia and Alaska, during the last great Ice Age the sea level may have been about 90m (300ft) lower, allowing a grassy patch of land to develop between the two continents. If the First Americans didn't cross on foot, it is suggested that they migrated by boat, then edged their way down the Pacific coast, before moving east and south across the continent. Whatever way they came, that is where they came from.

There were later migrations, too. The ancestors of the Inuit probably crossed the Bering Strait in boats about 5000 years ago, and, in around 1000AD, Leif Erikson established a Norse settlement that we now know as Vinland on the tip of Newfoundland. His, however, would be a less successful migration. Within a century Vinland had been abandoned.

OPPOSITE: Christopher Columbus was attempting to find a western route to Asia when in 1492 he chanced upon the Bahamas. His subsequent voyages explored the Caribbean and parts of Central and South America, but never North America.

OPPOSITE: Popularly known as the discoverer of America, Christopher Columbus died in 1506 – still maintaining that the Americas were not a separate continent, but part of Asia.

Estimates vary wildly, but it is now believed that there were between five and 12 million Native Americans north of Mexico by the end of the fifteenth century. They were not a single society, but numerous tribes that, while connected through trading networks, spoke different languages and were often hostile to each other.

There were also whole societies that had risen and fallen by 1300AD, long before the Europeans appeared. The sophisticated people who built the Cahokia mounds in Illinois or the settlement in Pueblo Pintado, New Mexico – works quite unlike anything constructed by the surviving tribes – still puzzle archaeologists today.

Then, in 1492, the North American continent changed forever when Genoese explorer Christopher Columbus crossed the Atlantic Ocean seeking a new sea route to the Far East – and stumbled across the Caribbean. The first waves of exploration, conquest and colonization by the Spanish, French and English that followed may have been led by greed, guns or God, but in all cases the newcomers brought the same weapon, and one they didn't realize they possessed: germs.

Disease

Isolated from the rest of the world, the peoples of the Americas had never been exposed to the common cold, influenza, leprosy, typhoid, the bubonic plague, measles, cholera and, most importantly, the smallpox virus. While many people in Europe still died of smallpox, Europeans had, over centuries of exposure, built up

POTATOES, HORSES AND COWS

The transfer of plant and animal life between the Americas and the rest of the world after 1492 was not just mutually beneficial; it was revolutionary. Not only did it change what people ate, but also how much they ate, how they farmed and how many people they could feed. That meant it changed how societies developed.

The Spanish and English explorers brought home the potato, tomatoes, avocado, chillies, turkeys and tobacco; in America, the changes were even greater. Horses had died out there around 10,000BC, but were reintroduced by the Europeans, who also brought rice, sugar cane, alcohol, pigs, sheep, donkeys, cattle and wheat – which allowed the previously unpromising soil of American prairies to become agricultural land.

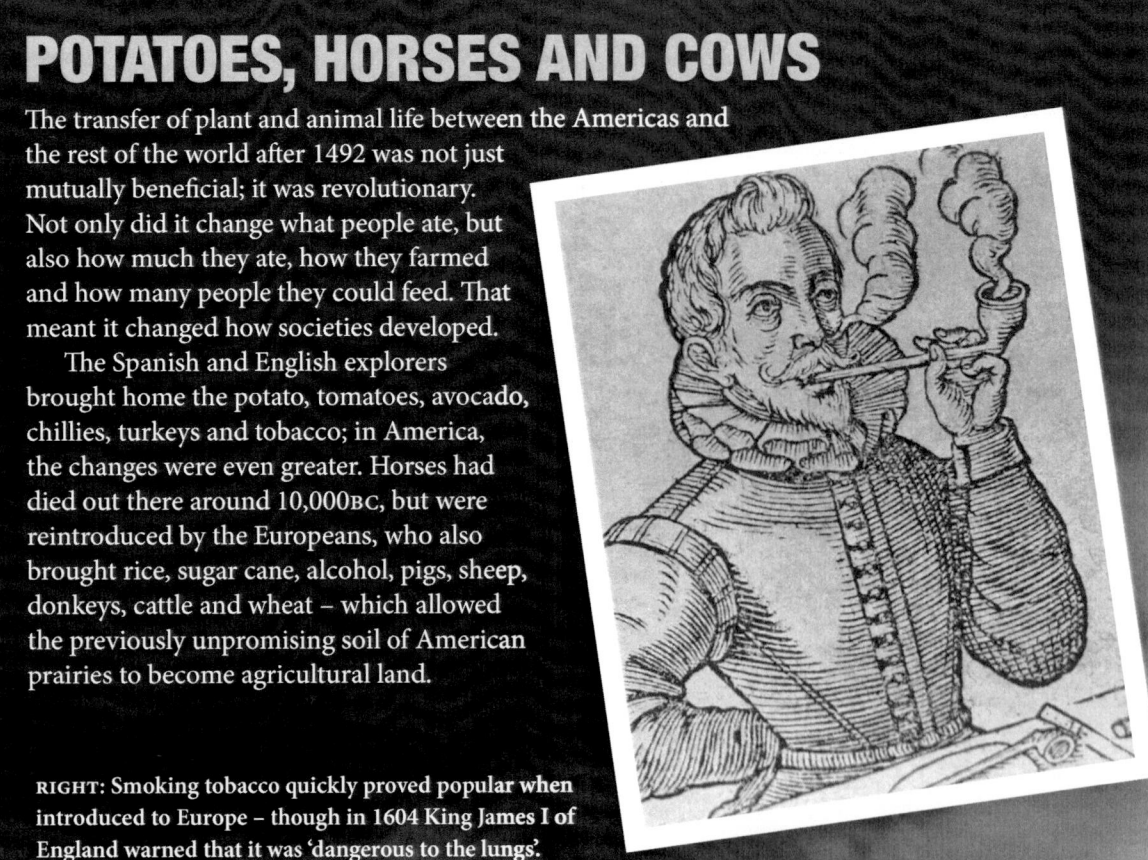

RIGHT: Smoking tobacco quickly proved popular when introduced to Europe – though in 1604 King James I of England warned that it was 'dangerous to the lungs'.

A NEW WORLD 13

some immunity to the virus. The Native Americans had no such immunity.

While the Spanish first carried their diseases into Florida and Mississippi, in the north, the French presence in the St Lawrence Valley eradicated most of the Huron Indians and Iroquois during the seventeenth century. The English played their part, too, the settlement of Plymouth being built by the *Mayflower* pilgrims on the site of an Indian village that English-borne viruses had wiped out.

> 'As late as the 1760s, smallpox remained a major killer among Native Americans.'

Even as late as the 1760s, smallpox remained a major killer among Native Americans. Using it as a form of germ warfare during the Pontiac rebellion, British commander Jeffrey Amherst gave Indian chiefs infected blankets from a smallpox hospital, urging his men to 'to try every other method that can serve to extirpate this execrable race.'

Did the Europeans catch any diseases in return? It has been argued that they carried back from America the syphilis bacterium, but the debate on whether this was the origin of syphilis in the Old World is still ongoing.

Certainly most of the deadliest infections went one way; by 1650, it is estimated that the Native American population was reduced to one-tenth its number before European contact. For North America, this could have meant a reduction from five million people down to just 500,000.

BELOW: In tackling diseases contracted from Europeans, Native Americans in Florida tended their sick by, on the left, cutting into the skull to remove diseased blood, and, on the right, fumigating to remove toxins.

NAMING THE NEW WORLD

Christopher Columbus, although celebrated across the US, never actually set foot on what is today the United States. His four voyages were to the Caribbean islands, Central and South America, and he always maintained that the Americas were part of Asia.

Although the continent is named after Florentine traveller Amerigo Vespucci, he didn't discover America either, being no more than a lowly member of expeditions to the New World after Columbus. So, how did Vespucci come to have a continent named after him? In short, by dint of a lie that got lucky.

In 1504–5, letters titled *Mundus Novus* ('New World') began circulating in Florence. The letters were forgeries, but were attributed to Vespucci, stating that he had not only been the captain of his voyages, but had discovered the New World. Elsewhere, Vespucci had written factually about his travels, but because the forgeries included sensational material about the sexual and dietary habits of the natives they became very popular. Meanwhile, in France, Martin Waldseemüller was creating a new map of the world; using the forged Vespucci letters as his source, he named the newly described landmass after the Florentine. By the time Waldseemüller learned that Vespucci was not the pioneer the letters claimed him to be, and removed Vespucci's name from his subsequent maps, the name 'America' had already begun to take hold.

RIGHT: Despite the Americas being named after him, Amerigo Vespucci neither discovered the continents nor led the voyages in which he sailed to the New World.

The Spanish Inroads

As in South America, the Spanish ventured into North America in search of silver and gold. They would be disappointed. What little gold a pioneer called Hernando de Soto found among the natives in Florida had, he failed to realize, been taken by them from earlier Spanish shipwrecks. Repeatedly, Native Americans fed the Spanish dream of a northern El Dorado located… 'just a few more days' away. Perhaps this was their way of getting rid of the troublesome Spanish and passing them on to a neighbour.

De Soto, who was rich from expeditions among the Incas, had landed at Tampa Bay in 1539 with 500 soldiers, dozens of horses and war dogs (mastiffs and Irish wolfhounds), along with hundreds of pigs to eat. It was his good fortune to encounter Juan Ortiz, a survivor from an earlier expedition who had been living among the Indians for 12 years. Ortiz would be an interpreter, along with kidnapped Indians, as De Soto crossed the southeast in search of booty. At times

16　CHAPTER 1

RIGHT: Leading the first European expedition to venture deep into what today is the United States, Hernando de Soto and his men tortured villagers in their fruitless search for gold in Florida. In response, the Native Americans became increasingly belligerent towards the Spanish.

they abducted village chiefs, demanding ransom in food, women and slaves. But as word spread about De Soto, so resistance grew. In 1540, his force was attacked by the chiefdom of Tazcaluza: 22 Spaniards were killed and 148 wounded, while about 1000 Indians died.

Becoming more brutal after this, De Soto's forces attacked and plundered villages. However, wintering among the Chickasaws in northern Mississippi in 1541, low on supplies and not having found any riches, the decision was made to return to Mexico. Soon after that, De Soto died and, after building boats and setting off down the Mississippi River, his men were further attacked by

hundreds of Indians. Alive but with no bounty, the survivors made it back to Mexico City in 1543.

De Soto's expedition was just one of many throughout the sixteenth century that explored the South. Inflicting great damage, the explorers also suffered from disease and conflict with Indian tribes. Attacked by New Mexico's Acoma Pueblo Indians in 1598, Juan de Oñate saw his nephew's body thrown off a cliff. Deciding to make an example of his enemy, De Oñate not only killed hundreds in open battle, but, following Spanish practice at the time, cut one foot off each of the adult male prisoners.

The Spanish did succeed in establishing the town of San Agustín in Florida in 1565, and missions led by Franciscan friars were built, where missionaries set about trying to develop peaceful relations with the tribes. The Spanish also often took Indian wives. The situation remained precarious, however, and, by the early 1600s, the Guale Indians were in revolt and the Spanish in retreat. By 1706, only San Agustín and a few villages survived under Spanish control in Florida.

'It would be 16 years before the Spanish recovered New Mexico.'

The Pueblo Revolt

In converting some Indians to Christianity, the Spanish created a new division among Native Americans and, during the seventeenth century, there were frequent raids in New Mexico from the Apache and Navajo on Christianized Pueblo Indians. Later, suffering from a drought and under threat from other tribes, the Pueblo lost heart in their Christian rituals and returned to their old faith. The Franciscans' response was to arrest 47 Pueblo spiritual healers, executing three in 1675 for witchcraft, while the rest were flogged and briefly imprisoned. Five years later, the Pueblo revolted, directing their ire against 21 priests and missionaries, whom they killed, along with 380 other Spaniards. Churches were destroyed and Pueblo religious leaders, in a reversal of baptism, bathed Christianized Indians in rivers to wash away the stain of Christianity.

After that, Spanish communities retreated to Mexico. It would be 16 years before the Spanish recovered New Mexico. When they returned, they did so with greater humility, no longer trying to impose their religion and culture with force, and accepting a cultural compromise. Despite all their efforts, however, the colonies of Florida, New Mexico and Texas remained large but isolated outposts for Spain.

The French

While the Spanish pushed into North America from the Gulf of Mexico, the French approached from the northeast, establishing a settlement on the St Lawrence River in 1541. Although quickly abandoned, the settlers did give a name to the St Lawrence region: they called it 'Canada' after a local Indian word for 'village'.

For the rest of the century, the French resorted to fishing expeditions and bartering with the Indians in the Gulf of the St Lawrence. Then, in the early seventeenth century, when trade was secure enough, they built a trading post – Quebec – from where French fur traders established alliances with Indian tribes, particularly the Huron. This, though, made them enemies of the Huron's own enemies, the Five Nation Iroquois. The Iroquois, in turn, allied with and secured arms from France's enemies, the Dutch, who had settled further south. In this way, both Europeans and Native Americans took advantage of the others' allegiances and hostilities.

BELOW: The Taos Canyon in New Mexico was the scene of the 1680 revolt by Pueblo Indians against the Spanish settlers. Four hundred settlers were killed and the remaining 4000 were driven out of the province.

ABOVE: A late seventeenth century map of North America, showing how well the eastern seaboard had been mapped. In contrast, territory west of the Mississippi River is described as a 'tract of land full of wild bulls'.

By 1650, New France had a population of only 657, while over the same period New England had grown to 33,000. Situated more northerly, New France had a harsher climate than New England, and the taxes to be paid from the colony to the home country discouraged many from settling. So, although by the early eighteenth century, the French had claims on land from the Gulf of St Lawrence down to the Gulf of Mexico, New France remained a weaker territory than its rivals.

The English

What distinguished the English colonies from the Spanish and French was their relative autonomy, the opportunity of property ownership and the benefit of excellent farming land, although their initial efforts were not promising. The first settlement, at Roanoke Island, North Carolina, in the 1580s, quickly disappeared, and the Jamestown settlement in 1607 in Virginia was nearly wiped out by starvation. One man, as the settlement's Captain John Smith reported, 'did kill his

CANOEING DOWN THE MISSISSIPPI

A major change in France's fortunes came with René-Robert Cavelier, Sieur de La Salle, a lapsed Jesuit turned explorer. With a troop of Frenchmen and Indians, he established forts in the Great Lakes, before, in 1682, canoeing down the Mississippi River to the Gulf of Mexico – although this was not the destination he was seeking. He'd been hoping to find a route to the Pacific and so on to Asia – but he claimed the new territory for France, anyway, naming it Louisiana after his king, Louis XIV.

La Salle's next expedition from France approached America from the Gulf of Mexico. After a troubled voyage that saw three of his four ships lost, he landed too far west; his men then spent three years trying to find the mouth of the Mississippi. In 1687, with no end in sight, his troops mutinied and shot him. A sorry end, but today La Salle's achievements as an explorer are commemorated across France, Canada and the US.

LEFT: Explorer René-Robert Cavelier, Sieur de La Salle, claims possession of the Mississippi region, naming it 'Louisiana' after his king, Louis XIV.

wife, powdered her [with salt], and had eaten part of her before it was knowne.' Once discovered, he was executed.

Like the Spanish in Florida, the English had arrived in Virginia with the hope of finding gold, and also of navigating a passage through the continent to Asia. Instead, there was no gold and they soon proved that they weren't capable of feeding themselves. Help came from the local Powhatan Indians, but the tribe's good will was soon tested. By 1620, the colonists were taking land from the Powhatans without any attempt at payment. This led, in 1622, to the Powhatans killing 347 settlers – more than a quarter of the colony. Following further disputes, in 1644 the Powhatans butchered a further 400 colonists in a single day.

It might seem surprising that the Native Americans, who had no guns unless they had obtained them from Europeans, could inflict such losses on the English. However, a skilled bowman could fire six well-aimed arrows a minute, whereas someone wielding a musket could, at best, fire it three times a minute. Even then, the aim was uncertain at distance, and the musket often liable to malfunction.

> 'A skilled bowman could fire six well-aimed arrows a minute.'

ABOVE: Despite having guns, the Europeans could still be overrun by the Native Americans. Unlike a bow and arrow, a musket could, at best, be fired three times a minute, while its aim was uncertain at distance.

Tobacco

Although the English had not found gold in Virginia, they had come across a palatable strain of tobacco smoked by the Indians, which, when business took off, sold in England for up to ten times what it cost to produce in the colony. The problem was securing sufficient manpower to farm it. While in New France the difficulty was attracting migrants, in Virginia the trouble was keeping them alive. Between 1607 and 1624, about 7600 people had emigrated from England to Virginia, but, after almost 20 years, Virginia's English population was still only about 1200 – with disease killing off many of the settlers. The local Indian population, too, was being depleted through disease, as well as being driven away in the land grab.

Indentured servants were introduced to work on the farms. Given a free passage to Virginia from England, the workers contracted themselves to a master for seven years. After that, they were free to work as wage earners, and, if they saved enough money, to buy their own land – something easier to achieve in Virginia than in Europe. Not that life was easy: in the early years the chance of survival for indentured servants was 50 per cent.

Nor were things getting any easier. With the end of the English Civil War

ABOVE: The English settlers did not find gold in Virginia, but the Native Americans did introduce them to tobacco. Cultivating it for export to the European market proved to be the making of the colony.

(1642–51), wages rose in the old country and emigration to Virginia became less appealing, while attempts at using captive Native Americans to work the fields proved unsuccessful, too. Knowing the terrain better than the English, the local tribespeople could easily escape, and enslaving a population with whom the English also needed to trade was poor for business relations. Therefore, the plantation owners looked to how manpower shortages had been resolved in another English colony in Barbados: African slave labour.

Slavery

Virginia and the Carolinas became England's first slave colonies in America. In the very early years, slaves were treated as indentured servants and were freed after completing the years of their terms. In a rather extreme example, for instance, in 1651 former slave Anthony Johnson owned 250 acres of land and had slaves of his own.

Over time, however, conditions for the slaves became harsher and more rigid. In 1662, Virginia adopted the principle that the children of slave mothers were also slaves, regardless of paternity. Following this, in 1705 the colony formalized its slave code, identifying slaves as those 'who were not Christians in their native country', forbidding intermarriage with slaves, and freeing a master of punishment should he accidentally kill a slave whom he had to discipline. Whipping and violence were common, and workers would be pushed to keep up with the rate set by the fastest labourer.

Slave numbers grew rapidly. In 1680, there were roughly 4000 people of African descent in Maryland and Virginia; 30 years later, there were 31,000. That said, in the 1730s in Virginia, only about 30 per cent of slaves lived on plantations where there were 10 or more slaves; more frequently, there were only a couple of slaves per plantation. Consequently, slaves lived closely with the plantation owner and white servants. It was their status as much as their colour that defined them, as historian Ira Berlin writes: 'Throughout the 17th century and into the first decades of the 18th century, black and white servants ran away together, slept together, and upon occasion, stood shoulder to shoulder against… established authority.'

Some slave owners raped their slaves or used them as sexual playthings, but, in South Carolina at least, the situation became more nuanced: the more integrated lives of slaves and slaveholders meant that the holders were more inclined to recognize their sexual relations with black slave women and sometimes free from slavery the offspring of these unions. From this emerged a free caste of light-skinned people of colour.

> 'Some slave owners raped their slaves or used them as sexual playthings.'

BELOW: Violence was the lubricant of the entire slave system. Slaves could be whipped for suspected minor thefts or for trying to run away. To make their bondage more bearable, slaves could deliberately misunderstand orders, feign ignorance or work slowly.

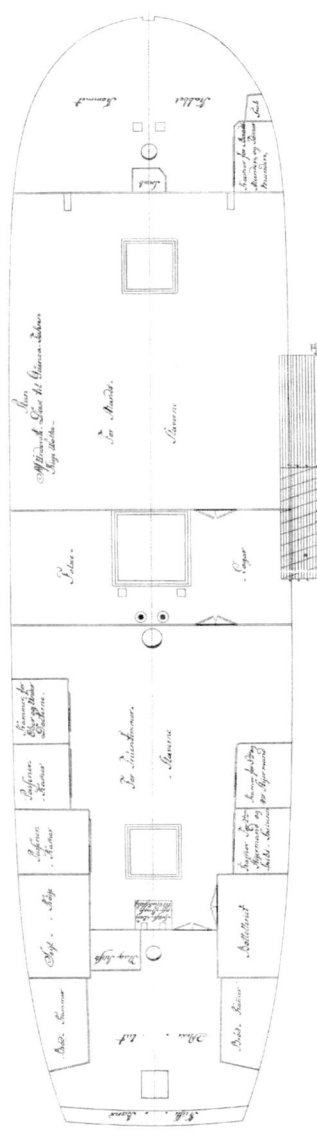
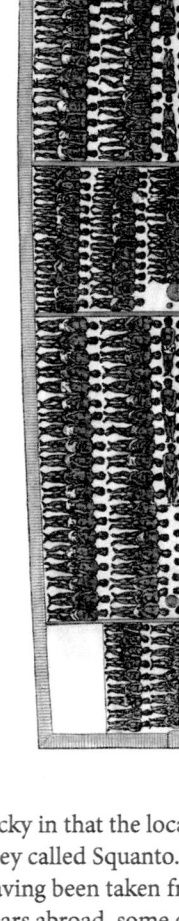

ABOVE: The deck plan of a slave ship in the 1700s. With around 200 slaves shackled closely together, slave ships developed a stink that could be smelt miles downwind.

The Atlantic Slave Trade

Between 1700 and 1775, 250,000 African slaves were transported to North America, making up about six per cent of all the slaves shipped across the Atlantic – far more were transported to the Caribbean and Brazil. Although it doesn't lessen the barbarity of the Atlantic slave trade, there were probably as many slaves – between three and five million – held within Africa by Africans as there were in the Americas.

Slaves were acquired through raids, through African tribal chiefs selling their captives and prisoners of war, and from African slave traders. Onboard ships, the captives were chained at the neck and stacked on wooden shelves about 75cm (30in) high. Lying in their own excrement and urine, many died of dysentery. Some starved themselves to death, while others tried to jump overboard when brought on deck for food and exercise. Occasionally there were rebellions on board – even more occasionally these were successful.

Conditions improved during the eighteenth century as crossing times were reduced by a few weeks to no more than two months; by the 1780s, nine out of ten slaves were surviving the voyage.

A New England

The *Mayflower* may be romantically remembered as the beginning of New England, but within a year of arriving half its 102 passengers were dead. Even so, as families of artisans and craftsmen, largely unused to working the land, they were lucky in that the local Wampanoag tribe helped them, not least a Wampanoag they called Squanto. New England was not completely uncharted territory and, having been taken from the coast by English fishermen, Squanto had spent 15 years abroad, some of that time working in London, and some in slavery in Spain, before returning home on another exploratory expedition. He was a good man for the newcomers to know.

Unlike the gold-seekers in the South, the first settlers in New England in 1620 had been primarily motivated by religion – they were Separatists from the Church of England. Believing Judgement was nearing, John Winthrop, a Puritan who led the first large wave of immigrants to New England 10 years later, proclaimed: 'God hathe provided this place [New England] to be a refuge for manye whom he meanes to save.' New England, they believed, was destined for them, and they were not going to tolerate dissenters: accordingly, they hanged several Quakers

THE STONO REBELLION

In contrast with British colonies, slavery in Spanish Florida was usually less harsh: there slaves often had the right to marry and to hold property – and the territory welcomed runaways from other parts of east coast America. With this in mind, in 1739, 20 slaves at Stono Bridge, near Charles Town (Charleston), South Carolina, stole guns and began marching towards Florida.

Attacking plantations and killing more than 20 colonists along the way, their numbers soon swelled to around a hundred. But within a day, the plantation owners had caught up with them, shot them and, just as the rebels had done to some of the whites, decapitated many.

Often in the slave states, this was more complicated than just a case of black against white: 30 slaves, mainly assimilated Creoles, had remained loyal to their white masters and had killed some of the black insurgents.

Although swiftly dealt with, the Stono Rebellion sent shock waves through the white population in South Carolina, which was outnumbered two to one by its slaves. Consequently, slave laws were tightened.

who repeatedly tried to proselytize, and they excommunicated Anne Hutchinson for preaching, banishing her from Massachusetts in 1638.

Although New England did not become a major slave-owning colony, that wasn't down to the Puritans' faith, but because tobacco and rice didn't grow in the cooler northern climate – so there was no need for such a large workforce as there was on the plantations in the South. Some slaves worked as farm labourers and domestic servants in New England, although, at most, in Rhode Island in 1710, they made up only five per cent of the population. In contrast, by 1775 in Virginia, two out of five people were black slaves.

Not only were there fewer slaves in the North compared with the South, they had better rights, too, not being classified as property in Massachusetts, and, following conversion to Christianity in New Amsterdam, in some cases they were given their freedom. When New Amsterdam was acquired by England in 1664, 75 of the town's 375 blacks were free.

BELOW: Unlike other early settlers, the Pilgrim Fathers were not seeking commercial gain in America, but a promised land free to practise their religion.

SCALPING

Long taken by warring Indians as battlefield trophies, it was the Europeans that turned scalping into a business. As an indication of the hostility between the colonies and the Indians and also among Indian tribes themselves, scalp bounties began appearing in the 1670s. Lacking much of an army, Massachusetts paid £10 per scalp to scalp hunters during Queen Anne's War in 1702, while during the 1711 war with the Tuscarora in North Carolina, John Barnwell led an expedition that scalped 52 Indians, including ten women. But scalping worked the other way, too: during the Seven Years' War, the French offered bounties for British scalps.

New England may have been founded on Puritan spirit, but, as the story of Hannah Dustan demonstrates, it proved to be a brutal frontier. In 1698, an Abenaki war party captured Dustan, along with her newborn child and her nurse, Mary Neff, in Haverhill, Massachusetts. The following day, one of the Abenaki warriors killed Dustan's baby, before forcing her and Neff to join another warrior, Abenaki women and children on a 240km (150-mile) trek towards Canada. After some days, Dustan took a tomahawk from a sleeping Abenaki and, with the help of Neff and a teenage boy who had been captured, crushed the skulls of the Abenaki men. Nor did Dustan stop there. She scalped her victims and others in the war party, later presenting the Massachusetts General Assembly with ten scalps – for which she was rewarded £50.

By embracing scalp hunting, writes historian John Grenier, American society had not only commercialized war, but 'made the killing of non-combatants a legitimate act of war'.

ABOVE: An American propaganda cartoon from the 1812 war with Britain, criticizing the 'humane' British and their 'worthy' Indian allies who scalp Americans.

ABOVE: The attack by English, Narragansett and Mohegan forces against Pequot men, women and children in New England in 1637. Many of the Indians not killed in the Pequot War (1636–38) were sold into slavery in the West Indies.

Indian Revolts and Rebellions

The arrival of Europeans seldom prompted unity among Indian tribes against a common enemy. With tension building between the Puritans and Indians in New England in the 1630s, the Pequot Indians sought an alliance with the Narragansetts. But rather than seizing an opportunity for Indian solidarity, the Narragansetts saw a chance to remove a rival tribe: they sided with the English.

The most notable event of the Pequot War (1636–48) was the 1637 attack by English, Narragansett and Mohegan forces on Fort Mystic. Most of the Pequot warriors were away raiding English settlements, but this didn't stop the English-led force setting fire to the fort and killing the women, children and old men who tried to escape. It is estimated that around 600 Pequots died in the attack; the Puritans lost two people.

Two months later, when the English defeated the remaining Pequot, their chief, Sassacus, fled to Mohawk territory, where he was beheaded. The Mohawks weren't going to involve themselves in the war, or side with non-Iroquoian people. Meanwhile, the remaining Pequots were sold into slavery in Bermuda or divided up among the Narragansetts and Mohegans as payment. As a political force in the seventeenth century, the Pequot were extinguished, as the Narragansetts had hoped – not that they would last much longer, either.

'Massachusetts paid £10 per scalp to scalp hunters during Queen Anne's War in 1702.'

When the English executed three Wampanoag men for murdering a Christianized Indian who had warned the English of a planned Wampanoag attack, revenge attacks from Wampanoag, and other Native tribes, ensued. This was the first time that the Puritans had prosecuted an Indian for an Indian

ABOVE: In 1729, the Natchez in Mississippi rebelled against French encroachments, killing more than 200 settlers. With the French military response being to sell hundreds of Natchez prisoners into slavery, by the late 1730s the tribe had ceased to exist as an independent people.

OPPOSITE: Unusually, Pontiac's Rebellion in 1763 saw Native Americans uniting against the Europeans. In the uprising, a loose confederation of northern Indian tribes captured nine British forts and attacked ships on the Detroit River.

crime – and it led to a massacre. The English retaliated, butchering hundreds of Narragansett men, women and children – as well as English men who had Indian wives.

It would get worse. When Metacom, the Wampanoag chief, and his followers sought help from the Iroquois, the Iroquois attacked them, while the Mohegans backed the English. In August 1676, the English caught Metacom, decapitating him. His wife and hundreds of survivors were sold into slavery in the West Indies. With 3000 Indians killed in the short war (600 English died), the Wampanoags and Narragansetts were virtually exterminated.

This treatment wasn't limited to the English. In the South in 1729, Natchez Indians rebelled with slaves, freeing other slaves and killing more than 200 French settlers – almost all the French men in the area. In response, the French sent slaves and Choctaw Indians against the Natchez, massacring hundreds and selling the Natchez survivors into slavery. By 1736, the few remaining Natchez had dispersed to live among the Cherokee and Cree. As with many conflicts between Europeans and Indians, the French had managed to exploit local enmities and employ one tribe of Indians against another.

Thirty years later, one rebellion would prove the exception to this rule. In Pontiac's Rebellion, northern tribes united in a large pan-Indian movement against the British, capturing nine British forts and besieging Detroit for three years. Finally crushing the rebellion, the British took the uprising seriously enough to issue a proclamation to the colonists to remain east of the Appalachians to avoid further conflict. This, though, wasn't respected and tensions between the colonists and Indians would remain high.

THE SALEM WITCH TRIALS

Up until 1692, a total of 12 women had been hanged as witches in Massachusetts and Connecticut, but in the period between February 1692 and May 1693, 20 people were executed for witchcraft in or around Salem, Massachusetts. A further 156 were imprisoned. What was going on? Probably nothing more satanic, but no less sinister, than mass hysteria.

Most accusations of witchcraft in New England at that time were dismissed, but when in Salem Village (present-day Danvers), Betty Paris, aged nine, and her cousin, Abigail Williams, aged 11, fell ill with convulsions and screaming fits, and no medical cause could be found, people began to wonder if the children were under a magic spell. Three years earlier, there had been a case in Boston of children convulsing and accusations of witchcraft, of which the people of Salem would have been aware.

By now the two girls had been joined by two more cases of convulsions: 12-year-old Ann Putnam and Elizabeth Hubbard, who was probably 17. Pressed to reveal their tormentors, the girls described how witches had appeared to them in spirit form and had caused the convulsions.

The first women to be accused of witchcraft were, unsurprisingly for witch trials, three social outsiders: Tituba, a slave who was either black or Native American; Sarah Good, a beggar known to curse those who crossed her; and Sarah Osborne, a woman who had damned herself in the eyes of the community by living with a man before marrying.

But, rather than remaining limited to these three suspects, the accusations grew. Believing the girls' testimony, more suspects were hauled into court, where they usually confessed to protect themselves and named accomplices, thus fuelling the hysteria. The accusations spread from Salem to neighbouring Andover, and although new colonial magistrates were sent for, in the hope of throwing cold water on the matter, they, too, believed the girls' testimonies and further fanned the flames.

By May 1692, 62 people were in custody. With any sense of justice temporarily abandoned, if the accused refused to admit any guilt, he or she was found guilty anyway and executed. Sarah Good, whose four-year-old daughter even gave evidence as a prosecution witness, was hanged. Sarah Osborne, whom Good accused of being a witch, died in prison. Tituba, who confessed under trial, was imprisoned but released after the scare had passed.

Meanwhile, the accusations climbed the social ranks, reaching Mary Phips, the wife of Massachusetts's Governor Phips. But when Samuel Willard, pastor of the First Church of Boston and president of Harvard University, was accused, the magistrates' credulity snapped.

Beginning to doubt all the testimony they had heard, the magistrates dismissed the girls' evidence and the governor called a new hearing. Fifty-two people were retried, only three of

Convicts

Of the 80,000 English migrants to America between 1700 and 1775, around 50,000 of them were convicts. Not only did transporting criminals put them out of sight and mind of the authorities, but there was plenty of work to be done in the colonies' plantations. Most convicts were young, male, unskilled labourers who had been found guilty of theft, but those sentenced to death in England for murder could petition the king and might, if they were lucky, receive a transportation pardon.

whom were found guilty – and they were reprieved, along with all those already in prison.

Of the 20 who had been executed, 19 had been hanged and one, Giles Corey, was gradually tortured to death by being crushed by ever-heavier stones in an attempt to make him offer a plea.

Whether the girls were attention-seeking frauds, affected by a kind of social epidemic following the incident in Boston, or afflicted with a psychological or physical illness, is not known. Successive generations of historians have offered varying theories for what happened in Salem. Was it about class, gender, rivalry among Puritan families, or an expression of the violence felt from the wars with Indians? Or was it a combination of all these factors at that time that allowed the mania to take hold?

ABOVE: Twenty people were executed in the Salem Witch Trials of 1692–93 before the accusations of witchcraft began to be doubted and the mass hysteria was extinguished.

As on slave ships, convicts were chained at the neck for most of the journey, although they had slightly more space than slaves. Once in the colonies, they were sold. 'They searched us there as the dealers in horses do those animals,' remembered convict William Green, 'looking at our teeth, viewing our limbs, to see if they are sound and fit for their labour.' Convicts sold at a third the price of adult male slaves and could be worked for more years than indentured servants. Whippings were commonplace, as were iron collars and chains, if the convict was considered unruly.

As criminals they arrived, but as historian A. Roger Ekirch has noted, convicts in America 'committed surprisingly few crimes'. There were cases of runaways, some even making it back to Britain, but after most had served their terms, the men usually moved to a new neighbourhood in an effort to distance themselves from the stigma of their servitude. Then they could try to begin a new life.

Europe's War in America

In the eighteenth century, British colonies were surging ahead in wealth and

ABOVE: While most transported criminals were thieves or had been found guilty of violent crime, in 1732 inmates from Britain's debtors' prisons – including members of the aristocracy – were sent to Georgia.

population, with settlers from Virginia and Pennsylvania starting to expand into the Ohio Valley. This area reached from the Appalachians up to the Great Lakes, and, although largely unoccupied by Europeans, it had long been claimed as part of New France. So, in response to the British encroachment (Great Britain having formally come into existence in 1707 with the Act of Union between the kingdoms of England and Scotland), the French began building a chain of forts from Lake Erie down to Fort Duquesne (present-day Pittsburgh).

> 'To fight in America, the British and French needed the help of the local Indians.'

By 1754, the two European powers were at war over Ohio County, a part of a broader global conflict between Britain and France, and their allies, in the Seven Years' War (1756–63). To fight in America, both the British and French needed the help of the local Indians. A confederacy of Iroquois tribes had kept a peaceful alliance with the French in the Ohio County, but the British now disrupted this by drawing the Mohawks away.

French forces based at Fort Duquesne defeated the English in 1754 and also in 1755, when the English ranks of conspicuous redcoats were easily picked off by French and Indian troops unseen in the trees. Worse was to come in a botched

LEFT: George Washington (on horseback) during the Seven Years' War. One outcome of the war determined whether the people of North America would mainly speak English or French.

ABOVE: The Battle of Quebec in September 1759 was not quite the decisive triumph remembered by the British. Although quickly victorious, the British garrison was subsequently marooned in the city, the starving, disease-ridden survivors only being rescued the following spring.

assault on Fort Carillon (Ticonderoga) on the Hudson River three years later. It would be the bloodiest battle in this conflict (known in the US as the French and Indian War) with 1000 losses on the British side. In 1758, the British succeeded in taking the now abandoned Fort Duquesne, only to find a line of stakes each topped with the skull of a British soldier – a grim reminder of their earlier defeat.

The Battle of Quebec

The key to French America was the fort at Quebec, which stands 91m (300ft) above the St Lawrence River. It is popularly remembered – in Britain, at least – that although the fort was near impregnable, the British, under General James Wolfe, managed a swift, surprising victory. By scaling a steep path at night, the British engaged the French on the Plains of Abraham and eliminated them with just two volleys. Within 10 minutes, the battle was over.

If that sounds too good to be true, it is. In fact, there were two battles at Quebec: Wolfe's victory in September 1759 was succeeded by a more decisive one the following year. But first, the 7000 British troops who had conquered the city now had to survive the winter where food shortages led to scurvy. By the spring, when 7000 refreshed French forces headed down the St Lawrence, there were only 3000 British troops who were battle worthy.

Again the troops met on the Plains of Abraham, but this time the battle was not resolved quickly. After two hours of hand-to-hand combat, half the British were dead or wounded, and the able-bodied were fleeing back behind the city walls. Still unresolved, Quebec was not won by the British until the main fleet arrived the following month and the French retreated. By the end of the year, all the French forts were in British hands.

The battle had been fought over land, but it was sea power that settled the victory. By 1763, the Seven Years' War was over, New France formally becoming part of the British colonies. In an act of eighteenth-century ethnic cleansing, 7000 French-Canadian settlers were deported from Nova Scotia down to France's remaining colony at Louisiana. However, France's hand in the future of America was not over yet.

> 'In the space of just over 250 years, Europeans had colonized eastern America.'

The New World

In the space of just over 250 years, Europeans had colonized eastern America, decimating the Native American population through disease and war and dispossessing a great many. Along with convicts from Britain, the Europeans had brought thousands of slaves from Africa, and fought their own imperial wars over American territory. But the colonies were now a major part of Atlantic trade, and the more successful and established they became, the more they prized their importance, and, in time, their independence.

With the fall of New France, members of the British colonies had celebrated by erecting statues to Britain's King George III and his leading politician, William Pitt. Yet within 12 years, the colonists would be at war with Britain – the war that would create the United States.

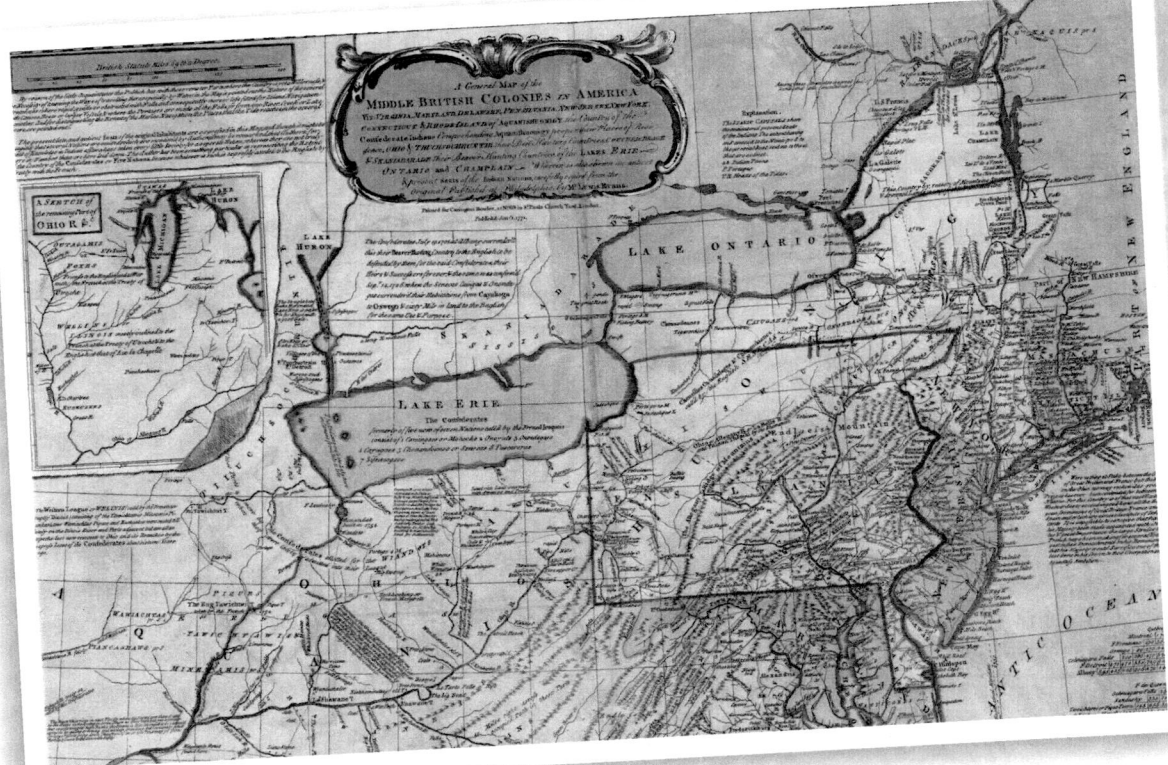

BELOW: This 1771 map of the **middle British colonies was designed to** spur **westward expansion following French encroachments. Its text warns that George III risks losing 'one of the best gems in his Crown to [French] usurpation and boundless ambition!'**

2

THE AMERICAN REVOLUTION

What began in 1765 as a tax dispute with Britain escalated through war to see the United States emerge as an independent nation. But, although the infant republic embraced ideals of liberty and equality, it would refuse to extend these rights to its slaves and its Native Americans.

The Seven Years' War (1756–63) with France had not just doubled Britain's national debt, it had also made running the 13 colonies of North America five times more expensive. For this, London wanted to make the colonists pay their share, not least because Great Britain was now keeping a standing army in North America. What followed between 1763 and 1776 was a series of efforts by Britain to extract revenue from the American colonies – a plan that was countered by increasingly violent resistance by colonists on the grounds that they shouldn't pay taxes if they were not represented at Parliament in London. As the famous slogan went: 'No taxation without representation'.

Not that representation was widely given in Britain, either. At the time, only around one in six adult British males had the right to vote, compared with two in three in the American colonies. Indeed Britain's electoral districts were an unreformed, corrupt hodgepodge that allowed districts with barely any inhabitants a representative at Parliament while new cities such as Manchester had none.

OPPOSITE: Although a veteran of the Seven Years' War, George Washington was not highly experienced in battle. Nevertheless, as commander-in-chief during the Revolutionary War, he led the Continental Army to pivotal victories at Trenton in 1776 and Princeton in 1777.

OPPOSITE: 'Unhappy Boston! See thy sons deplore, thy hallowed walks besmeared with guiltless gore,' begins Paul Revere's propaganda poster 'The Bloody Massacre', which reported the shooting by the British Army of five civilians in Boston in March 1770.

But then, just as electoral reform in Britain lagged behind population change, so the country's management of its colonies was also out of touch. In 1700, the population of the American colonies had been one-twentieth the size of that of Britain and Ireland combined; by 1770, however, it was a fifth – 2.1 million compared with more than 10 million in the British Isles. However, apart from efforts to extract taxes, London did not treat this rapidly emerging people any differently than it had always done. To London, the American colonies, like other parts of the empire, were unsophisticated, lesser entities. Showing its lack of consideration for American opinion, Parliament passed the Quebec Act in 1774, granting freedom of worship for Catholics in the largely French-speaking territories, ceded to Britain by the Treaty of Paris in 1763, and giving the governor of Quebec control over the vast Indian lands of the Ohio Valley. Enlightened though it may have been in its attitude towards the defeated French population, this managed to provoke American Protestants, land speculators and traders.

Sons of Liberty and Boston Tea

In March 1765, the British Parliament approved a stamp duty on legal documents and newspapers in the American colonies. Distinct from duties on trade, this was the first 'direct' tax introduced to the colonies – and it was resisted. In August that year, leaders of the opposition to the Stamp Act roused Boston's city mobs. Having, it was said, plied them with drink, they sent them against representatives of the British government, a riot that included the ransacking of the house of the lieutenant-governor of Massachusetts.

Rioting then spread across the 13 colonies, led not by thugs but mostly by middle-ranking people – mechanics, small merchants and shopkeepers – who commonly called themselves 'Sons of Liberty'. Having blocked imports of British goods, the protests died down only when London repealed the Stamp Act the following February.

In June 1767, Charles Townshend, the British Chancellor of the Exchequer, tried a different method of extracting more revenue out of the colonies by imposing higher duties on glass, paper and tea. Once more, this met resistance from local committees, with boycotts placed on British goods in return. Despite voices in Parliament arguing that using force would undermine any goodwill with Americans, more troops were sent from Britain to be garrisoned in Boston. By 1769, there were nearly 4000 British soldiers in a town of 15,000 people. Then, in March 1770, in a clash involving a mob that had harassed soldiers, five civilians were killed – the first fatalities in the developing conflict.

> 'The notion of independence was now being discussed in colonial newspapers.'

The protests and resistance had proved their point. With the little revenue collected by the Townshend Duties far overshadowed by the loss in trade through boycotts, the duties were largely repealed.

Britain, however, still didn't see the danger it was provoking. When, in May 1773, it disregarded American merchants' concerns and gave the ailing East India Company a monopoly to sell tea in North America, protests soon followed. The most remarkable of these has become known as the Boston Tea Party. On 16 December 1773, a group of 60 men, including apprentices, sailors and merchants – some vaguely disguised as Native Americans – dumped 340 chests of newly imported tea into Boston Harbor.

The British immediately responded with the Intolerable Acts (or Coercive Acts) of 1774, putting Boston under martial law, closing the port and asserting greater authority over local appointments. This worked in the protesters' favour, as the colonies began to unite against Britain by sending donations to Boston. For the first time, the notion of independence was being discussed in colonial newspapers.

The Continental Congress

Openly rebelling, the colonies now pushed aside royal authority and allowed new local administrators to levy taxes, supervise courts and organize militias. Meeting in Philadelphia, a Continental Congress of around 50 men from 12 colonies (Georgia didn't take part) discussed the colonies' future, agreeing to block imports from Britain, but holding in reserve a ban of exports to Britain, which would have ruined the economy in the South. Most delegates, though, still hoped for reconciliation with the mother country.

There were voices of support in London, too, such as that of Edward Burke, MP, who called for the Americans to be represented at Parliament and for a relaxing of the tax legislation. The prevailing opinion there, however, was for punishing the upstart colonies.

From Lexington to Bunker Hill

On 19 April 1775, a force of British soldiers from Boston marched into the village of Lexington, Massachusetts, in search of illegal arms. They were confronted by 70 local militiamen, a shot rang out – it's not clear from which side – and the British charged, killing eight Americans within a few minutes. Moving on to Concord the same day, the British didn't find any guns, but the town was set ablaze anyway. Then, while returning the 26km (16-mile) journey to Boston, they were attacked. By the end of the day, 70 British soldiers had been killed and 200 wounded; on the colonists' side the wounded or dead totalled 95. Worse was to come. Two months later, the British dislodged the colonists fortifying Bunker Hill outside Boston, but it cost them 250 lives and a further 750 wounded. With the fighting escalating, the Continental Congress decided to create a Continental Army with George Washington as commander.

LEFT: 'The rebels are not the despicable rabble too many have supposed them to be,' wrote British commander George Gage after his victory at Bunker Hill in June 1775 had cost him 250 men.

THE UNITED STATES OF COLUMBIA

What, though, were the 13 colonies going to call their new nation? The Declaration of Independence had stated 'The Unanimous Declaration of the Thirteen United States of America', and, that same year, Thomas Paine in *Common Sense*, his influential book arguing for independence, had first referred to 'the United States of America'. There was, however, some hesitation in Congress, not least because the word 'America' could, they thought, refer to anyone from all the Americas, not just the 13 colonies. Congress debated the matter, even considering the name 'United States of Columbia'. As Columbus's voyages had been financed by the Spanish crown, his reputation in the 13 colonies had not been cultivated by the British and his name had faded. But when the colonies began to look for new figureheads separate from Britain, his reputation saw a revival.

In the end, Congress decided to embrace the word 'America', leaving Columbus to live on in the names of US colleges, territories, towns and cities.

The Declaration of Independence

While moderates were still calling for representation in Parliament, in June 1776, John Adams, a Boston lawyer active in the protests, and Richard Henry Lee of Virginia proposed a resolution in the Congress: 'That these United States are, and of right ought to be, free and independent States, and that they are absolved from all allegiance to the British Crown…'.

Approving the motion, the Continental Congress appointed Thomas Jefferson, a committee member from Virginia, to draft a formal declaration of independence. While holding King George III accountable for all of America's grievances, the final 1300-word Declaration is very much an expression of the Enlightenment ideals of its day: 'We hold these truths to be self-evident; that all men are created equal; that they are endowed by their Creator with certain inalienable rights; that among these are life, liberty and the pursuit of happiness…'. The equality and liberty of white men, that is. In their eyes, women and slaves were not equal.

On 4 July 1776, the Continental Congress approved the Declaration of Independence. John Adams wrote to his wife Abigail that Independence Day 'will be celebrated by succeeding generations as the great annual festival'. He was right. Where 13 years earlier statues of George III had been erected across the colonies after the victory in the Seven Years' War, now the king's effigy was torn down.

The Armies

Independence might have been declared, but now the colonists had to realize it by breaking away from the world's most powerful nation. In 1776 alone, Britain sent 30,000 troops to North America, whereas the Continental Army usually numbered fewer than 5000 men, supplemented by state militia. After a season, America's soldiers would mostly return to their farms. There was another problem, too, in that about a fifth of white Americans remained loyal to the crown, with thousands fighting on the British side.

> 'Their ideals of equality and liberty didn't extend to women and slaves.'

OPPOSITE: **The Declaration of Independence** pronounced that governments derive 'their just powers from the consent of the governed', and that, as the British were seeking 'an absolute tyranny', the political connection between the United States and Britain was dissolved.

FIGHTING SLAVES

With war approaching, some slaves began to support their enemy's enemy – the British. In September 1774, Boston slaves offered to serve General Thomas Gage against their American masters; the following year, slaves in Rhode Island joined a group of Loyalists. Virginia's governor, John Murray, the Earl of Dunmore, seeing his white population turn against him, declared that he would free all slaves who were willing to fight for him. Between 800 and 1000 slaves, including families, slipped away from their jobs and joined what Dunmore called the Ethiopian Regiment. Their military efforts were largely unsuccessful, but Dunmore managed to disperse the survivors, sending the battle-worthy ones north to join Loyalist forces in New York and the rest to friendly territory in Florida and the West Indies.

Although the Americans lacked resources, the British faced other difficulties. Their war was 4828km (3000 miles) from home and they were fighting not to crush an enemy, but to win it over. Also, America was vast and lacked a capital to conquer. As a consequence, the British efforts focused on attacking the Congress's main army, in the hope that the colonies would lose faith in the rebellion.

With a smaller and weaker army, George Washington decided to fight defensively and avoid full-scale action, relying on skirmishes to disrupt the British supply chain. Reporting after Bunker Hill that American riflemen had concealed themselves behind trees before sneakily taking shots, one British soldier

BELOW: American forces try to hold their ground at Brandywine, Pennsylvania, in September 1777. With more than 14,000 troops on each side, it was the largest engagement in the Revolutionary War.

complained: 'What an unfair method of carrying on a war!' Like much of the British effort, he was missing the point. 'The British never really understood what they were up against,' writes historian Gordon S. Wood. 'Hence they continually underestimated the staying power of the rebels and overestimated the strength of the Loyalists.'

Reaching Saratoga

During the British campaign to occupy Philadelphia, George Washington was defeated twice in Pennsylvania in the autumn of 1777. However, the defeats were not disastrous and instead proved how well the Americans could stand up to superior forces. Meanwhile, a British force led by John Burgoyne had moved south from Canada in an effort to control the Hudson River. With an overextended supply train, and following skirmishes with the colonists, his 6000 troops found themselves surrounded by superior numbers at Saratoga, New York State, and fought two small battles before surrendering.

More significant than the outcome at Saratoga was its wider impact. Encouraged by the American victory, the French, who had already secretly been supplying the Americans with money and arms, signed a treaty with the United States, recognizing their independence and simultaneously declaring war on Britain. The Spanish and the Dutch then joined in on the French side. The 13 colonies now had major European might on their side.

Heading South

Having failed in New England in 1777, the British turned their efforts towards the South. Charleston, South Carolina, was won in May 1780 by the British after a three-month siege – although the following year the Americans regained control of most of that area. Then Washington marched south, trapping the British on Virginia's York peninsula. Usually, the British, with the world's largest navy, had the upper hand in sea power, but here their troops on land were denied any escape because the French fleet was blockading them.

Unable to manoeuvre and facing a force of 17,000 to his own 8000 troops, Lord Cornwallis was besieged at Yorktown. After three weeks, with smallpox spreading and his men beginning to starve, Cornwallis was forced to

> 'With war approaching, some slaves began to support their enemy's enemy – the British.'

BELOW: Pleading illness, British General Charles Cornwallis did not attend the surrender ceremony at Yorktown in October 1781, leaving his second-in-command, General Charles O'Hara, to carry Cornwallis's sword to the American and French commanders.

INOCULATIONS AND MUTINIES

With a smallpox epidemic decimating the American army in 1777, George Washington stepped up what had previously been a haphazard policy of inoculations. This was 20 years before Edward Jenner in England demonstrated the use of cowpox as a form of vaccination and set the course for widespread treatment of smallpox – so Washington's efforts were rudimentary and sometimes disastrous. He had, however, little choice, and established a quarantine unit where every soldier would have some smallpox pustules from an earlier victim inserted into an incision in his arm, thus transferring a mild dose of the virus in the hope of building immunity rather than killing the patient.

Apart from disease, the American soldiers often struggled financially because Congress lacked the organization to support its soldiers and the individual states proved unwilling to group together to pay for the war. Unpaid and barely fed, several American units mutinied in the winter of 1779–80. As mutineer Joseph Martin from Connecticut explained: 'The men saw no other alternative but to starve to death, or break up the army…'

RIGHT: General Anthony Wayne trying to quell the Pennsylvania Line Mutiny in 1781. During the Revolutionary War, American soldiers repeatedly mutinied over lack of food or pay.

surrender. Support finally came to the British in the form of 25 ships and 7000 men, but it arrived on the day terms were concluded.

The war wasn't over, but, writes historian Gordon S. Wood, 'everyone knew that Yorktown meant American independence.' Peace finally came in September 1783, with the British signing the Treaty of Paris, acknowledging the full independence of the United States.

The Aftermath

The war was experienced very differently across the colonies: while the Carolinas and Georgia saw much of the fighting, Massachusetts's moment happened in 1776 and Virginia's with Yorktown in 1781, but both were otherwise little touched by the conflict. Slave experiences varied, too, as slaves fought on both sides. After the war, those who had been freed by the British were relocated to Canada or the West Indies, just as white Loyalists moved to Canada or Britain.

Although the war may not have seen immense battles or long campaigns, 25,000 Americans died in it – in proportion to the population, the greatest loss of life after the Civil War. Of these deaths, only a third were lost in battle, the rest dying of disease.

Unsurprisingly, the war was waged at huge financial cost to the Americans. To fund it, Congress had printed money, leading to high inflation, as well as having borrowed massively from the French and Dutch. The United States was born heavily in debt. Now unprotected by the British flag, many American ships were attacked and their crews sold into slavery by corsairs from Muslim states in North Africa. With little money to spare, Congress could not pay any ransoms or tribute. Independence may have carried great enthusiasm, but there were immense problems to be addressed.

The Constitution

The Americans had declared their independence, and then gone on to win it. Now the Founding Fathers had to build a workable nation. During the war, each of the colonies had rewritten their constitutions as independent states, largely restricting the role of their British-sanctioned governors, and increasing the authority of local elected assemblies. The Revolution, though, hadn't only been about shaking off British tyranny, but blocking any future kind of tyranny. As property qualifications for voters were reduced, many more people became enfranchised, thus allowing farmers, merchants and lawyers to join what had previously been the exclusive domain of wealthy gentlemen. Rule by monarchy and aristocracy was now a thing of the colonial past.

However, this could create its own problems at the other extreme, with too much power concentrated locally. Thomas Jefferson complained that when 'all the powers of government, legislative, executive, and judiciary, result to the legislative body' the government in Virginia had turned 'despotic'. Another future president, James Madison of Virginia, said that 'a spirit of locality' in the state legislatures was the states, destroying 'the aggregate interests of the community'.

Added to this, in their uneasy alliance, the states were fighting commercial and territorial wars among themselves, with, for example, Connecticut charging higher tariffs on goods from Massachusetts than it did on imports from Britain, New York arguing with Rhode Island over land, and Vermont already threatening to leave the union.

When, by 1787, the government was unable to repay its debts or reliably levy taxes, it was uncertain as to whether it could honour its treaty obligations or ensure that its laws would be obeyed. 'It was not clear,' wrote historian Charles L. Mee, 'that it could be called a government at all.'

BELOW: George Washington presiding over the Constitutional Convention in 1787. For four months, the 55 delegates debated the content of the new republic's Constitution. Notably, neither John Adams nor Thomas Jefferson was present, as both were serving as US ambassadors in Europe.

In an effort to reach an agreement across the country, the Constitutional Convention met over the summer of 1787, from which emerged a national Constitution. Three major issues for the Convention were the differences in influence between small and large states, slavery, and state power versus that of a new federal government.

As small states feared that they wouldn't have a voice in a national government, a compromise was struck: while in the lower house of the legislature, a state's presence would be determined by its population – so, Rhode Island would have only a single seat, while Virginia would have 10 – this would be counterbalanced in the Senate, where each state, regardless of size, would have two seats.

On the matter of slaves, the Southern states regarded them as property and did not allow them to be part of the electorate. They did, however, count each slave as three-fifths of a person when it came to arguing the size of their population, which therefore decided how many seats they deserved in the House of Representatives. While viewed as 'cruel bondage' and inhumane by many, slavery wasn't something about which the Southern states would negotiate: it had to be accepted as peculiar to them if the Constitution was to be ratified.

BELOW: Addressing the objections of anti-Federalists, the Bill of Rights amendments to the Constitution declared that all powers not specifically delegated to Congress are reserved for the states or the people.

As for the federal government, it would have responsibility for war, diplomacy, taxation, borrowing, coining money and the regulation of trade, while its power would be controlled with a series of checks and balances. The executive, legislature and judiciary would all be separate; senators would be chosen by the legislature, and members of the House of Representatives by the electorate.

The Bill of Rights

The Constitution was ratified state by state in 1787–88, with George Washington unanimously elected president – not by the public, but by senior figures appointed by the individual states. Still, opponents in many states, fearing a loss of basic freedoms to the national government, demanded a Bill of Rights.

Ten amendments to the Constitution were ratified in 1791. Of these, the First Amendment affirms freedom of speech, of the Press and that 'Congress shall make no law respecting an establishment of religion', while the Tenth addresses the essential balance in the US between the federal government and the individual states, clarifying that the government possesses only those powers delegated to it by the states or the people through the Constitution.

OPPOSITE: Thomas Paine's pamphlet *Common Sense*, published in January 1776, was enormously influential in arguing for independence. Paine, though, wasn't from the colonies, but had arrived from England just two years earlier.

It is the Second Amendment of these original 10 that today provokes the most emotional response. It states: 'A well-regulated militia being necessary to the security of a free state, the right of the people to bear arms shall not be infringed.' It would seem that in the late eighteenth century this meant citizens should own weapons and know how to use them to serve their state militia. That is no longer true today when there is a professional army, the FBI and police forces throughout the country. Whether the Second Amendment should be interpreted more broadly, as it is by many, to mean an individual's unconditional right to possess firearms to defend himself or herself, remains at the heart of the ongoing debate about gun control.

ABOVE: Slaves working on a cotton plantation. Slavery was the cornerstone of the Southern economy – both George Washington and Thomas Jefferson owned slaves on their Virginia plantations.

OPPOSITE: In the Massacre of Wyoming Valley in Pennsylvania in July 1778, Iroquois Indians fought alongside the British in defeating the Revolutionaries. The following year, 40 Iroquois villages were destroyed in an effort to crush their morale and their loyalty to the British.

Slavery and Liberty

Shortly after arriving in America from England in 1774, Thomas Paine witnessed a slave auction in Philadelphia – the city of brotherly love. 'With what consistency of decency,' he would write, could American slaveholders 'complain so loudly of attempts to enslave them, while they hold so many hundred thousand in slavery?'

So how did Americans reconcile their calls for liberty on the one hand with their ownership of slaves on the other? Many, particularly in the North, did not: Vermont's 1777 constitution, for instance, called slavery a violation of 'natural, inherent and inalienable rights'. And, partly through conscience and partly because uncertainty in the economy favoured free labour, some Philadelphia masters began to free their slaves in 1774. The same year, the northern colonies, as well as Virginia and Carolina, banned the Atlantic slave trade at the urging of the Continental Congress.

However, even though it violated the ideals behind the Revolution – and many realized that – totally abolishing slavery was at that time unthinkable: it was the cornerstone of the Southern economy and all white Americans, both north and south, benefited from it directly or indirectly.

'Although it violated the Revolution's ideals, abolishing slavery was unthinkable.'

Also, in parts of the South where black populations were much larger, free blacks were feared. In Georgia in November 1774, six male and four female slaves were burned alive at the stake after murdering their plantation overseer, his wife and several whites on neighbouring plantations. The punishment wasn't just torturous vengeance for the crime, but a warning against other potential rebellions.

Through the continued Atlantic slave trade in some states and through children being born into slavery, there were far more blacks enslaved at the end of the Revolutionary era than at the beginning. One thing had changed, however. The Revolution had brought an end to a different era: that of slavery's *unquestioned* existence.

A Revolution for Native Americans?

Native Americans fought on both sides in the war: the Oneidas and Tuscaroras, for instance, stayed with the Americans, while the Seneca and many other tribes, wanting to defend their lands from American encroachment, sided with the British. Inevitably, after the war, many Indians who had allied with Britain saw their lands passed to the United States. 'In endeavouring to assist you,' said a

BUILDING A CAPITAL

After independence, Congress moved from town to town at first, but it was soon decided that the new country needed a capital. America's largest city, Philadelphia – with a population of 50,000 – was the obvious contender, but no other states were willing to concede to a dominant Pennsylvania. Virginians argued that, as the Potomac River led deep into America's interior, it would make a practical and symbolic location for a new capital. So it was decided, after some political wrangling, that the capital should be built there as the gateway to America's future in the West.

In 1791, a 16km (10 mile) square piece of land was carved out of Virginia and Maryland, creating the District of Columbia, where the capital Washington would be built, although for many years it remained a squalid place, marginal to most Americans.

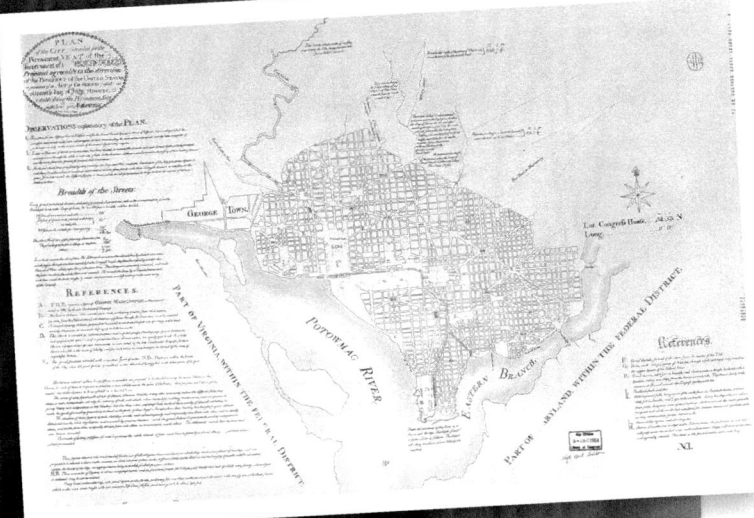

ABOVE: The plan for the capital of Washington on the Potomac River, which, Thomas Jefferson wrote, 'offers to pour into our lap the whole commerce of the Western world'.

member of the Wea tribe, 'it seems we have wrought our own ruin.' As so many Native Americans had supported Britain, almost all were now treated as enemies. The Confederation Congress of 1787 might have promised to recognize and protect Indian land rights, but in practice land speculators moved in. American independence was, in the words of historian Gordon S. Wood, 'a disaster for the Indians'.

The American Future

With support from France, the 13 colonies had managed to defeat the mother country and had gone on to forge a modern republic. To the east, conflict with Britain and even France was not yet over, while looking westward vast lands lay to be explored and exploited, fought over and conquered.

3

GOING WEST

Through wars and land purchases, the United States would more than double in size in the first half of the nineteenth century. More space, however, did not mean better treatment for Native Americans, while North and South would become further divided over slavery.

A T THE END of the War of Independence in 1783, Britain ceded to America land west of the Appalachians and north of the Ohio River. Mapping this new territory, Thomas Jefferson, in the Land Ordinance of 1785 and the Northwest Ordinance of 1787, devised a system that said when territories reached populations of 60,000 they could apply to join the Union as a state.

But, were new states to be slave states or free states? This was an issue that would last from the early years of independence until the end of slavery after the Civil War. Despite protests from the South, Congress did prohibit slavery in the new northwest states, although it conceded that slave owners could maintain the right to hunt down fugitive slaves in the new territories.

Beyond the United States, large chunks of North America were still occupied by Britain, France and Spain. Florida was in Spanish hands, as was the Louisiana Territory, which fanned out in a northwesterly direction from New Orleans and reached right up to the Canadian border. Originally French, the vast area

OPPOSITE: 'Old America seems to be breaking up, and moving westward,' wrote English traveller Morris Birkbeck in Pennsylvania in 1817. 'We are seldom out of sight, as we travel towards the Ohio River, of family groups behind and before us.'

ABOVE: Before 1803, the United States reached as far west as the Mississippi and Ohio rivers. In buying Louisiana from France, America doubled in size, gaining most of what would become 12 US states.

had in 1763 been ceded to Spain, but in 1800 it passed back to the French. Jefferson wanted New Orleans for America, however, because, as Louisiana's port, it controlled US exports, including tobacco, which passed down the Mississippi. With this in mind, $10 million was offered to France for New Orleans. It soon became clear that France's Emperor Napoleon, who was in need of funds for a planned invasion of Britain, was willing to sell not just the city but the whole of the Louisiana Territory. So, in 1803, Louisiana was sold to the United States for $15 million. How big the territory was, the Americans didn't know exactly, but they understood that they had bought a vast area from the Mississippi to the Rockies. When eventually measured, it turned out to be more than 1,300,000 square kilometres (800,000 square miles). At a stroke, the United States had doubled in size.

'The Lewis and Clark party were the first US citizens to cross the Continental Divide.'

The Lewis and Clark Expedition

Having bought Louisiana, Jefferson sent a team to explore it. The expedition was led by his protégé, Captain Meriwether Lewis, and Lewis's friend, Lieutenant William Clark. They were to travel up the Missouri River, map the new territory and find a passage across to the Pacific coast.

Setting off in 1804 with a party of 32 soldiers, 10 civilians, Clark's slave and a few Native American guides and interpreters, they navigated their way up the Missouri and crossed the Rocky Mountains at Lemhi Pass (on the present-day Montana–Idaho border). This was the US frontier. French and British fur trappers had been active in the American interior since the eighteenth century, but the Lewis and Clark party were the first US citizens to cross the Continental Divide. From the Rockies, they made their way by canoe down to the Pacific coast, building a fort at the mouth of the Columbia River in Oregon. This was not just to protect themselves, but also for political reasons. It was important to establish an American presence in the area before the British or French did.

Returning to St Louis after two and a half years, both men became governors – Clark of Missouri, Lewis of Louisiana – but within three years Lewis would be dead. Having suffered for a long time from psychotic episodes, one evening he began raging and before the morning he had shot himself.

The mission, though, had been a great success. Although they had travelled 12,875km (8000 miles) into wild and sometimes hostile territory, their journey is remarkable for how well they fared, with their party suffering just one fatality – from a ruptured appendix. They had also had largely friendly encounters with

BELOW: Meriwether Lewis (centre) and William Clark (left) with Indian guide Sacagawea on their expedition's 12,875km (8000 mile) journey up the Missouri River, across the Rocky Mountains and on to the Pacific Ocean.

more than 70 native tribes. Only when Blackfeet Indians in Montana tried to steal guns did the situation end with two of the Native Americans being shot. Furthermore, although neither Lewis nor Clark was well educated, they had mapped new terrain, written studies of Native American tribes, and had coined almost a thousand terms for places, plants and animals. Without them we might know the 'Great Plains' and 'grizzly bear' by very different names.

A DUEL WITH THE VICE PRESIDENT

Duelling had been declared illegal in New Jersey, but that didn't stop Jefferson's vice president, Aaron Burr, and the former secretary of the Treasury, Alexander Hamilton, drawing pistols in July 1804.

Political rivals, their differences escalated when Hamilton was quoted in a newspaper as saying that he didn't believe Burr should be 'trusted with the reins of government'. When Hamilton refused to recant his words and other slurs, Burr made his challenge.

At the duel, both men fired and Hamilton was mortally wounded. Indicted for murder, Burr fled back to Washington where, beyond the jurisdiction of New Jersey, he was able to see out the final months of his vice presidency in peace. Never brought to trial for the murder, he spent the rest of his life in relative obscurity.

BELOW: Vice president Aaron Burr kills one of the Founding Fathers, Alexander Hamilton, in a duel in 1804.

LEFT: In an effort to suppress Indian tribes opposed to US expansion, General Arthur St Clair led troops into the Ohio Valley in 1791, where many were massacred by Indian warriors.

First nations, foreign nations

As America pushed west, Indians were repeatedly nudged off the map, or considered 'foreign nations' within the new republic. Jefferson saw them as 'noble savages' who, at best, would learn to live and farm like white Americans rather than roam as nomadic hunters. Failing that, they would have to remove themselves beyond the Mississippi.

Where the Indians weren't willing to give up their ancestral lands, violence broke out. Settlers told stories of Indian scalpings and massacres, and, tellingly, in 1789, the US government placed Indian affairs under the jurisdiction of the War Department. Then, in 1791, General Arthur St Clair led an army of 2000 enlistees into the Ohio Valley to pacify tribes opposed to the expansion. With many of St Clair's men deserting due to lack of provisions, pay and training, Indian warriors defeated the Americans, killing around 600 of them, wounding 300 more and forcing the remainder to flee. To ritually finish the affair, the Indians stuffed the mouths of dead soldiers with soil. It was the largest defeat in history of a US Army unit by Native Americans.

Although significant, their victory was short-lived. George Washington sent greater numbers of troops against the Ohio Valley Indians, and, in August 1794, at Fallen Timbers in northern Ohio, the tribesmen were driven from the field, with hundreds being killed. When the surviving Indians fled to Fort Miami (now Maumee, Ohio), the British refused to open the gates as it risked provoking further conflict with the US. Defeated, the Indians ceded nearly all of present-day Ohio along with part of Indiana.

> 'To ritually finish the affair, the Indians stuffed the mouths of dead soldiers with soil.'

ABOVE: Thirty years after winning independence from Britain, the United States declared war on its former European ruler. During the conflict, the British set Washington's public buildings on fire – the only time that the capital has been occupied by a foreign power.

In 1809, however, an inspirational chief, Tecumseh, emerged from the Shawnee and pulled together a union of tribes in Ohio country and further south among the Creek. In their thousands, the Native Americans successfully resisted the US until their cause became muddied with international affairs – when the US went to war with Britain.

The British on Capitol Hill

How was it that within 30 years of Britain recognizing American independence, the US would declare war on the European power and British redcoats would sack Washington?

At first, the Napoleonic Wars had proved a good commercial opportunity for the US. Jefferson's approach was to let the Europeans have their war and trade with both sides without getting hurt or involved. Both Britain and France, however, saw that as undermining their war efforts and each routinely intercepted American merchant ships they believed to be trading with the other. Once on board the ships, the British not only confiscated goods, but frequently pressganged sailors to serve with them. In all, the Royal Navy kidnapped 3800 American sailors during this period.

While Britain blocked America's trade with Europe and the West Indies, the US imposed embargoes on Britain, too – although this hurt America more than Britain. In time, France agreed to respect US shipping, but Britain's blockade continued. So, in 1812, President James Madison presented the case for war: either the US would fight or accept subordination in international affairs to the British. Congress chose war.

In the two-and-a-half-year conflict there was no major front and most of the land fighting involved American attempts to secure control of Canada. The British, with so many troops tied up in Europe, turned to the Shawnee chief Tecumseh for support. Together, the British and Indian forces occupied Detroit and Fort Dearborn (present-day Chicago), before pulling back to the north side of the Great Lakes. When Tecumseh was killed in battle in 1813, however, his confederacy, lacking his charismatic leadership, fell apart.

> 'The Americans killed 300 British soldiers while losing just 13 lives on their side.'

Opening a new front the following year, the British attacked Washington, before burning its public buildings, including Capitol Hill and the presidential mansion – which, when painted white after the war, became known as the White House. The last major battle came with the British assault on New Orleans in January 1815. Having launched an attack on the earthworks outside the city, the British had failed to bring any ladders, and their troops were picked off as they clambered over each other's shoulders. Easily victorious, the Americans killed 300 British soldiers while losing just 13 lives on their side. As it happened, the whole assault was in vain: the two countries had already signed a peace treaty a month earlier in Ghent in the United Netherlands, but the news had not yet reached America.

Peace re-established the status quo: the borders remained unchanged and the embargoes were no longer an issue as the Anglo–French wars had ended, while the protection of Indian lands, which the British had called for just months earlier, was not secured.

The Indian Removal Act

In the southeast, Native Americans had made a great effort to assimilate, accepting Protestant missionaries, establishing schools and even owning slaves. With long traditions of agriculture and settlement rather than nomadic life, they were better suited than other tribes to follow European models. After three centuries of European presence, blood was now often mixed. John Ross, chief of the Cherokee, for instance, was the son of a Scottish trader and a part-Indian mother. A successful cotton producer and slave owner, in politics he encouraged assimilation. Among their own people, the Cherokee adopted a two-house legislature and a judicial system. But Ross also argued for Cherokee rights, to the extent that in 1827 the Cherokee, largely located in Georgia, declared their independence from the US.

Not only was this anathema to the white people of Georgia, the following year gold was discovered on Cherokee land and Georgia's state legislature passed a law affirming that all the Cherokee came under its jurisdiction. The Cherokee responded that their sovereignty was negotiated with the federal government, not state law.

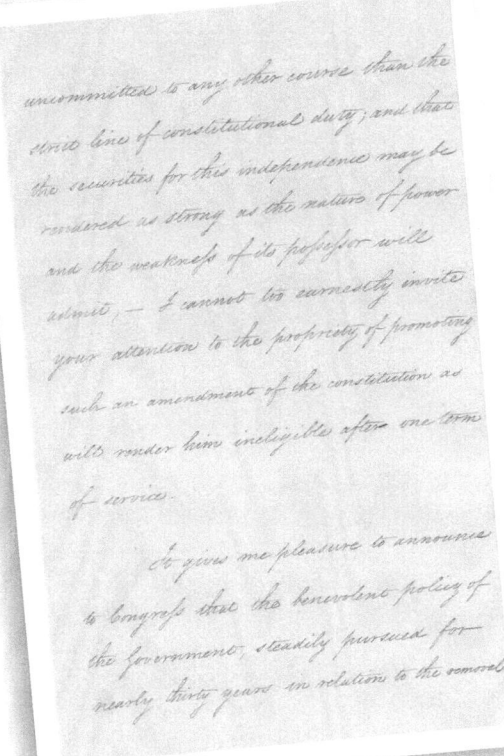

BELOW: Despite protestations from Northern states, the Indian Removal Act was passed in 1830, paving the way for the forced expulsion of tens of thousands of Indians from their homelands in America's southeast.

Making it a federal matter did not help the Cherokee – President Andrew Jackson was fully in favour of Indian removal. In his first State of the Union message in December 1829, Jackson asked: 'What good man would prefer a country covered with forest and ranged by a few thousand savages to our extensive republic, studded with cities, towns and prospective farms?' He requested that Congress set aside 'an ample district west of the Mississippi' for Indian tribes to live in under their own governments with minimal control from Washington. If they were to remain, the Indians would have to be subject to state laws.

To the Protestant North, where there were few Native Americans left, the suggestion of removing the Indians westwards, and failing to convert them to Christianity, was received with horror. Was that the behaviour of a country founded on 'life, liberty and the pursuit of happiness'? As Senator Theodore Frelinghuysen of New Jersey pointed out: 'We successfully and triumphantly contended for the very rights and privileges that our Indian neighbours now implore us to protect.' Nevertheless, the Indian Removal Act was passed in 1830.

Of the 'Five Civilized Tribes' in the Southeast, the Chickasaw Nation, Choctaw and Creek were the first to sign up for removal and swap their territory for land further west. The Seminole in Florida, however, fought back, claiming that the treaty had been forced upon them. It would take six years and 1500 American dead before they were crushed, with many Indians dead or forcibly removed, leaving just pockets of tribespeople who had been joined by runaway slaves.

Meanwhile the Cherokee, led by John Ross, fought on, but through the courts rather than on the battlefield. In 1831, Ross took his suit, that it was a federal not a state matter, to the Supreme Court. Two justices agreed with him; the other five did not. With legal channels exhausted, the Cherokee were finally pushed out of their homes at gunpoint. Herded into stockades, hundreds died of malnutrition and dysentery. The survivors, about 13,000, were marched west of the Mississippi, with a quarter dying on the way. The new land in the west was guaranteed by the US government – but the same had been said about the land the Indians had just lost.

OPPOSITE: **John Ross, Chief of the Cherokee, was the son of a Scottish trader and a part-Indian mother. A successful cotton producer, he attempted to resist the removal of his tribe westwards, not by waging war, but through the US courts.**

> **'Herded into stockades, hundreds died of malnutrition and dysentery.'**

In the 1820s, about 125,000 Indians lived east of the Mississippi. Twenty years later there were only 30,000, mostly on reservations around the Great Lakes. Freed up, the land in the southeast could now be exploited for an industry that was surging ahead: cotton production.

Slaves

What kind of future did this new, optimistic republic promise its slaves? Although Pennsylvania became the first state to abolish slavery, in 1780, that did not spell immediate liberty. Slaves were economic assets to be exploited, so the new law meant that no slave born before 1 March of that year in the state was freed, and that any slave born after 1 March would not be freed until the age of 28. That way, there would not be any free slaves in Pennsylvania until 1808 at the earliest.

Still, by 1804, all the Northern states, where there were about 30,000 slaves, had introduced similar laws that would gradually abolish slavery. In 1808, Congress voted to end US participation in the African slave trade within two years. Despite more than 150,000 slaves being shipped to the US between 1801 and 1810 – the highest figure for any decade in American history – it must have seemed that, with the new legislation, slavery was about to die out in the US.

DENMARK VESEY AND NAT TURNER

If lottery winners are usually remembered for their frivolous spending, slave Denmark Vesey was the exception: in 1800, he won $1500 on a lottery and with it bought his freedom. A carpenter by trade, Vesey went on to lead a breakaway black Methodist church in Charleston, South Carolina. His fiery rhetoric called for slaves to fight for their freedom, but in 1822 Vesey was convicted of plotting a slave revolt. What was really being planned is unclear and was probably exaggerated by white leaders, but Vesey and 30 others were hanged.

Nine years later, slave Nat Turner did lead a rebellion of more than 70 slaves and free blacks in Virginia. As they moved from plantation to plantation freeing slaves, more than 55 white men, women and children were killed. The retaliation, however, was even bloodier. Although the rebellion was crushed within two days, more than 200 black people, many uninvolved in the rebellion, were subsequently killed by a white mob. Convicted, Turner was hanged, beheaded and quartered. Fifteen other slaves and one free black man were also hanged, while 12 slaves were sold out of state.

After the successful anti-slavery revolution in Haiti (1791–1804), Nat Turner's rising had confirmed Southern fears of a slave insurrection and states now passed laws restricting slaves, like Vesey, from gaining their freedom.

RIGHT: Captured after his slave rebellion was crushed, Nat Turner was tried and executed.
BELOW: A statue of Denmark Vesey, erected in Charleston, South Carolina, in 2014.

In fact, the opposite was true. The ending of America's involvement in the Atlantic trade only increased the value in the domestic slave market. Owners now bred slaves for sale and, as the Southern states introduced slavery into new states, demand increased. Across the Americas as a whole, the US had imported the smallest proportion of African slaves, but by the time of the Civil War in 1861 it would be home to four million, the largest slave population in both North and South America.

The demand for slaves was driven by cotton production. With mechanical innovations, short-staple cotton could now be produced 50 times more quickly than in the eighteenth century – if there were the hands to pick it. Using slave labour, it could be a profitable product for the world market, and production expanded right across the South.

Jefferson certainly appreciated the injustice of slavery, but he also understood the economy of the South and depended on 200 slaves to work his own Virginia plantation. Although he believed that Indians could be 'civilized' to become Americans, he felt that blacks and whites were bound by their slave–master relationship, and that the best future for black people would be to establish their own nations in Africa, even though many of them had never been there.

An auction house in Atlanta, Georgia, photographed by George N. Barnard during the Union occupation of the city in the Civil War. The man reading is an African-American soldier from the Union Army.

So, at the same time that slaves in the North were beginning to experience their freedom, slavery in the South was being strengthened. After months of political debate as to whether new states would be slave states or free, in 1820 Congress drew an east–west line through the country, stating that all new states north of 36 degrees 30, would be barred to slavery. Known as the Missouri Compromise, this may have temporarily settled the matter, but it effectively partitioned the country, reinforcing the divisions between North and South. Jefferson prophetically referred to it as 'a fire bell in the night'.

Texas and Mexico

By 1821, the US was no longer the only United States in North America. The United States of Mexico had just gained its independence from colonial Spain and, reaching across the southwest of North America and far up the Pacific Coast, it was roughly the same size as the US. But it was Catholic and didn't permit slavery, which proved to be a problem for the American settlers pushing into its states of Texas and California. With slaves making up 20 per cent of the US population, the 40,000 settlers in Texas had no intention of changing their ways – so much so that in 1835 they declared Texas an independent state.

It was a bold move, but Mexico wasn't going to let Texas go. Troops were sent in, skirmishes followed and, after a 13-day siege, on 6 March 1836, numerically superior Mexican forces stormed the Alamo fort near San Antonio. In the battle, 600 Mexicans died and all the Texan and American defenders, more than 180 of them, were killed. The following month, a Texan-American force led by Sam Houston – with the famous rallying cry of 'Remember the Alamo!' – surprised the Mexican Army, defeating the enemy in 20 minutes at the Battle of San Jacinto.

BELOW: Former congressman and frontiersman Davy Crockett wields his rifle like a club as the Texan defenders are overrun by Mexican soldiers at the Alamo.

Although Mexico now conceded independence to the new Republic of Texas, this didn't mean that the territory would automatically become part of the US. That would have upset the delicate balance struck between the number of slave and free states, which had been maintained by only allowing them to enter in pairs: one slave state with one free state. Therefore, Texas's destiny remained uncertain for almost a decade.

Promised Land
During this period, America was changing – it was building, and very quickly. In 1825, its first manmade waterway, the 584km (363-mile) Erie Canal, connecting the Hudson River with Lake Erie, was opened; within 15 years, America would have more than 5311km (3300 miles) of canals. In the same period, it built just as many kilometres of railway, almost double that of Europe. As well as transport, the telegraph, which was pioneered in the US in the 1830s, offered a rapid form of long-distance communication.

The result was that the idea of a nation reaching from the Atlantic to the Pacific became both conceivable and within reach. Internationally, the US were pioneers, too, dominating the whaling industry and establishing links with China as early as 1784, where they undercut the British East India Company.

> 'Finally, the US invaded Mexico, blockaded its ports and occupied Mexico City.'

While the population of the US nearly doubled over these years, Mexico remained largely agrarian, its fragile union of states near to collapse, and its population only increasing slightly to seven million.

With expansionist fervour at full rein, in 1844 the emerging American Democrat Party began campaigning for the 're-annexation of Texas' – although, in truth, Texas had never been properly annexed in the first place. Legislation was pushed through Congress and, in 1845, Texas became a state, with US troops asserting a claim of a border with Mexico along the Rio Grande, much further south than the existing frontier. At the same time, an envoy was sent to Mexico City offering up to $40 million for New Mexico and California.

The envoy's offers were flatly rejected. But, when Mexican troops crossed the Rio Grande and left 16 US soldiers dead or wounded, the new Democrat president, James K. Polk, used the pretext to call for military action, claiming that Mexico had 'invaded our territory and shed American blood on American soil'.

Mexican resistance in Texas proved stronger than anticipated, however, and the war dragged on for two years (1846–48). Finally, the US invaded Mexico, blockaded its ports and occupied Mexico City, forcing the Mexicans to the negotiating table. The ensuing Treaty of Guadalupe Hidalgo, signed in February 1848, gave the US all of the provinces of New Mexico and California in exchange for $15 million – the same price that they had paid for the Louisiana Territory almost 50 years earlier, but for even more land. Mexico lost half of its landmass, while the land the US gained – what would become the states of Arizona, New Mexico, Nevada, Utah and California – makes up roughly a quarter of the nation today.

The shape of modern America was now taking form. Two years earlier, the US had come to an agreement with Britain over the northern border, dividing the Northwest along the 49th Parallel. This pushed the British out of Oregon County, but gave both countries access to the Juan de Fuca Strait, allowing Britain to build an ice-free port at Vancouver.

RIGHT: The California Gold Rush of 1849 was followed by later mineral discoveries across the West – silver in Nevada, gold in Colorado, copper in Montana and zinc in Idaho. Here prospectors wash and pan for gold in the Dakota Territory in 1889.

"357. "We have It Rich." - Washing and panning gold, Rockerville, Dak. Old timers, Spriggs, Lamb and Dillon at work. Photo and copyright by Crabill, 1889.

THE DONNER PARTY

Going west full of the pioneering spirit of 'manifest destiny' – the mid-century concept that the land was America's God-given right to inhabit – wasn't, understandably, sufficient to ensure a safe arrival. Many people perished on the journey, either from hostile encounters with Indians, drowning at river crossings, thirst or starvation. Some of the worst hardships were suffered by the Donner Party. In May 1846, a loose train of pioneering families, led by George Donner and numbering 90 adults and children, left Independence, Missouri, for California, a journey of more than 2253km (1400 miles). Rather than taking the established Oregon Trail, they followed a new route plotted by adventurer and author Lansford W. Hastings, which crossed Utah's Wasatch Mountains and the Great Salt Lake Desert. Instead of saving time, as Hastings had boasted, this added 240km (150 miles) to their journey, meaning that it was already November when they reached the Sierra Nevada mountains.

With snow falling unusually early, the families soon found themselves snowbound. Seeking help, a party of the 17 strongest members set out for Sutter's Fort near Sacramento, California, more than 160km (100 miles) away. With only six days of provisions – the most the party could afford to spare – they were soon starving. When members began to die, the others resorted to cannibalism, labelling the human meat so that no one would eat their own kin. After six weeks crossing the mountains, just seven survivors reached the fort and found help.

Those who had remained at the mountain camps also cannibalized their dead before the rescue party reached them in the spring. In all, 47 of the original 90 members of the Donner Party survived the crossing.

California could be bountiful, but reaching it was largely a journey into the unknown, trusting, in this case, Hastings's unfounded claims of a shortcut. J. Quinn Thornton, who had travelled part of the route with the Donner Party, later dubbed Hastings the 'Baron Munchausen of travellers'.

ABOVE: Stranded crossing the Sierra Nevada mountains in the winter of 1846, some members of the Donner Party began to die of starvation. Others were later forced to cannibalize the dead to survive.

The Gold Rush

The drive of people westwards surged with the discovery of gold in California in 1848. Two years earlier, there had been about 10,000 people in California; by 1849, there were 80,000, and, by 1860, there were 380,000 non-Indian people. But the newcomers weren't all from the US: within two years, 25,000 Chinese had arrived, along with Latin Americans, Australians and Europeans.

With California not yet a state, it was a near-lawless place allowing prospectors to take what land they wanted for free, rather than having to buy land off the government as they did elsewhere. That said, few of the prospectors got really rich; canny merchants supplying the miners did better. Levi Strauss, for instance, had gone west with the intention of selling canvas for tents before realizing that the biggest demand lay in hard-wearing denim trousers, while laundries, boarding houses and brothels sprang up to cater for the new population. Boomtowns quickly developed, but could just as quickly become ghost towns once the gold ore was exhausted or easier pickings were found elsewhere. Ships in the port of San Francisco were even abandoned by their crews, who, on arrival, joined the rush. With the unmanned boats clogging up the harbour, many were broken up and the wood used for new housing in the rapidly expanding city.

Native Americans once again suffered as the prospectors pushed them off their land or allowed the silt from mines to poison their crops. This led to violent conflicts. One of the bloodiest was the 1852 Bridge Gulch Massacre in California, when more than 150 Wintu were killed by about 70 Americans led by the sheriff of Trinity County. A revenge attack after the Wintu had killed a US colonel, it later emerged that the Wintu that the Americans butchered were not the ones responsible for the colonel's death.

ABOVE: Despite protestations from abolitionists, when California entered the Union as a free state, a concession was made to slave states: henceforth, runaway slaves caught in free states had to be returned to their Southern owners.

The Compromise of 1850

The growth in population in California led by the Gold Rush once again unsettled the balance between North and South. As the population in the more urbanized North and in the West was increasing at a far greater rate than in the South, free states would have more seats in the House of Representatives – seats being based on each state's population. If this trend were to continue, argued Senator John C. Calhoun of South Carolina in 1850, a Congress dominated by free states would force the South to choose 'between abolition and secession'. He was right.

To avert abolition or secession – for the time being, at least – when California entered the Union as a free state in 1850, a concession was made to the South in the form of the Fugitive Slave Law. Citizens were forbidden from helping fugitive slaves, and Northern states would be required to assist the South in returning fleeing slaves to their masters.

Land of the Free

By 1850, the US reached east–west from the Atlantic to the Pacific, its borders were largely settled, its cities growing, its industries thriving. However, the division between North and South, between slave states and free states, had only become more entrenched as the first half of the nineteenth century progressed. Soon it would pitch the nation into civil war.

4

THE CIVIL WAR

Given the long-standing differences between North and South over slavery, it is less remarkable that they eventually went to war than that violent conflict was avoided for so long. But when war did erupt, the conflict would be particularly bloody, with more American lives lost than in both World Wars combined.

In Georgia in 1848, a slave called Ellen Craft cut her hair short, put on men's clothes and, being light-skinned enough to pass for white, posed as a sickly white gentleman heading north for medical treatment. To complete the picture, accompanying 'him' was a black male servant – who was in fact Craft's slave husband, William. In that way, Ellen and William Craft escaped to freedom. Their tale is one of the more remarkable and celebrated regarding fugitive slaves, but throughout the nineteenth century several hundred slaves a year fled north, assisted by the 'underground railroad' of sympathizers.

The Crafts settled in Boston, where William found work as a cabinetmaker. However, two years after their escape, the Fugitive Slave Bill was passed and the Crafts' former slave owner sent two agents to recapture them. With blacks and whites in Boston vehemently opposed to slavery, the Crafts were protected, while the agents were harassed in the streets. After a couple of days, the pursuers gave up. To some this was 'mob law', and President Millard Fillmore denounced the

OPPOSITE: During the Civil War, the North had a larger population, more industry, control of the US Navy and more than three times the number of white men of military age. The South, though, had some international support, notably from Britain.

RIGHT: Fugitive slave Ellen Craft – disguised as a sickly white man as part of the escape she and her husband made when they fled to Boston in 1848. When agents were sent to recapture them, the Crafts were protected by free blacks and white sympathizers.

actions of the Bostonians. Meanwhile, the Crafts' friends helped them onto a ship bound for England.

The Crafts had escaped again, but in the 1850s there were 332 cases of alleged former slaves being forcibly returned to the South. Some had fled north years earlier, but in February 1851, a black man was taken from his wife and family in southern Indiana and returned to an owner who claimed that he was a slave who had run away nearly 20 years before. The burden of proof lay with the man to prove that he was free, not with the agents to prove he was the slave they were seeking. In response to the new law, many people in northern black communities fled across the border to Canada – an estimated 3000 moving there in 1850 alone.

Violent Protests

'*Civil War – The First Blow Struck*' read a headline in a Lancaster, Pennsylvania, newspaper in September 1851 – more than a decade before the Civil War broke out. The story reported how a slave owner had ventured north to recapture two slaves and had been shot dead on encountering armed resistance from 24 free blacks. To the South, this was an act of insurrection supported by fanatics, and President Fillmore sent in the Marines. Although several arrests were made of both black and white men, charges were later dropped.

Not that the North was universally in favour of abolition. Former slaves moving into free communities in northern cities were repeatedly attacked by mobs, as in Providence, Rhode Island, in 1831; a decade later the black population was expelled from Cincinnati.

While defenders of slavery in the South argued that, unlike wage earners who might risk unemployment and even starvation, slaves were looked after for life, the abolitionist movement in the North among whites and blacks continued to grow.

RIGHT: A $500 reward offered for a runaway slave from Missouri named 'Aaron or Ape'. In the 1850s, there were 332 cases of alleged former slaves being forcibly returned from free states to the South under the Fugitive Slave Law.

Not that everything was straightforward among some abolitionists. While slavery might well be considered a moral abomination, self-interest could complicate anti-slavery feeling. Would the spread of slavery result in more slaves fleeing to free states, and, thus, in competing for jobs, push down wages, some people worried. Would slave states develop more competitive manufacturing industries than Northern states? Or would slave plantations become established in the West to rival free farms? The debate raged back and forth across the states.

Bleeding Kansas

The Missouri Compromise of 1820 had stated that all states north of the 36 degrees 30 line were barred from slavery, but by the 1850s this was being undermined. The Compromise of 1850 allowed Utah Territory, all of which was north of the line, to choose whether or not it should be a 'free' state. Meanwhile, California, most of which lay *south* of the line, had chosen to enter the Union as such.

Then, in 1853, Democratic Senator Stephen A. Douglas's Kansas-Nebraska Act allowed the new territories of Kansas and Nebraska – both of which were north of the line and had been carved out of what had previously been termed 'permanent' Indian territory – to settle their slavery issue by popular vote. Many in the North feared that slavery would now expand across the West.

In response to the act, a new political player, the Republican Party, emerged. While Whigs and Democrats had support across North and South, Republicans were dedicated to stopping slavery's further expansion. In time, the party would be joined by Abraham Lincoln, a former Whig Congressman and lawyer working in Illinois.

With both pro-slavery and anti-slavery factions moving into Kansas to swing the state their way, violent conflict erupted there, with pro-slavery forces burning the free-soil town of Lawrence in 1856. In response, Massachusetts abolitionist John Brown led a group that killed five pro-slavery settlers near Pottawatomie Creek, in Franklin County. Armed anti-abolitionists took over polling stations, casting fraudulent ballots to elect a pro-slavery legislature, and guerrilla fighting spread quickly across the state, resulting in 200 deaths.

The question was, could, or would, the Supreme Court reinforce the Missouri Compromise? Alas, no. In 1857, the case of Dred Scott came up. As a slave who had been taken to the free territory of Minnesota, was he free and therefore exempt from later sale as a chattel? The Supreme Court decided that not only was Scott not free, but that Congress had no right to forbid slavery in the territories, and that, as a non-citizen, Scott had no right to sue. With that decision, slavery was free to expand. The Missouri Compromise had been repealed.

BELOW: Dred Scott's case arguing for his freedom from slavery caused public outrage and deepened tensions between North and South when it was rejected by the Supreme Court in 1857.

'Armed anti-abolitionists took over polling stations, casting fraudulent ballots.'

John Brown's Body

Fanatic? Murderer? Prophet? John Brown's violent protests against slavery were condemned by some in both the North and the South. His final action was an attempt to establish liberated zones in the hills of western Virginia, by leading 18 followers, five of whom were black, against a federal arsenal at Harper's Ferry in October 1859. Hoping to spark a slave revolt, his raid was a mess; within two days, most of his men had been killed or captured. He received the death penalty, a punishment that inevitably made him a martyr for the abolitionist cause.

Tensions rose across the country in 1860, with mob attacks on suspected abolitionists, and boycotts against northern goods, while in Texas a vigilante outbreak resulted in the deaths of a hundred suspected dissidents. In November of that year, Republican candidate Abraham Lincoln won the presidential election – unsurprisingly gaining virtually no seats in the South. With an anti-slavery party now in power, South Carolina seceded from the Union, followed by the Deep South states of Mississippi, Alabama, Louisiana, Georgia, Florida and Texas. In February 1861, the Confederate States of America were born.

> 'John Brown's raid was a mess and most of his men were soon killed or captured.'

President Lincoln

Lincoln's presidency not only ended in an assassination, it began with his efforts to avoid one. Fearing an attack by pro-slavery vigilantes before his inauguration, he disguised himself as an invalid to travel on a special train through Philadelphia and Baltimore, arriving before dawn in the capital for the ceremony. It was an inauspicious beginning to a presidency that would see the Union torn apart and then be recast as free to all black people.

Not that Lincoln was a dogmatic abolitionist. His two basic aims in the war were to stop the further expansion of slavery westwards and to preserve the Union. 'I have no purpose, directly or indirectly, to interfere with the institution of slavery in the States where it exists,' he said in his inaugural address in March 1861. 'We are not enemies,' he said of the Confederacy, 'but friends...', even though the new Confederacy had already elected Jefferson Davis as its president.

Going to War

Statistically, the North had a huge advantage over the South. It had twice the population, vastly more industry, more railways, 75 per cent of the nation's farmland, 16,000 men in its army and 90 warships. In sum, it controlled 75 per cent of the country's wealth.

The only hope for the first seven Confederate states was in enlisting the help of the Upper South – the more northerly, industrialized states – in particular Virginia. That way, it might be able to drag out the conflict long enough for the North to become war weary and give in to secession.

However, even in a conflict about slavery, the issues were not always clear-cut: Kentucky, Maryland and Missouri were border states in the Union that were also slave-owning. Meanwhile, in areas of the South with few or no slaves, such as the Appalachian uplands, there was Unionist sentiment.

First Blood

The opening shots of the war were an artillery bombardment from Charleston, South Carolina, at Fort Sumter – a federal property commanded by Major Robert

OPPOSITE: **John Brown** was found guilty of murder, treason against the Commonwealth of Virginia and inciting a slave rebellion. Although fitting his character, it is a myth that he kissed a black child on his way to the gallows.

SLAVES IN THE CAPITAL

In the 1840s, the District of Columbia (D.C.) – which encompasses Washington – still had a thriving slave market in its city of Alexandria. Fearing abolition, D.C.'s pro-slavery residents petitioned Virginia to take back the land, including Alexandria, that it had donated to help form the District in the 1790s. With Congress in agreement, in July 1846 that land was returned to Virginia.

The Compromise of 1850 abolished the slave trade in D.C., though not slavery itself. That lasted until the Civil War, when, in 1862, slaves there were emancipated, with slaveholders receiving up to $300 per freed slave. Each newly freed slave was given $100 if he or she chose to settle in places such as Haiti or Liberia – the idea persisting that the US was a white society and blacks might be better off abroad. Some blacks were also compensated as slave owners, having once bought their family members away from other owners. In all, 3185 slaves in D.C. were freed.

Anderson. With few supplies, Anderson could hold out for only a day and a half before he had to surrender.

The fall of Fort Sumter was sufficient to persuade Virginia to secede. Arkansas, North Carolina and Tennessee followed, making a total of 11 Confederate states. Who, though, was to lead them?

Lincoln had offered command of the Union army to Robert E. Lee, but Lee found his loyalties divided: although devoted to the Union, he was a Virginian. After much anguish, he resigned his commission in the Union Army and rode south to Richmond, Virginia, the new Confederate capital, and little more than 160km (100 miles) from Washington. There he accepted the command of the Confederate Army.

RIGHT: Confederate soldiers occupy Fort Sumter, Charleston, South Carolina, after the surrender of the Union Army in the war's first engagement. Crucially for the Confederates, this victory persuaded the more industrialized state of Virginia to side with them.

Bull Run

The first true battle of the Civil War came in July 1861 at Bull Run Creek, just 40km (25 miles) from Washington. With ill-prepared Union soldiers, many of whom were nearing the end of the 90-day term for which they had signed up, the battle quickly turned into a rout when the Confederates surged forward. Many Union troops drowned trying to cross Bull Run Creek: it was a humiliating defeat for the Union. But Bull Run (or Manassas, as it is also known) did prompt the North to take the war more seriously.

Grant and Shiloh

Robert E. Lee had been lost to the Union when war broke out. Ulysses S. Grant, who would become the other great leader of the war, wasn't even in the Union Army, let alone leading a unit. Grant was a former soldier who had been thrown out of the army for drinking; failing to find any other purpose in life, he was selling leather goods in his father's shop in Illinois. Now the army needed him back.

By 1862, Grant was a brigadier general, making his name at the Battle of Shiloh in Tennessee – although it didn't begin well for him. On the first morning of the battle, 6 April, the Confederates surprised the Unionists, who, though fighting on, were driven back in disarray. It was a disaster for the North. However, thousands of reinforcements arrived overnight, and the following morning it was the Unionists' turn to push the exhausted Confederates off the battlefield. The death toll was immense: about 13,000 Union troops were killed, while the Confederates lost about 10,500. In fact, more Americans died at Shiloh than in all the country's previous wars combined.

> 'More Americans died at Shiloh than in all the country's previous wars combined.'

The Battle of Shiloh, in Tennessee in April 1862, began as a disaster for the Unionists when they were surprised by Confederate forces. But, having been reinforced overnight, the Unionists pushed the exhausted Confederates off the battlefield the following day.

Despite the Union victory at Shiloh, by the summer things were looking so promising for the South that Lee invaded the North, hoping that it might result in Britain recognizing the Confederacy. If, as Lincoln said, the war was about preserving the Union, not about freeing slaves, then secession could be regarded internationally as a fight for independence from an overbearing empire. Furthermore, Britain depended on plantation cotton to supply its textile industry and was already sufficiently sympathetic to the Confederate cause to allow it to build warships in British dockyards.

Lee's advance into Maryland, however, found the Unionists better prepared than expected. At the Battle of Antietam (Sharpsburg) on 17 September, the Union soldiers were victorious. However, losses were again huge on both sides – the combined casualties of killed and wounded reaching 23,000, making it the bloodiest single-day battle in American history. Lee's army was now too weak to continue its campaign. Emboldened, Lincoln elevated the conflict into something more than just preserving the Union.

ABOVE: 'If my name ever goes into history it will be for this act, and my whole soul is in it,' said Abraham Lincoln of the Emancipation Proclamation which, announced in September 1862, promised the freeing of blacks in rebel-held areas.

The Emancipation Proclamation

Before Antietam, there had been a chance that border states might switch to the Confederacy, but now the Unionists were on a stronger footing. Five days after the battle, Lincoln issued a preliminary emancipation proclamation, promising to free blacks in rebel-held areas from 1 January 1863. Internationally, this proved the death knell for any possible support for the Confederacy: while Britain might have backed the South in the name of freedom fighters, it definitely would not send troops to defend slavery.

Confederate President Jefferson Davis called the proclamation 'a measure by which several millions of human beings of an inferior race, peaceful and contented labourers in their sphere, are doomed to extermination, while at the same time they are encouraged to a general assassination of their masters.' That was, perhaps, an expected response. However, Lincoln had other worries when, in a backlash in the North, hundreds of soldiers deserted, and, in the 1862 elections, those Democrats pushing for a peace settlement with the Confederates leaped to 32 seats in the House.

Overall, though, across the South, the slave system was already beginning to crumble; with white masters away fighting, many slaves fled north or went on go-slows. To maintain order, when conscription was introduced in the South, those owning more than 20 slaves were exempt.

> 'Antietam remains the bloodiest single-day battle in American history.'

Black soldiers in the Union Army

In January 1863, Lincoln went a step further, declaring that freed slaves would be received into the Union's armed forces. While his motivations were partly to solve a manpower shortage, the move had wider ramifications. 'Once let the black man get upon his person the brass letter,' said former slave and campaigner Frederick Douglass, 'there is no power on earth that can deny that he has earned the right to citizenship.'

Free blacks and former slaves rushed to join up, amounting to nearly a tenth of the Union Army by the end of the war. Unsurprisingly, inequalities remained, and, until they complained, black soldiers earned $3 less a month than white ones, while, still suffering discrimination, they mostly fought in segregated units and in the lower ranks. Furthermore, if they were captured by the Confederates, they could be tried as slave insurrectionists – an offence that carried the death penalty.

BELOW: In 1863, African Americans were accepted into the Union forces. By the end of the war, more than 200,000 were serving in the Union Army and Navy.

The Battle of Gettysburg

Following a devastating defeat of Union forces at Fredericksburg in Virginia in December 1862, General Lee had a successful spring in 1863. He ran rings around the Union Army, before venturing into the North and invading Pennsylvania. What black civilians the Confederates found there were sent south into slavery.

At this point, however, Lee's army ran into General George Meade's Union forces near a small town called Gettysburg. Preparing for battle, Meade settled the Union line along low ridges. It was a strong position, but Lee, brimming with confidence after his recent victories, was not deterred. After two days of episodic fighting, on 3 July, Lee ordered his men to march forward towards the Union line, even though that meant moving across a mile of open farmland against an enemy dug in on higher ground and backed by artillery. As the Confederates advanced, the Union soldiers waited with their weapons loaded until the enemy was a couple of hundred yards away. They then fired 1700 rifles at the same time, backed by 11 cannon.

Barely any Confederate soldiers reached the Union lines – and only half of the 15,000 advancing men made it back to their own lines. Not only was the battle lost for the Confederates, after that day Lee's forces were unable to pursue the campaign. They turned back to Virginia.

> 'In just 272 words in the Gettysburg Address, Lincoln redefined the war.'

The Gettysburg Address

It took months to clear away the bodies at Gettysburg, but that November a special cemetery for Union dead was opened. Edward Everett, a celebrated orator, gave a two-hour speech, which Lincoln was requested to follow with 'a few appropriate remarks'. In all, he spoke 272 words, including these: 'the world will little note nor long remember what we say here'. He was wrong about that. In the Gettysburg Address, as his speech became known, Lincoln, from the opening 'Four score and seven years ago' to the closing 'government of the people, by the people, for the people…', redefined the war. He didn't mention the Union or Confederacy once, but said 'nation' five times – a word not used in the Declaration of Independence, which had referred to 'Free and Independent States'. Also, he anchored the speech in the values of the American Revolution – a fight for equality and liberty – while not talking about slavery specifically. As historian James M. McPherson has noted, it was after the Gettysburg Address that people largely shifted from saying 'The United States are' to 'The United States is…'.

BELOW: Given at the opening of a cemetery for Union dead in November 1863, Lincoln's Gettysburg Address reaffirmed the republic's foundations in liberty, proclaiming that 'a new birth of freedom' would bring equality to all the nation's citizens.

SUBMARINES AND BALLOONS

The Civil War witnessed a number of technological advances that would change warfare. The immense number of casualties at Antietam in 1862, for instance, was due to new rifles that were far more accurate, and their range four times greater, than earlier muskets.

The conflict also prefigured World War I with drawn-out battles fought from trenches, such as at Vicksburg, Mississippi (May–July 1863), where the Confederates were starved into submission, and at Petersburg, Virginia (June 1864–March 1865).

In naval warfare, the conflict saw the first ironclads – steam-powered, iron-hulled ships. USS *Monitor* is best known for its central role in the Battle of Hampton Roads, Virginia, in March 1862, where it was the first ironclad to encounter and defeat another ironclad – CSS *Virginia*. With a revolving turret, *Monitor*'s design would establish a type of warship in its name.

ABOVE: An observation balloon at Seven Pines, Virginia, in May 1862. With the balloon connected to telegraph wires, enemy positions could be telegrammed back to commanders.

Although they might seem to be an invention of the twentieth century, early submarines played a small role in the conflict, too. CSS *Hunley* was a 12m (40ft) submarine, powered by a crew of seven hand-cranking the propeller. Reaching a speed of 7.4km/h (4.6mph) and armed with one torpedo, in February 1864 the *Hunley* attacked and sank the warship USS *Housatonic*, which had been part of the Union blockade of Charleston. On its way back to base, however, the *Hunley* sank, with all lives lost.

Existing technologies were also put to military use. Hot-air balloons would ascend over a battlefield; then, with wires hooked up to telegraph lines, positions could be telegraphed back to commanders.

There were non-military developments, too. The Union imposed the country's first income tax and issued the first paper currency, enabling it to endure the conflict with less inflation than the South. The war also led to the revoking of some US liberties: arrest without trial was allowed, while martial law was imposed in war areas in both North and South.

BATTLE OF FORT PILLOW

In April 1864, Confederate General Bedford Forrest led his forces in attacking Fort Pillow, Tennessee, where the Union garrison consisted of 585 men, half of them black. While some on both sides claimed that the Union Army never gave in and fought to the end, the majority view from Unionists and Confederates was that the battle turned into a massacre after the Union Army had surrendered.

The Confederates suffered only 14 fatalities, but the Union lost 277 men, 80 per cent of whom were black. Were more blacks killed in the fighting simply because of where they were positioned at the fort? Or was it a case that, fearing enslavement if they surrendered, they fought to the death? Or were they specifically targeted by the Confederates? Some certainly did surrender: one Confederate soldier, writing home soon after the battle, described how 'deluded negroes would run up to our men, fall upon their knees, and with uplifted hand scream for mercy, but were ordered to their feet and then shot down.' Would they have shot dead a white Union soldier who had surrendered?

Lincoln discussed the massacre with his Cabinet, wondering if he should enforce an Order of Retaliation, by which any Confederate prisoner of war would be executed if a Union prisoner were killed, and put on hard labour any POW if a Union soldier were enslaved.

In the end, no action was taken, although the Joint Committee on the Conduct of the War investigated the events. In the South, General Forrest regarded the losses at Fort Pillow as demonstrating 'to the Northern people that negro soldiers cannot cope with Southerners'. He later became the Grand Wizard of the Ku Klux Klan.

LEFT: At Fort Pillow, 80 per cent of the Union dead were black, although they represented only half of the Union forces present.

New York riots

John D. Rockefeller, J.P. Morgan and Andrew Carnegie all began making their names during the Civil War – but in business, not on the battlefield. With conscription introduced in the North in the spring of 1863, each legitimately paid at least $300 to be exempted from military service. For $850, Carnegie paid an Irish immigrant to take his place.

The inequality of the conscription laws did not go unnoticed, and, just weeks after the victory at Gettysburg, riots erupted in New York. In what was perhaps also an expression of war weariness, more than 100 people were killed when largely Irish crowds attacked the black population, abolitionists and draft offices. Other attacks rippled across the North.

BELOW: Protesting at the unfairness of the conscription laws – where the wealthy could pay to be exempt – riots erupted in New York in July 1863. Draft offices, blacks and abolitionists were attacked, with at least 100 lives lost.

Approaching Atlanta

Gettysburg may in hindsight be seen as a turning point in the war, but victory was by means certain for the North. Ulysses S. Grant was now in charge of the Union armies and was seeking a victory in Virginia, but at Cold Harbor in June 1864, thousands were lost in an advance on Confederate trenches, with 6000 killed in a single hour. In the same month, the Union suffered 50,000 dead or wounded in other battles, and the outskirts of Washington were attacked. At Petersburg, Grant's campaign turned into nine months of trench warfare with lines extending more than 48km (30 miles) to the outskirts of Richmond.

By the summer of 1864, it was unsurprising that Lincoln did not think he would be re-elected in November. As it happened, General William Tecumseh Sherman's force came to the rescue. Approaching from Tennessee, Sherman besieged Atlanta, before setting it on fire. He then continued a scorched earth policy until he reached the coast. The morale boost of Sherman's success helped Lincoln be re-elected.

> 'At Petersburg, Grant's campaign turned into nine months of trench warfare.'

Confederate Slave Soldiers

By 1864, the South was crumbling internally. The Northern blockade on European imports was having its effect, printing money was leading to roaring inflation, and starving soldiers were beginning to desert. The result was that by early 1865, the Confederates had begun to think the unthinkable: could they put slaves in the army in return for offering them their freedom? For four years they had fought to preserve slavery and now it was being suggested that they free the slaves. Southerners were bitterly divided on the matter, but General Lee was in favour of having them serve. 'We must decide whether slavery shall be extinguished by our enemies and the slaves be used against us,' he said, 'or use them ourselves at the risk of the effects.' Of course, by making black men soldiers, as Frederick Douglass had argued in the North, you made them citizens. As General Howell Cobb from Georgia pointed out: 'If slaves

ABOVE The hanging at Arsenal Prison, Washington, D.C., on 7 July 1865 of four of John Wilkes Booth's fellow conspirators in the assassination of President Lincoln.

will make good soldiers, our whole theory of slavery is wrong.' Desperation won the argument: blacks were accepted into the Confederate Army in March.

Two months earlier, Lincoln had succeeded in pushing the Thirteenth Amendment through Congress, ending slavery by just two votes. Many had defended slavery as part of their constitutional rights, but now the Constitution had been changed and those who might object – the Southerners – were not part of Congress to protest.

Appomattox

By April, the Confederates could no longer defend their capital, Richmond. Fires were lit as government papers were burned and supply depots were ignited. Confederate forces abandoned the city; on 4 April, Lincoln entered the smouldering ruins to a cheering crowd of black people. After a short battle in the village of Appomattox Court House five days later, General Robert E. Lee surrendered.

On 14 April, Lincoln and his wife Mary took their seats in the presidential box at Ford's Theatre in Washington to see a comedy. During the play, the president was shot in the back of the head at point-blank

> 'Between 620,000 and 750,000 lives were lost in the Civil War.'

IN INDIAN COUNTRY

As with the War of Independence, Native Americans fought – almost 29,000 of them – on both sides in the Civil War. Once again, they suffered greatly, with more than 10,000 killed. Despite the South having removed them West, generally the 'Five Civilized Tribes' retained strong ties with Southern states, directing their hostility towards the Union. The Cherokee, however, were divided and ended up fighting their own civil war. The primary dispute was between Chief John Ross and Stand Watie, both of whom were slave owners who represented different Cherokee populations: Ross's followers were poorer; Watie's were wealthier farmers. Watie became a brigadier-general in the Confederacy, while Ross's men, led by his nephew John Drew, defected north to Unionist Kansas in 1862. The following year Ross joined them and freed his own slaves.

Watie's forces fought many winning battles against Unionist Creek and Cherokee. But after the war, the Cherokee farmlands were in ruins and, devoid of a governing structure, remained violent and anarchic.

ABOVE: Slave-owning Cherokee Stand Watie became a Confederate general in the war – and didn't surrender until June 1865.

range by John Wilkes Booth. The assassin then jumped down to the stage, shouting '*Sic semper tyrannis!*' ('So is it always for tyrants') – the motto of Virginia – before fleeing. Booth, an actor who was part of a plot to save the Confederacy, was tracked down 12 days later and, refusing surrender, shot dead.

A national day of mourning marked Lincoln's funeral. After that, his coffin began the long, meandering journey back to his hometown of Springfield, Illinois, lying in state in cities along the way. It is estimated that half a million people in Philadelphia went to pay their respects.

Home of the Brave

In all, somewhere between 620,000 and 750,000 lives were lost in the Civil War, while hundreds of thousands of men were maimed. Although large parts of the Southern states were untouched by the fighting, Atlanta and Richmond were in ruins, as were many farms. The South had seceded from the Union over slavery, but rejoining it would mean accepting the Thirteenth Amendment.

Lincoln had been a moderate abolitionist, and not, originally, in favour of an equal standing between the races. In 1858, he had declared himself opposed to: 'the social and political equality of the white and black races… to making voters or jurors of negroes… nor to intermarry with white people.'

Now he had succeeded in making slaves free. But, killed at the pinnacle of his achievements, he would escape the burden of bringing the Union together again and making emancipation work.

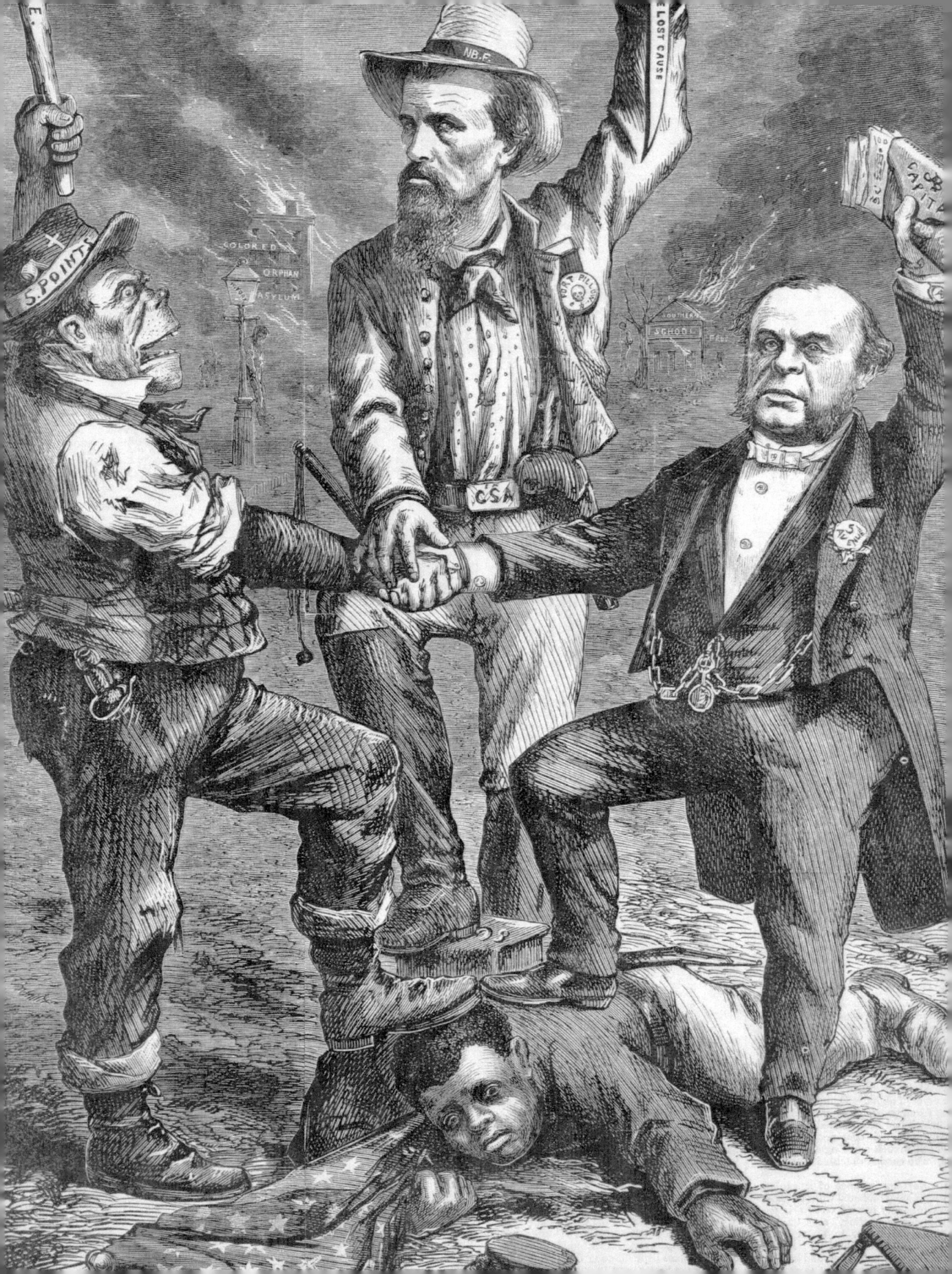

FREEDOM AND CLOSING THE FRONTIER

In the South, slaves were now free, but liberty would throw up new barriers. Meanwhile, in the North, corruption and the exploitation of the workers helped industry to boom, and, in the West, the days of being wild were nearing their end.

A THIRD OF the South had been badly affected by the Civil War, but the rest was largely untouched. The great challenge now lay in reconciling the South with the North politically, and in creating a new economy no longer based on slave labour. As it was impossible to try every Confederate as a traitor, it was agreed that a state could be readmitted to the Union once a certain proportion of its citizens had taken an oath of loyalty to the United States. By the end of 1865, state governments founded on these principles were in place in the South.

Freed slaves were happy to walk away from their plantations, but now four million free men and women – conditioned all their lives to slavery – had to find their way in the world with no property, no education and little or no money. A former slave was, said former abolitionist Frederick Douglass, 'free from the individual master but the slave of society.'

Although the Thirteenth Amendment had liberated slaves, within months most Southern states had passed legal codes aimed at keeping black people in

OPPOSITE: An 1868 campaign poster, portraying the Democratic Party as opposed to the Reconstruction and black rights while favouring the interests of: Irish Americans (left), Southern Confederates as represented by Nathan Bedford Forrest (centre), and northern businessmen, represented by financier August Belmont (right).

subordination. They were denied the right to vote or to serve on juries, nor could they testify against white people, while the Second Amendment was also refused to them – that is, they were not given the right to bear arms.

To counteract the behaviour of the states, Congress passed the Civil Rights Act, giving full citizenship to blacks, which became permanent in the Fourteenth Amendment in June 1866. Ten years earlier, the Supreme Court had declared that Dred Scott and all other blacks were not citizens. Now, according to American law, 'all persons born or naturalized in the United States were citizens'.

Still dominated by Northern states, Congress passed legislation to dissolve Southern state governments in 1867 and put the South under peacetime military rule until it was decided that they were co-operating. With such backing, all state legislatures in the South had, for the first time, black members. In the most extreme example, of the 123 members of South Carolina's House of Representatives in 1873, 100 were black. In elections, blacks had the vote, while whites who had supported the Confederacy did not. For a time, black votes outnumbered white ones. And free public education was introduced for all across the South.

> 'More than 3000 people, mainly black, were killed or wounded in battles and massacres in Louisiana.'

Ku Klux Klan

The reconstruction of the South became a great opportunity for political reform – but also, for some, for profiteering. Carpetbaggers – northerners who lived out of a suitcase and were only in town long enough to rip off someone, and scalawags – southern fellow travellers – together managed to exploit the public offices of the South through corruption and bribery.

Soon opposition to Republican rule, especially where crooks and conmen had moved in, led to the rise in Tennessee in 1866 of the Ku Klux Klan. With its members dressed in white robes and hoods, the Klan sought to terrorize black

and white supporters of the Republican Party and thereby help get a Democrat into the White House. The Klan was outlawed within five years, but in that time it had stretched its purpose to include that of police force, judge, jury and executioner. When former slave Cy Guy was believed to have made a 'scandalous insult' to a white woman in Orange County, North Carolina, the Klan came after him. 'They tries him there in the woods,' remembered former slave Ben Johnson. Then they strung him up, writing in Guy's own blood, 'that any nigger what takes down the body shall be hunged too'. Only after four days did the sheriff remove the body.

There were similar white revolutionary movements in other parts of the South. In 1874, several thousand supporters of the White League attempted an armed revolt in New Orleans. In total, in the decade to 1876, more than 3000 people, mainly black, were killed or wounded in battles and massacres in Louisiana.

One by one, the Republican state governments of the South began to fall, being replaced by regimes reflecting traditional Southern power: white landowners. By 1877, the Reconstruction that had begun at the end of the Civil War was ending. Then in 1883, the Supreme Court overturned the Civil Rights Act of 1875, which had guaranteed black access to public places. Blacks also lost their voting rights through devices such as literacy tests and poll taxes, meaning that between 1896 and 1904 the number of registered black voters in Louisiana fell from 130,000 to just 1350. Those imprisoned might find themselves labouring as convicts or on the chain gang – 'corporate public slavery in all but name', as historian Philip Jenkins describes it.

ABOVE: An 1868 political cartoon published in Alabama's *Tuscaloosa Independent Monitor*, which was edited by local Ku Klux Klan leader Ryland Randolph. The cartoon threatens that carpetbaggers and scalawags seeking to profit from the South will be hanged.

LEFT: A camp of freed slaves in the former Confederate capital of Richmond, Virginia, in 1865.

RIGHT: So-called 'Jim Crow Laws' replaced slavery with segregation. Here the Supreme Court ruled on the Plesy versus Ferguson case that separate railway carriages must be provided for blacks and whites.

JIM CROW LAW.

UPHELD BY THE UNITED STATES SUPREME COURT.

Statute Within the Competency of the Louisiana Legislature and Railroads—Must Furnish Separate Cars for Whites and Blacks.

Washington, May 18.—The Supreme Court today in an opinion read by Justice Brown, sustained the constitutionality of the law in Louisiana requiring the railroads of that State to provide separate cars for white and colored passengers. There was no interstate commerce feature in the case for the railroad upon which the incident occurred giving rise to case—Plessey vs. Ferguson—East Louisiana railroad, was and is operated wholly within the State, to the laws of Congress of many of the States. The opinion states that by the analogy of the laws of Congress, and of many of states requiring establishment of separate schools for children of two races and other similar laws, the statute in question was within competency of Louisiana Legislature, exercising the police power of the State. The judgment of the Supreme Court of State upholding law was therefore upheld.

Mr. Justice Harlan announced a very vigorous dissent saying that he saw nothing but mischief in all such laws. In his view of the case, no power in the land had right to regulate the enjoyment of civil rights upon the basis of race. It would be just as reasonable and proper, he said, for states to pass laws requiring separate cars to be furnished for Catholic and Protestants, or for descendants of those of Teutonic race and those of Latin race.

Sharecropping and Segregation

Most blacks and many whites could not afford to farm their own land, so they received plots from landowners, giving him half of their crop in a system known as sharecropping. As the former slaves lacked the cash to get started, the landowner loaned them seed and equipment on credit, driving them into debt. Furthermore, being illiterate, many former slaves were open to exploitation by the sharp practice of some landowners regarding the contracts they were asked to agree. Some virtually re-enslaved themselves through documents they unwittingly signed. 'For many black labourers and sharecroppers,' writes historian David Reynolds, 'the New South was little better than the Old.'

Where the old division had been between slave and free, in the New South the division came between black and white. 'Jim Crow' laws, as they became known, separated black and white people in public places. On trains, the 'Jim Crow' car was the hot, dirty one next to the engine. When, in 1895, Homer Plessy deliberately sat in a whites-only part of a Louisiana train, he was arrested and jailed.

Plessy managed to take his case to the Supreme Court, arguing equal rights for all citizens under the Fourteenth Amendment. However, his case was rejected, with the Court stating that the Amendment 'could not have been intended to abolish distinctions based upon color, or to enforce social, as distinguished from political, equality'. In the same ruling, the Court affirmed that segregation was legal as long as separate facilities were equal in quality, leaving it to individual states to ensure that standards of equality were maintained. They were not. Slavery had been replaced by segregation.

THE RE-ENACTMENT AT GETTYSBURG

Where today enthusiasts re-enact battles from long before they were born, at the 50th anniversary of the Battle of Gettysburg in 1913, the veterans played themselves. By then, the youngest veteran was 61 years old.

In the immediate years after the Civil War, few soldiers from North or South had taken part in veterans' events, but time is a great healer: the 1913 Gettysburg commemoration drew 50,000 people and lasted for six days.

How, though, would the two sides of combatants feel to be facing their former enemies once again? In recreating the assault of 3 July 1863 that had cost more than 7000 lives, the ageing Confederates helped each other across the fields, before reaching the Yankee line, where the Union veterans were waiting. Finally, the Union soldiers surged forward at their old foe – not in combat, but, as Philip Myers, a young observer, noticed, 'reunited in brotherly love and affection'.

There was still great ill feeling in the South about the war, but on this day, among these men, it was forgotten.

ABOVE: Union and Confederate flags held by veterans of the Battle of Gettysburg, 50,000 of whom returned for the action's 50-year commemoration in 1913.

Big City Corruption

The final third of the nineteenth century was, in the words of historian Philip Jenkins, a 'time of buccaneering capitalism at its most flagrant'. Andrew Carnegie and John D. Rockefeller may now be remembered as great philanthropists, but they were ruthless when it came to forging their way ahead in the American steel and oil industries. Similarly, the 'Erie Ring' of financiers Daniel Drew, Jim Fisk and Jay Gould – flush from their successes profiteering and blockade running during the Civil War – challenged Cornelius Vanderbilt over his efforts to monopolize the transportation systems of New York State. Both sides played dirty, fighting their battle with thugs, as well as through immense bribery of the courts, judges and public officials.

Politics had become corrupt, too. Between 1866 and 1871, New York City was controlled by a political syndicate known as the 'Tweed Ring'. Two years later, it was discovered that the Union Pacific Railroad had funded the construction of its western railway line at hugely inflated prices. To keep this quiet, shares had been distributed to US congressmen to avoid investigation.

Hard Times

With a manufacturing boom, America quickly became the factory of the world, and cities developed rapidly. The boom, however, came at a price for labourers. Shifts in Pittsburgh's steel mills could be 12 hours a day, seven days a week. And while the first skyscrapers celebrated new wealth, the poor lived in ever more confined conditions. In New York, it was not uncommon for 200 people to live in a single townhouse. By the 1880s, the slums of New York's East Side were said to be twice as densely populated as those of London.

OPPOSITE: Through ruthlessly driving competitors out of business and, at times, sanctioning violence and sabotage, John D. Rockefeller rose to dominance of the oil industry in the 1870s.

BELOW: An English coal-heaver's home in Poverty Gap on New York's Lower East Side, photographed by Jacob Riis in 1890. In good times, the father earned $5 a week at the city docks.

Despite everything, opportunities for work continued to draw immense numbers of immigrants to the US. But it is no surprise that there were labour disputes throughout the final decades of the century – often involving violent clashes with the Pinkerton Detective Agency, hired by the factory owners. In 1877, the bloodiest year, strikes by railroad workers spread to other industries, leading to protests from New York and Pittsburgh across to Ohio and Illinois, and resulting in at least 100 deaths.

In Chicago in 1893, workers at the Pullman rail plant went on strike when engineer and industrialist George Pullman made wage cuts, but refused a parallel reduction in rents for his workers in his company town. Hoodlums turned the strike into a riot, and the army was sent in, leading to 34 deaths. Then in 1914, the National Guard used the new weapon of machine guns against miners in Colorado, killing 70 people, including women and children.

> 'Hundreds of Navajo died of exhaustion on the forced march to their reservation.'

In addition to the harsh treatment from employers, the law was rarely of any help for workers; for example, the Supreme Court decided in the 1905 Lochner case that New York had no power to regulate the maximum working hours of employees. This was just one of many cases where government regulation of business activities was found to be an infringement of corporate civil rights. As historian David Reynolds writes: 'The cities were America's pride and shame, monuments to capital and capitalism, yet also the graveyard of labour.'

The Indian Wars

Across territory occupied by Native Americans, the story was repeatedly one of treaties being ignored and settlers encroaching on Indian land, leading to much bloodshed. Conflict with Native Americans in Texas, largely the Comanche, lasted for 50 years in the middle of the nineteenth century, only ending with the final Comanche moving to reservations in Oklahoma in 1875. In 1862, starving Santee Sioux rebelled against settlers in Minnesota when they had not received the provisions that they had been promised under a US treaty; they killed 700 settlers before the US Army could respond. Three hundred Indians were sentenced to death for the murders. Lincoln commuted most of the sentences, although 38 were hanged, making it the largest mass execution in US history.

In the subduing of the Navajo between 1864 and 1866, 9000 Native Americans were forced to march from their reservation in Arizona to the Bosque Redondo Reservation, 482km (300 miles) away in New Mexico. Hundreds died of exhaustion on the way, and it is said some were executed. When they arrived, Bosque Redondo turned out to be overcrowded and the Navajo were forced to join Apaches, not a tribe they were friendly with. The Navajo were also raided by the Comanche, who, in turn, raided them back.

With poor water supplies and with crops failing, the US Army began to incur huge costs in feeding the Indians; the Navajo began leaving in 1867, before the reservation was officially abandoned the following year. In a rare reversal, the US then permitted the Navajo to return to their traditional lands.

Where the Buffalo Roamed

Both white settlers and Plains Indians – with the warring Sioux acting almost like imperialists over other tribes – hunted buffalo to disastrous effect. In the middle

OPPOSITE: Although billed as Geronimo's last buffalo kill – at Fort Sill in Oklahoma around 1906 – this may also have been his first: his earlier hunting experiences in New Mexico and Arizona were unlikely to have brought him into contact with any.

of the century, there may have been 60 million buffalo; by 1883, there were fewer than a thousand. For the white Americans who ate some buffalo and hunted them for sport, the elimination of the animal made a perverse kind of sense, as Secretary of the Interior, Columbus Delano, explained to Congress in 1874: 'I regard the destruction of such game as Indians subsist upon as facilitating the policy of the Government, of destroying their hunting habits, coercing them on reservations, and compelling them to begin to adopt the habits of civilization.' Ridding the Plains of buffalo was a way of ridding them of Native Americans.

Little Big Horn and Wounded Knee

The names of the massacres involving Native Americans over the centuries have largely been forgotten, but 'Custer's Last Stand' at Little Big Horn is well known – because it is one of the few cases where white Americans were the victims. In Montana in June 1876, General George Custer's forces from the Seventh Cavalry, supported by Crow Indian scouts, were hugely outnumbered and outmanoeuvred by Northern Cheyenne and Arapaho tribes, including leaders Sitting Bull and Crazy Horse. Of more than 200 men whom Custer directly led into battle, none survived. The grim news of Custer's defeat reached the rest of America on 4 July – the centenary of the Declaration of Independence.

Little Big Horn, however, proved to be a pyrrhic victory for the Native Americans, as it stirred white Americans into settling 'the Indian problem'.

Over the next three years, the major Indian military forces were crushed, while new treaties confiscated vast pieces of land on a 'sell or starve' basis. In 1886, even Apache leader Geronimo in Arizona was forced to surrender.

A new religion suddenly emerged from the starving and desperate Lakota Indians of South Dakota – the Ghost Dance, one of the tenets of which was the eradication of white settlers. Fearing an attack, the US cavalry decided to hold some chiefs in custody. But in its effort to take Sitting Bull in December 1890, shots were fired, resulting in his death and those of eight of his supporters and six policemen.

Two hundred members of his band joined other Native Americans heading for safety on a reservation, but on the way they were intercepted by US cavalry at Wounded Knee Creek. When the troops tried to search them, a scuffle developed, a shot rang out and the cavalry began firing. In the shooting, the cavalry killed 150 Indian men, women and children, including those who tried to flee, while also accidentally firing on their own troops. Twenty-five soldiers died and 39 were wounded in the fighting.

> 'In the shooting, the cavalry killed 150 Indian men, women and children.'

Such massacres had not been uncommon, but Wounded Knee would be one of the last as the Native Americans, their numbers depleted through disease and war, were now limited to scattered reservations. 'When I look back from this high hill of my old age, I can still see the butchered women and children lying heaped and scattered all along the crooked gulch,' wrote Wounded Knee survivor Black Elk years later. 'And I can see that something else died there in the bloody mud, and was buried in the blizzard. A people's dream died there. It was a beautiful dream.'

Throughout the nineteenth century, Native Americans had repeatedly been uprooted and shunted onto less productive, more cramped land. As historian Howard Zinn observed, the United States made 400 treaties with the Indians – and broke every one of them.

OPPOSITE: Collecting the bodies of the 150 Indian men, women and children who had been shot by US troops in the Wounded Knee massacre in South Dakota in 1890. In the confusion, the troops had also killed 25 US soldiers.

Searching for Cynthia Ann Parker

Founding Father Benjamin Franklin wondered in 1753 why it was that a Native American child raised by settlers would, if ever allowed to see its Indian relatives, refuse to return to a settler family. But if a settler child were taken prisoner by Indians and 'lived awhile among them' it would, having been returned to its white family, 'become disgusted with our manner of life' and 'take the first good opportunity of escaping again into the woods'.

So it was with Cynthia Ann Parker, one of the kidnapped children whose story inspired the movie *The Searchers*. When she was a child, her extended family moved to Texas, building Fort Parker. There, in 1836, a Comanche-led war raid massacred five men in her family, raping the women and cutting the genitals off her grandfather, John Parker, before scalping him. Two women and three children were kidnapped, including Cynthia, aged about 10, and her two-year-old brother, John Richard. The women were gang raped and treated as slaves, but children were regarded as a way to increase the tribe's size and were accepted as tribal members.

After many months, the captive women were freed when Cynthia's uncle, James W. Parker, tracked down the Comanche party and paid ransoms. After six years, John Richard was freed, though he proved unable to adapt to white society and ran away to rejoin his Comanche family.

Cynthia was not found and stayed with different Comanche for 24 years, marrying a chieftain and having three children, one of whom, Quanah, became the last free Comanche chief. When she was about 34, Cynthia was 'rescued' by Texas Rangers, but she spent the remaining decade of her life refusing to adjust to life in white society, once escaping temporarily back to her Comanche family. Heartbroken at being separated from her part-Comanche children, she refused to eat and died in 1871.

> **'The United States was a young country in need of a national mythology.'**

BELOW: Cynthia Ann Parker with her daughter Topasannah in 1861, shortly after they was 'rescued' from the Comanche. Separated from her other part-Comanche children, Parker refused to adjust back to life in white society.

How the West was Spun

In 1889, the previously Indian land of the Oklahoma territory was opened up to the last great western land rush. On 22 April alone, 50,000 people surged across two million acres of newly available land, staking their claim on what would become their new farmland. With the settlement of Oklahoma, argued historian Frederick Jackson Turner in 1893, the frontier was closed, and so the first period of American history was at an end.

Just over a century old, the United States was a young country in need of a national mythology. It found it in the West. The pioneer spirit had looked to a future in the West; now life in the West could begin to pass into the realm of myths of a recent past. Where old Europe had heroes in medieval knights and honest outlaws like Robin Hood, America's heroes would be cowboys – which was odd, given how unheroic the life of a cattle herdsman usually was. But, as historian William W. Savage notes: 'Everything that has been done to the cowboy has been done, consciously or unconsciously, to make him usable as a myth.'

In fiction, in the romantic paintings of Albert Bierstadt and Frederic Remington, and later in movies and on television, cowboys became honourable, courageous and chivalric, their actions reaching far beyond looking after their bovine charges.

Shotgun Hospitality

Cowboys did not really exist until after the Civil War; it was only then, with the buffalo population almost extinguished, that the cattle industry took off. Cowboys would drive cattle north to railheads, where the cows would be loaded on to trains to take them to the cities of the Midwest for slaughter. Dodge City in Kansas developed as a railhead and was for 10 years the largest cow town in the world. In popular culture, it has a reputation for its outlaw activity. In reality, for all its cowboys and gamblers, saloons and brothels, as well as merchants, bankers and families, there were very few unnatural deaths.

True Western incidents, such as Wyatt Earp's gunfight at the OK Corral in Tombstone, Arizona, in 1881, became famous because they were so uncommon. Villains, saloons and stagecoaches, let alone ones being held up, were seldom seen. In fact, the racial conflicts in Louisiana and the South were more violent than the romanticized West during this period.

Admittedly, the West could be lawless – in places there were no lawmen – so communities established committees of vigilance to deal with desperadoes. Sometimes this did descend into mob rule, but usually it involved responsible citizens working against horse thieves, cattle rustlers and robbers. The most active vigilance committee was at Fort Griffin in Texas, where, in April 1876, they caught a man stealing a horse. Meting out their own form of justice, they promptly hanged him from a tree, leaving below the swinging body a pick and shovel for anyone who might want to bury him.

The feuds of the West, of Billy the Kid and Wyatt Earp, were, as historian Philip Jenkins notes, essentially factional struggles for economic and political power, just like the conflicts in the cities back east. Just as the courts had favoured big business in industrial disputes, so they often failed to convict the powerful in the West – such as the Stock Growers Association in their 1892 'war' against homesteaders in Johnson County, Wyoming. In this way, the myths of the Wild West, in which justice was found for the little man outside the law, proved a corrective to the historical injustices often handed down.

The End of the West

By the late 1880s, the open land had largely been fenced off by homesteaders. Cattle driving gave way to wheat fields, and towns ironed out the wilderness and lawlessness. With the Wild West ending, its survivors could move on, some finding work in the myth industry – Wyatt Earp spent his final years advising on Westerns in 1920s' Hollywood. William F. Cody, who had been an army scout, buffalo hunter and Indian fighter, established 'Buffalo Bill's Wild West Show', featuring Annie Oakley, which toured America and Britain, performing Western-style circus stunts and historical scenes.

The Wild West, as much as it ever existed, was over. In 1900, artist Frederic Remington wrote to his wife: 'I shall never come to the West again – it is all brick buildings.'

ABOVE: The Dodge City Peace Commission of 1883, with Wyatt Earp seated second left. Earp has entered the mythology of the West as a celebrated lawman, but he had had several run-ins with the law himself.

OVERLEAF: William F. Cody had been an army scout and buffalo hunter before turning his skills to circus entertainment in staging 'Buffalo Bill's Wild West'. A supporter of Native Americans, Cody called them: 'the former foe, present friend, the American'.

SHOOTING THE PRESIDENT

James A. Garfield did not survive for long in the White House. Inaugurated in March 1881, by September he was out of office. On 2 July, while heading for a train at the Baltimore and Potomac Railroad Station in Washington, he was shot by Charles J. Guiteau, a disturbed dropout. Garfield fought for his life for three months before dying; Guiteau, who had remained beside the president after the shooting, was hanged the following year.

Twenty years after Garfield's death, on 6 September 1901, President William McKinley was at a public event in Buffalo, New York, when he was shot by 28-year-old anarchist Leon Czolgosz. McKinley's wounds turned gangrenous and he died before his assassin was sent to the electric chair the following month.

The Imperial Age

In 1867, Russia sold Alaska to the United States for $7 million, ending its imperial stake in North America. The US, on the other hand, was about to emerge into its own imperialist era. When, in 1895, the people of Cuba launched a nationalist revolution against the Spanish empire, the Spanish suppressed the Cubans, stripping the countryside to deny the revolutionaries access to food and shelter, and herding the people into the towns and cities. US newspapers, particularly popular ones owned by William Randolph Hearst and the Pulitzer chain, were heavily critical of the Spanish action, stirring up popular opinion against the Spanish Empire.

This wasn't just exotic international news for Americans; there was a commercial interest here, too. Cuba, only 145km (90 miles) from Florida, was home to American sugar and tobacco plantations, and with the Cuban cities rioting, US Marines were sent to protect American residents and property. When, in February 1898, the USS *Maine* exploded in Havana harbour, the same newspapers, feeding war fever, promptly blamed enemy action. A naval court of inquiry concluded that a submarine mine was responsible, although it could also have been caused by a technical fault on the ship. Nonetheless, war was declared on the Spanish Empire and Cuba soon fell into American hands.

The following month, the US intervened in nationalist movements against the Spanish in the Philippines, taking control of the islands. By the end of the year, America had formally acquired possession of Hawaii, along with the former Spanish colonies of Puerto Rico, the Pacific island of Guam and the Philippines.

The brief Spanish–American War had seen relatively few American lives lost. But the fighting in the Philippines was not over yet. The next year, the native people of the Philippines began a revolt against the Americans that would take three further years to suppress. Efforts to crush this were brutal, including water torture, prison deaths and concentration camps. By 1900, 70,000 US troops were stationed in the Philippines; when the conflict was over, 4000 US troops had died, while Filipino fatalities may have reached as many as 250,000.

BELOW: The explosion of the USS *Maine* while in Havana harbour in 1898 helped trigger America's war with Spain. An inquiry ruled that the blast was caused by a mine, though it could well have been a technical fault.

The Panama Canal

Despite the casualties in the Philippines, the Spanish–American War had introduced America as a player on the world stage. Realizing the importance of being able to move warships quickly from the Pacific to the Atlantic, in 1903, President Theodore Roosevelt negotiated to lease land to build a canal in Panama, a region at that time controlled by Colombia. Negotiations were helped by the presence of a US gunboat, followed by an engineered rebellion to create the puppet state of Panama. After that, within two weeks the US had signed the Canal Treaty, winning the right in perpetuity to build and operate a canal through Panama.

To some Americans, acquiring overseas colonies was an extension of the process by which the US had reached across North America, bringing disorganized or weak areas under the protective American wing. But this new position was not universally popular at home. Ben Tillman, a senator from South Carolina, criticized efforts to replace Spanish rule in Cuba with American control, calling the US – in a term subsequently hurled, rightly or wrongly, many times at America – 'the policeman' of the area.

Nevertheless, when US forces withdrew from Cuba in 1901, the terms of departure effectively made the island an American protectorate, including allowing America to build bases there. One of them would be Guantánamo Bay.

America, America

In the generation after the Civil War, America had become the largest economy in the world, and, with its involvement in Latin America and in the Philippines, it had launched itself as an imperial power. Now the twentieth century would see it involved in huge conflicts on the global stage.

ABOVE: Having been started by France in the 1880s, construction of the Panama Canal was taken over by the United States in 1904. By the time it was completed 10 years later, the 77km (48 mile) project had claimed the lives of 5600 workers.

6

THE NEW AGE

Although determined not to become involved in World War I, by 1918 American troops were fighting in the trenches in Europe. The United States would, however, emerge dominant from the war, with its industries booming, while mobsters thrived during Prohibition. Then, in 1929, the bubble would burst.

I N AUGUST 1914, war broke out in Europe, with Britain, France and Russia in conflict with the Central Powers of Germany, Austro-Hungary and the Ottoman Empire. The United States was not involved. As in the Napoleonic Wars in the early nineteenth century, it sought only to maintain its neutrality and continue its existing trading patterns with European powers on both sides of the conflict. Furthermore, if it did go to war, which side would America be on? Its population was a melting pot of different people, including Germans, British, Irish, Italians, Czechs, Serbs and many others – but chiefly, as President Woodrow Wilson observed, 'the nations now at war'. Neutrality was the obvious path.

However, as with the war of 1812, it proved impossible to remain neutral, and to trade with countries that were at war, because America's merchant ships became military targets. In 1915, Germany abandoned the recognized policy of 'stop and search' of civilian ships and began firing indiscriminately at them. Most famously it torpedoed the British Cunard liner *Lusitania*, sailing from New York

OPPOSITE: Dorothea Lange's photograph of a migrant farm worker and two of her seven children in Nipomo, California, in March 1936, has become one of the best-known images of the Great Depression.

ABOVE: The torpedoing of the liner *Lusitania* by a German U-boat off the coast of Ireland in 1915 caused the deaths of 1198 passengers and crew, including 128 Americans. Despite the international outcry, President Wilson remained determined, at that time, not to be drawn into World War I.

to Liverpool, killing 1198 passengers and crew. While Germany claimed, correctly, that the ship had secretly been carrying arms and ammunition to Britain, the sinking prompted an international outcry. Despite the loss of 128 American lives, Wilson remained determined not to be dragged into the war.

For a time, Germany ceased targeting civilian ships, but in early 1917 it resumed torpedoing vessels bound for Britain and France. This was a gamble: would these attacks exhaust British supplies and force Britain to surrender before America could mobilize against Germany? They didn't. In March 1917, the interception of the so-called Zimmermann Telegram from the German foreign ministry to the government of Mexico, suggesting a German–Mexican alliance against the US and the reoccupation of Texas and other states that had been lost to America, fuelled war fever. On 6 April 1917, Congress voted to declare war on Germany.

> **'A million Americans were part of the Allied Meuse-Argonne campaign.'**

Bravery in the Trenches

Two million American soldiers served in the trenches in France, but because of the training required for new conscripts and a shortage of ships, it was not until summer 1918 that significant numbers of American troops arrived in Europe. Still, in September 1918, a million Americans were part of the Allied Meuse-Argonne campaign, which broke the German lines.

AFRICAN-AMERICAN SOLDIERS

Segregation and racial tension in America did not stop with the country going to war. Violence erupted in August 1917 in Houston, Texas, when black soldiers stationed at Camp Logan retaliated against discrimination and abuse from white residents and the police. Marching on the city, the soldiers killed 16 white civilians and police, while four black soldiers died in the fighting. For the offences, more than 100 soldiers were court-martialled, 63 received life sentences and 13 were hanged.

Of those who did serve in Europe, most were given service roles rather than combat ones. There were, however, two black combat divisions, the 92nd and 93rd, made up of approximately 40,000 troops. Unease about white Americans fighting alongside black Americans led to the 93rd being loaned to the French Army. Issued with French helmets and weapons, but keeping their US Army uniforms, the 369th Infantry Regiment of the 93rd never lost a trench, retreated or had a soldier taken prisoner, and only once failed to take an objective.

Private Henry Johnson of the 369th, a former Albany station porter, became the first American to be awarded France's military decoration the Croix de Guerre. By the end of the war, 171 members of the 369th had received the Croix de Guerre or other French military decorations.

As Native Americans living on reservations had largely been denied citizenship, they couldn't be drafted for military service, but 6500 Indian men enlisted and served in every major US Army engagement of the war. In 1919, Congress granted automatic citizenship to all Indian war veterans, and in 1924 citizenship was granted to all Indians who had not yet received it.

LEFT: African-American soldiers in France in 1918.

Suddenly in November, the war was over, with Germany and its allies exhausted by the economic blockade and crushed by recent offensives. For the US it had been a fairly brief involvement, but casualties had been high – as they were for all belligerents – with 116,000 American deaths, fewer than half of them in battle.

The League of Nations

The war left Europe exhausted but America a dominant world player. For President Wilson, this was his opportunity to create a new world order of collective security – his 'fourteen points' including open seas, limited arms, a recognition of people living under colonial rule and a 'general association of nations' recognizing each country's political independence and territorial integrity.

After lengthy negotiations in Europe, this initiative became the League of Nations, but, despite the war, or as a consequence of it, American feeling remained opposed to becoming entangled in foreign alliances or wars. Ironically, Wilson failed to get US membership of the League of Nations through Congress. It had been his idea and it existed, but he couldn't persuade his own people to sign up for it.

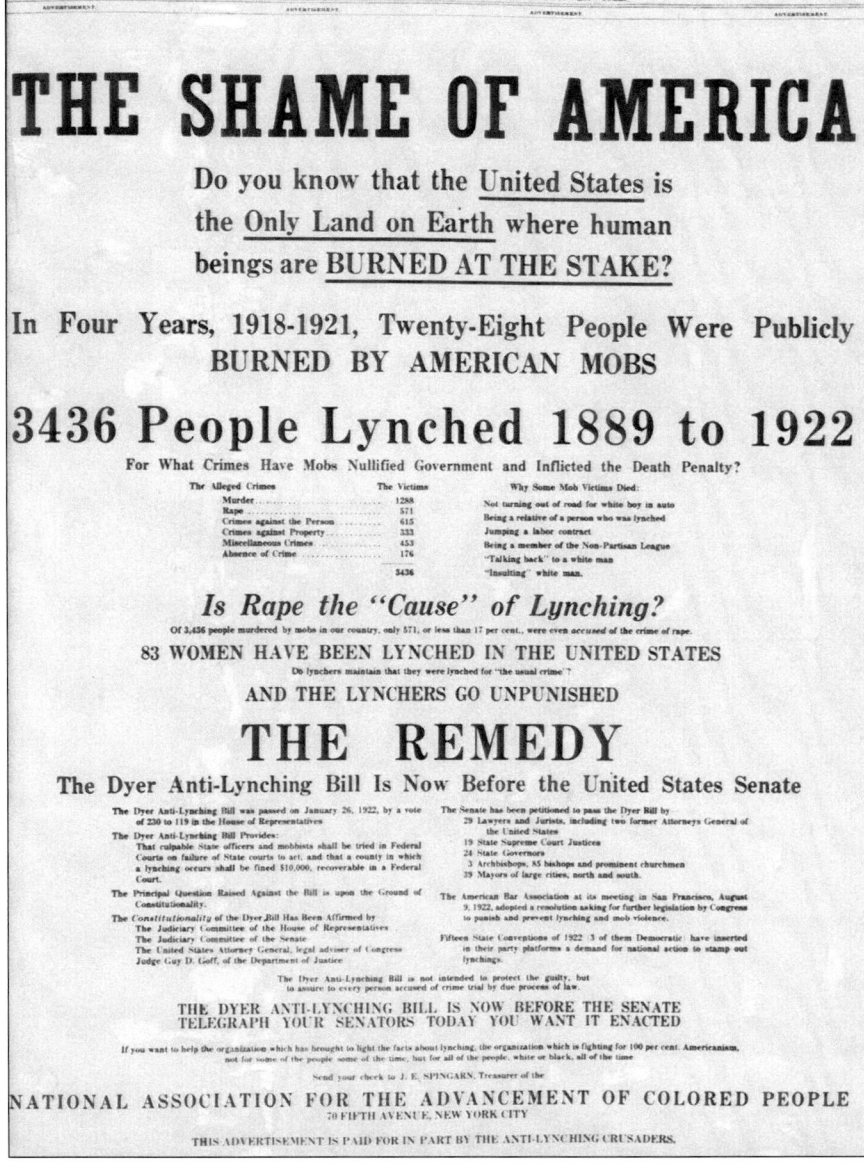

BELOW: An advertisement by the National Association for the Advancement of Colored People (NAACP) urging the US Senate to pass the 1922 Dyer Anti-Lynching Bill. The bill didn't make it through the Senate, being repeatedly blocked by Southern Democrats.

Lynchings

The war years proved good for American industry, and black Southerners were now increasingly attracted north by better-paid jobs in manufacturing and a chance to escape the South's 'Jim Crow' segregation laws. By 1920, 500,000 black Southerners had headed north as part of the Great Migration. During the war years, the black population of Chicago almost doubled, reaching 110,000, but blacks were still discriminated against. In July 1919, a race riot there left 38 people dead. In East St Louis two years earlier, black strike-breakers had been blamed for the failure of a labour protest, with 100 black people dying in the ensuing violence.

Meanwhile, in the South, the Ku Klux Klan saw a revival; by the early 1920s, the movement had a membership in excess of four million. Blacks were usually the victims of lynchings and burnings,

but Asians, Catholics, Jews and anyone foreign-born could be targeted. The Klan had become an extreme expression of a conservative Southern Protestant backlash against multicultural America.

In May 1916 in Waco, Texas, Jessie Washington, a black teenager, pleaded guilty to murdering his employer, Lucy Fry, a white English farmer. Having received the death sentence, Washington was being led from the dock in Waco's courthouse when spectators surged forward and dragged him outside. Watched by a crowd in front of city hall, Washington was doused in oil, hung from a tree and repeatedly lowered into the flames of a bonfire, which burned him alive. Although the case was condemned across the country, no one was ever prosecuted for his killing.

Nor were lynchings limited to the South. In 1930 in Marion, Indiana, Thomas Shipp and Abram Smith were lynched – the photograph of their dangling bodies inspiring the song 'Strange Fruit'. As far north as Duluth, Minnesota, in 1920, three black circus workers were lynched by a mob after a white 19-year-old girl, Irene Tusken, had accused them of raping and robbing her. Her doctor could find no evidence of sexual assault, but the same day a mob broke into the jail where the arrested men – Elias Clayton, Elmer Jackson and Isaac McGhie – were being held. After a sham trial, the men were beaten and hanged. Trial proceedings of the mob opened two days later. Of 25 indictments for rioting, three received convictions and two were tried for rape, with one found guilty. But as with other lynchings, no one was ever convicted for the murders of the lynched men.

ABOVE: Thomas Shipp and Abram Smith were arrested in Marion, Indiana, in 1930, for murdering a white man and raping his white girlfriend. The following evening, they were dragged out of the jail by a mob and lynched.

> 'Jessie Washington was doused in oil, hung from a tree and lowered into the flames of a bonfire.'

Anti-immigration and 100 per cent Americanism

Looking inwardly, the war had generated waves of both patriotism in America and anti-German feeling. Then, with the Bolsheviks taking power in Russia in 1917, there was a small Red Scare in the US (1919–20), when workers, often immigrants, went on strike and vigilante groups emerged to rough them up.

A small anarchist movement also had a violent impact. One parcel bomb sent to a former US senator in May 1919 blew the hands off the maid who opened it. The following month, bombs were let off outside the homes of politicians, with the front of the house of attorney general, Mitchell Palmer, being blown in. No one inside was seriously hurt, but the bomber, Italian anarchist Carlo Valdinoci, lost his life in the explosion.

Tightening up security, Palmer created a new Bureau of Investigation – a forerunner of the FBI. Raids were made on alien radicals – with 4000 seized across the country in one night in 1920 – and people were held without charge. Although these actions were criticized as a breach of civil liberties, 800 were still deported.

Anti-immigrant feeling, even in a nation of immigrants, led to the closure of the open-door policy in the early 1920s – with some exceptions. Latin Americans were still allowed, as migrant Mexican farm labour was needed, and immigration from China and Japan was not completely banned. European immigration, however, fell drastically.

BELOW: The home of Attorney General Mitchell Palmer after anarchist Carlo Valdinoci let off a bomb, killing himself in the blast.

ABOVE: The St Valentine's Day Massacre, Chicago, 1929. In a turf war, Al Capone's South Side Italian-American bootleggers shot dead seven members of Bugs Moran's North Side Irish gang.

A Drink to Prohibition

For decades, evangelical Protestants had campaigned against the sale of alcohol, while Catholics of Irish and German descent had opposed it. But with the anti-German mood during and after the war, the Prohibitionist case was strengthened. Consequently, in January 1920, the Eighteenth Amendment came into force, banning the manufacture, import and sale of 'intoxicating liquors'.

Not that Prohibition stopped all America drinking – it just drove it underground, from where organized criminals moved in to manage it. For them, Prohibition was a golden opportunity, the profits enabling bootleggers to extend their influence. Unsurprisingly, turf wars broke out, with mass shootings, such as that in Philadelphia in 1928 and on St Valentine's Day in Chicago in 1929, where seven members of the North Side Irish gang were shot dead by four of Al Capone's South Side Italian-American gang. The perpetrators escaped easily: with two dressed as policemen, they 'escorted' the other two – with their hands up – from the garage, and disappeared into the city before the real police arrived.

In all, Capone may have been responsible for ordering 300 deaths, but it was for tax evasion that he was eventually convicted in 1931. Already suffering from neurosyphilis, he gradually lost his mind while in prison. He died at his Florida home in 1947.

> 'Not that Prohibition stopped all America drinking – it just drove it underground.'

Chicago had been Capone's domain, but in New York by the end of the 1920s, two other factions of Italian-American gangsters had emerged for dominance, one led by Joe Masseria and the other by Salvatore Maranzano. In 1931, Masseria was murdered, leaving Maranzano dominant. To limit disputes, he divided the city's underworld into five families, each with its own turf. But in setting himself up as boss of all bosses, Maranzano seems to have gone a step too far. Within six months he was murdered on the orders of Charles 'Lucky' Luciano – who was supposedly one of his followers.

Luciano brought in a new era of collaboration with other criminal groups, such as Jewish mobsters Meyer Lansky and Ben 'Bugsy' Siegel. Elsewhere, racketeer and political boss Enoch L. 'Nucky' Johnson rose to power in Atlantic City, New Jersey, where the liquor laws went largely unenforced.

When Prohibition ended in 1933, the mobsters sought new ventures. Some worked their way into unions and labour rackets, others moved into narcotics, gambling and prostitution. They didn't go away; they just diversified.

Fire and Water in California

Far more destructive than the earthquake in San Francisco in 1906 were the fires that followed it. Caused by ruptured gas mains, the fires burned for four days and nights, destroying, along with the earthquake, 80 per cent of the city's mainly wooden buildings and killing 3000 people. In a few cases, residents were motivated not to put the fires out, some even starting them – as insurers didn't indemnify against earthquakes, but did against fire damage. San Francisco was quickly rebuilt, but in the following decades it lost its standing as the West Coast's largest city to Los Angeles.

With oil and, from 1914, a rapidly expanding movie industry, L.A. was growing quickly, but it lacked one vital natural resource: fresh water. Dry in summer and not much wetter in winter, Los Angeles

> 'Caused by ruptured gas mains, the San Francisco fires burned for four days.'

LEFT: The 1906 San Francisco Earthquake and the fires that followed left at least 227,000 people – more than half the city's population – without homes. The earthquake also permanently diverted the lower course of the Salinas River by 9.6km (6 miles).

ABOVE: Part of the system that brought water across the desert to supply the city of Los Angeles, the St Francis Dam collapsed in 1928, flooding the valley beneath it and causing the deaths of 425 people.

receives less rainfall than some deserts. So where does the city get its water?

The answer, of course, is that it pipes it in. The man largely responsible was William Mulholland, the Belfast-born, self-taught chief engineer of Los Angeles's Bureau of Water Works and Supply. His name is memorialized in Mulholland Drive, the city's winding, tree-lined road and the home to some of Hollywood's biggest stars. But in bringing the water to L.A., and therefore enabling the city to grow and its gardens to look so wonderfully verdant, a great price was paid elsewhere in California.

That was in the Owens Valley, 370km (230 miles) north of L.A., where the snow melt from the Sierra Nevada provided plenty of surplus water for local farmlands. Quietly, in the first decade of the twentieth century, Mulholland's men began buying up farmland – and the water rights that went with each plot – not letting on that this was on behalf of the City of Los Angeles. With the land acquired, Mulholland then began building an aqueduct to link the Owens Valley with Los Angeles.

Completed in 1913, the Los Angeles Aqueduct remains a feat of civil engineering, using gravity to carry water down through the Mojave Desert to L.A. But the more the city grew, the more water it demanded. Farmers in the Owens Valley realized that it was taking the water they needed for their farms and that the Owens Lake – originally 19km (12 miles) long and 13km (8 miles) wide – was emptying. In protest, the aqueduct was dynamited a number of times. Nevertheless, by 1926 the Owens Lake was dry. Today, noxious soda ash and carcinogenic nickel blow off the lakebed. It is America's largest single source of dust pollution, and a large clean-up operation has been running since the 1990s.

Despite the ill feeling in the Owens Valley, in the 1920s Mulholland was still fêted in L.A. – until his reputation was shaken by a disaster closer to home. In the San Francisquito Canyon, 64km (40 miles) north of Los Angeles, Mulholland and his team built the St Francis Dam. Copying their design from a textbook, but not modifying it when they increased the dam's capacity without strengthening its walls, their structure was unsound. Opened in 1926, the dam collapsed one night two years later, flooding the valley beneath it and killing 425 people. The disaster remains California's second greatest loss of life after the San Francisco earthquake. Although no one was found to be individually responsible, Mulholland blamed himself, retiring the following year and withdrawing from public life.

Today, with a population of more than four million, a third of Los Angeles's water is still provided by Mulholland's aqueduct – but the city's environmental position remains precarious, with droughts and forest fires persistent concerns.

> 'The dam collapsed, flooding the valley beneath it and killing 425 people.'

Hollywood

Having opened its first studio in 1914, Hollywood was the heart of American film-making by the end of the decade. While other cities were mass-producing cars or consumer goods, Los Angeles' mass production was movies. The first stars, such as Mary Pickford and Charlie Chaplin, emerged – and, soon learning the value of their popular appeal, they negotiated lucrative contracts for themselves.

But, being highly paid, loved by the masses, fawned over by employers and, at heart, acutely aware of the fickle nature of fame, made stardom a volatile mix. It should be little surprise that just as Hollywood magnifies its stars' faces across the big screen, it also magnifies their lives, making them more vulnerable to excesses, whether alcohol, drugs or sex, or fame and failure. When a star's moment has passed, the downfall can be brutal. With the coming of sound films in 1928, silent comedy star Karl Dane's career faltered. With his strong Danish accent unpopular with audiences, he was dropped by MGM and by 1934 was selling hotdogs outside Paramount Pictures. He shot himself soon after.

Many went west to Tinseltown seeking fame and fortune, only to be disappointed. Successful stage actress Peg Entwistle did manage to become known in Hollywood, but not for her movies. Not having been signed by a studio in 1924, she climbed to the top of the Hollywood sign and threw herself off.

BELOW: Karl Dane was a silent comedy Hollywood star, but, with the coming of sound movies in 1928, his Danish accent proved unpopular and his career collapsed. With subsequent ventures failing, he shot himself in 1934.

Tinseltown's Greatest Scandal

We don't know his movies anymore, but Roscoe 'Fatty' Arbuckle is notorious for his involvement in one of Hollywood's most famous scandals. An immensely popular silent movie comedian earning $1 million a year, Arbuckle is remembered for the story that he killed an actress in a sordid sex act. Except that he didn't.

When Virginia Rappe fell ill at a party that Arbuckle was holding in San Francisco in 1921, she was seen by a doctor, who diagnosed no complaint other than her being drunk. Two days later, Rappe died of peritonitis caused by a ruptured bladder. Bambina Maude Delmont, who had attended the party with Rappe, went on the offensive, claiming that Arbuckle had raped Rappe, who

allegedly had said that Arbuckle had hurt her. Was Delmont hoping to extort the movie star? Well, she did have previous convictions for extortion.

Rappe's manager embellished the tale, stating that Arbuckle had used a piece of ice to simulate sex with Rappe. By the time this was reported in the Press, the ice had become a bottle that broke, inflicting fatal internal wounds. Even before the final verdict, Delmont was profiting from the case, touring the country with a show about the scandal. With so much misinformation being circulated, could Arbuckle receive a fair trial?

> 'Delmont was already profiting from the Arbuckle case, touring the country with a show about the scandal.'

Not until it was too late. Although the rape and murder charges were quickly dropped, a manslaughter charge remained. Arbuckle went through three trials; the first two juries reached deadlock, with mistrials declared. The third trial found him not guilty, its jury even writing a letter of apology to the star, finding him 'entirely innocent'.

Innocent, yes, but Hollywood had already washed its hands of the sullied star. Arbuckle did later return to occasional work, but, a broken man and now an alcoholic, he died of a heart attack in 1933.

After stories like Arbuckle's, Hollywood made an effort to clean up its act – not by behaving better, but by hushing things up. Whereas today public access to stars' lives is closely controlled by publicists, from the 1920s to the 1950s it was the studios who guarded the stars on their books. Studio fixers, such as MGM's Eddie Mannix, kept scandals out of the public eye by maintaining close relations with Los Angeles's District Attorney Buron Fitts – MGM's head Louis B. Mayer was the top donor to Fitts's re-election campaign – and in buying silence by putting bartenders, hospital staff and policemen on the studio payroll. It is also believed that the fixers may have even covered up murders, with the alleged suicides of Jean Harlow's husband, Paul Bern, in 1932, and George Reeves, star of TV's *The Adventures of Superman*, in 1959, never being wholly convincing.

The Wall Street Crash

After World War I, the US may have become politically inward-looking, but financially it was open to the world. It invested heavily in Europe, while in trade America became the world's leading exporter and, after Britain, the second largest importer. The automobile and its related industries in petrol and rubber for tyres, in particular, were booming.

By the mid-1920s, the economy was growing at around seven per cent a year, while share values

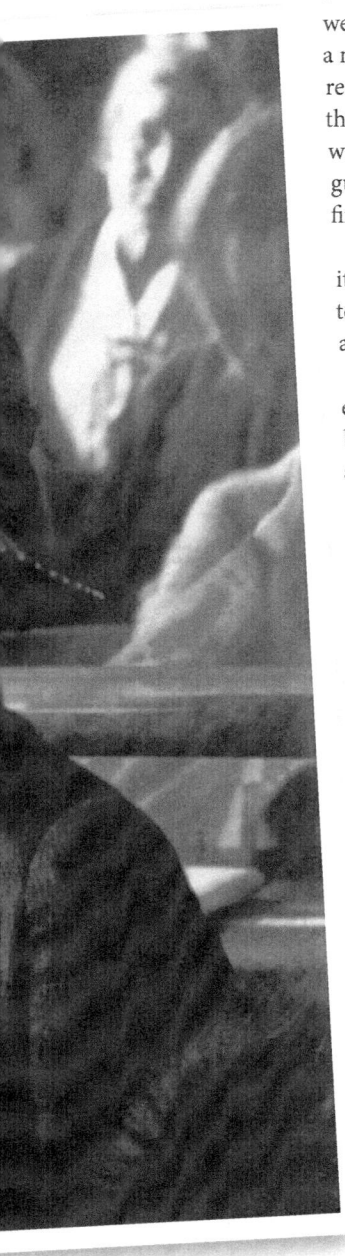

LEFT: Movie star Roscoe 'Fatty' Arbuckle supported by his wife Minta Durfee during his trial for manslaughter in 1921. In all, Arbuckle went through three trials before being found not guilty, but the scandal had already ruined his career.

ABOVE: A crowd outside the New York Stock Exchange on 24 October 1929, as selling intensified in the days preceding the Wall Street Crash. In the Depression that followed, unemployment would reach almost 24 per cent.

on the New York Stock Exchange increased 15-fold between 1923 and 1929. There were warnings that the market was overheating, but, with things going so well, they were ignored. Then in October 1929 the bubble burst. A week of panic selling cut a third off the value of the market. This in itself didn't sink America into depression, because only one per cent of the population owned shares, but it was an indicator of the changing economic climate. People began tightening their belts.

With spending on consumer goods falling by 20 per cent in 1930 alone, factories closed and workers were laid off, leading to people defaulting on mortgage payments and loans. This exposed another weakness in the US: with no central bank, local banks were allowed only limited reserves and were highly vulnerable. When the crash caused a run on the banks, they had no one to turn to and closed – with millions of Americans seeing their savings disappear. Between 1929 and 1933 – Herbert Hoover's presidency – 20 per cent of America's banks closed. In some places, people resorted to a barter economy.

Nor did it stop there. With America cutting back on lending overseas and raising tariffs on foreign imports, the Depression deepened around the world. In the US, shantytowns for the homeless – nicknamed 'hoovervilles' after President Hoover – grew up around major cities.

In 1933–35, Depression conditions worsened when drought and high winds hit the farms of the Midwest. With newly mechanized farming methods having already caused soil erosion, parts of the Great Plains were turned into a dust bowl. Some people died from dust pneumonia, others starved and, by 1940, 2.5 million people had left the Plains states. Thousands of ruined farmers trekked west from Arkansas and Oklahoma to seek work in California.

THE BONUS MARCHERS

During the summer of 1932, 20,000 unemployed war veterans moved on Washington, setting up temporary shacks in the city and demanding that the government pay them now a bonus that had been promised for 1945. It was largely peaceful until some agitators whipped things up. The army sent in tanks and tear gas, setting fire to the shacks and leaving two veterans shot dead and two infants asphyxiated by the gas. There was widespread outrage at the heavy-handed response, but Army Chief of Staff, Douglas MacArthur, argued that his actions had stopped more damaging situations developing.

LEFT: The Bonus Marchers camping out on the Capitol lawn in Washington, D.C., in June 1932.

THE MOB IN THE DREAM FACTORY

Hollywood could be corrupting, but it could also be corrupted. After the ending of Prohibition, some mobsters moved west, looking for a new racket. First they infiltrated the projectionists' union, causing strikes, and later they moved in on the movie technicians' union, the 12,000-strong IATSE (International Alliance of Theatrical Stage Employees). With Chicago mobster muscle having ensured they were voted in to run the union, George Browne and Willie Bioff established themselves in their new roles by leaning on the Hollywood studios for backhanders. With the major Hollywood studios each paying the duo $50,000 a year and smaller studios each paying $25,000, Browne and Bioff only pushed for minimal advances in their workers' rights. Meanwhile, union members would have to contribute two per cent of wages to a union fund: two-thirds of this went to the Chicago mob, and the rest to Bioff and Browne's own pockets.

What brought Bioff and Browne down was their effort to expand and take over the Screen Actors' Guild (SAG). When Robert Montgomery, the guild's president, hired private detectives to investigate Bioff, it quickly came to light that Bioff had not served a sentence for procuring a prostitute in Chicago in 1922, and that Joe Schenck, Chairman of 20th Century Fox, had paid him $100,000. What, the public might wonder, was the chairman of a movie studio doing paying a union leader $100,000?

After more investigations, Schenck and Bioff were brought to trial in 1941. Agreeing to give evidence against Bioff, Schenck served only four months for bribery, before being released back to Fox. There, aged 69, he began a relationship with teenage starlet Marilyn Monroe. To escape a long sentence in Alcatraz for tax evasion and racketeering, Bioff, in turn, agreed to testify against the Chicago Mafia. This led to indictments against a number of mobsters, including Frank 'the Enforcer' Nitti, who shot himself the day his indictment was handed down. Others received 10-year sentences, while Bioff and Browne were paroled after three. Bioff went to live quietly in Phoenix, Arizona, where, one day in 1955, someone left a bomb under his car. The murder has never been solved.

RIGHT: The wreckage after mobster Willie Bioff was killed in a car bomb in Phoenix, Arizona, in 1955.

The New Deal

When Franklin D. Roosevelt was inaugurated as president in March 1933, a quarter of the US workforce was unemployed and banks had closed in 38 states. Quickly, Roosevelt repealed Prohibition and managed to get many of the banks reopened, reassuring the country that their money was better in banks than under the mattress. Already, the mood was looking a little more buoyant. That summer, the Glass-Steagall Act separated investment banks from those handling loans and deposits, the blurring of the two having contributed to the Crash and the Depression – as it would in the financial crisis of 2008. In taking America off the gold standard, Roosevelt devalued the dollar, generating a demand for now cheaper US exports.

To counteract the effects of the Dust Bowl, laws were put in place to conserve soil and to plant more than 200 million trees from Canada to Texas. The federal government began a massive programme of work relief, employing people in construction projects, in teaching and in public libraries. In 1935, unemployment pay was introduced – with, across the decade, more than a third of the population receiving public aid of some kind. America was getting back on its feet.

> 'Hollywood could be corrupting, but it could also be corrupted.'

The Winds of War

Internationally, the mid-1930s saw America at its most isolationist. Where Woodrow Wilson had hoped and failed to make the US a major player in maintaining world peace, the 1935–37 Neutrality Acts worked to keep America out of any foreign entanglements, making it illegal to sell arms or make loans to belligerent nations.

Once again American neutrality was declared when war broke out in Europe in September 1939. But the United States had said that in 1914, too. Then, on 7 December 1941, the Japanese attacked the US naval base at Pearl Harbor in Hawaii, and America went to war once more.

BELOW: President Franklin D. Roosevelt (left), with Secretary of Agriculture Henry A. Wallace, during a White House radio broadcast about the New Deal Farm Programs in July 1940.

7

WORLD WAR II

Although America proclaimed its neutrality when World War II broke out in Europe in 1939, in just a few years it would not only be forced into the bloodiest conflict in world history, but also determine the war's outcome. Then, in 1945, it would signal the birth of the nuclear age when it dropped atomic bombs on Japan.

T**HE UNITED STATES** declared war against Japan the day after the attacks on Pearl Harbor in 1941. However, America hadn't, despite its claims, been wholly neutral since the war had begun in September 1939. Although there was much anti-war sentiment in the US, President Roosevelt was staunchly anti-fascist and was soon quietly providing Britain and France with aid and support in their fight against Adolf Hitler's Germany. Within three months of Britain and France going to war, America's Neutrality Act had been revised to permit them to buy munitions on a 'cash and carry' basis. The following September, the US gave Britain 50 ageing destroyers, while making sure that this was presented as a business deal rather than aid, with Britain, in return, offering America long leases on naval bases. Similarly, by 1941, the Lend-Lease Bill pretended that vast amounts of weaponry were only being loaned to Britain and the Soviet Union – for return after use.

Domestically, rearmament had been stepped up and conscription

OPPOSITE: US infantrymen in a liberated part of France, August 1944. When the US entered the war in 1941, there were fewer than two million Americans in the armed forces; by 1945, there were more than 12 million.

ATTACKS ON AMERICA

With Japanese expansion across the Pacific and attacks on US merchant shipping, fears grew of an invasion of the American West Coast. No attempt at invasion happened, but there were some isolated assaults. In February 1942, a Japanese submarine fired shells at the Ellwood Oil Field near Santa Barbara, southern California. That June, another Japanese submarine fired shells at Fort Stevens on the Columbia River, Oregon – though without causing significant damage. Three months later, the continental US saw its only air raid of the war when a floatplane launched from a submarine dropped two incendiary bombs on the mountains of Oregon. Due to poor weather and the actions of fire patrols, the fires were put out with minimal damage.

Between November 1944 and April 1945, the Japanese Navy launched more than 9000 fire balloons towards North America. Most were ineffective, but five children and a woman were killed in Oregon when one of the children tampered with a bomb that one of the balloons had been carrying – they would be the war's only deaths in mainland America due to enemy action.

Worries about traitors in the nation's midst after the attack on the Ellwood Oil Field had led to the justification of the internment of almost 120,000 Japanese-Americans in mainland America – nearly two-thirds of whom were US citizens. Of course, Germany and Italy were also at war with the US, but there was no internment of the many Americans from German or Italian families. As the proportion of Japanese-Americans in Hawaii was too large for mass internment, martial law was imposed on the islands instead.

However, a number of Japanese-Americans from Hawaii, some of whom had been in the Hawaii National Guard, successfully petitioned to be allowed to serve in the US armed forces, and in 1943 the 442nd Infantry Regimental Combat Team of Japanese-American soldiers was formed. Generally forbidden from front-line action in the Pacific War, some used their language skills in intelligence work, while others fought in Europe. In total, about 14,000 men served with the 442nd. With 9486 Purple Heart military honours awarded, it became, considering its size, the most decorated unit in the war.

ABOVE:
Japanese-American families assembling in Turlock, California, in May 1942, before being sent to internment camps in Arizona.

reintroduced. 'Vicariously at least,' writes historian Philip Jenkins, 'the United States was in all essential ways a combatant power for most of 1941.'

The mass raid on Pearl Harbor may have come out of the blue, but an attack of some kind had been expected, although Malaya or the Philippines had been thought more likely targets. Back in 1937, Japanese aircraft had sunk the US gunboat *Panay* while it was anchored on the Yangtze River, China, and, concerned about Japan's imperialistic expansion in China and southeast Asia, America was already offering covert aid to the Chinese war effort, including the use of American pilots. Following the sinking, commercial treaties with Japan had been annulled and economic restrictions imposed – including, crucially, access to American oil.

> 'All eight battleships in port were damaged, with four of them sunk.'

Pearl Harbor

Beginning at 7.48am, the attack at Pearl Harbor on 7 December 1941 consisted of two waves of 353 Japanese aircraft – fighters, bombers and torpedo planes – launched from six aircraft carriers, which the US had failed to spot manoeuvring into range. All eight US battleships in port were damaged, with four of them sunk, while three destroyers and three cruisers were also damaged or sunk.

BELOW: USS *Shaw* under attack during the Japanese raids on Pearl Harbor on 7 December 1941. Within months, the destroyer had been repaired and went on to serve in the Pacific for the rest of the war.

Within a couple of hours, 2400 Americans were dead. Fortunately for America, its aircraft carriers were not in the base at the time and, therefore, not hit. Furthermore, six of the battleships damaged at Pearl Harbor were returned to service.

Would America now join Britain in the European war against Germany? The question was swiftly resolved when Hitler declared war on the US four days later.

The Pacific Campaign

In the first months of the war, America's main military concern was to stop the Japanese expansion across the Pacific. Malaya had fallen the day after the attack on Pearl Harbor, to be followed by the Dutch East Indies in March, and Burma and the Philippines in May. Australia, too, was threatened, with Darwin's port and airfields attacked in a large air raid in February.

> 'Some died of hunger or dysentery in the cramped, unsanitary conditions.'

Bataan Death March

With the Japanese advancing in the Philippines, as many as 76,000 starving American and Filipino soldiers were caught in Bataan province. Surrendering in April 1942, they were forced to march 97km (60 miles), before being transported by train to a prison camp. Some died of hunger or dysentery in the cramped, unsanitary conditions on the trains or at the prison camp. Others, regarded by the Japanese as sub-human for having surrendered, were beaten, bayoneted and even beheaded on the march – between 7000 and 10,000 POWs were killed.

After the war, Masaharu Homma, the military commander of the Philippines during the Japanese occupation, was tried as a war criminal and executed, along with seven other senior-ranking soldiers.

BELOW: American prisoners of war in Bataan in the Philippines in 1942. Shortly afterwards, they were marched 97km (60 miles) by the Japanese to a prison camp, with many POWs dying en route from exhaustion or disease. Others were executed.

ABOVE: US Navy aircraft attacking Japanese ships at the Battle of Midway in June 1942. With the sinking of all four of Japan's large aircraft carriers, the battle was a major turning point in the war in the Pacific.

Turning the Tide in the Pacific

In May 1942, America reasserted itself in the Pacific with its first major victory at the Battle of the Coral Sea. This also marked a change in warfare: it was the first battle in which aircraft carriers engaged each other through their aircraft, but where the ships neither directly sighted nor fired on each other. Battleships would become a thing of the past, and future naval battles would be led by aircraft carriers.

The following month saw an even more significant victory for the US. The Japanese had hoped to lure the American fleet into a trap at Midway Atoll – located, as its name suggests, halfway across the Pacific. But American cryptographers had learned the planned date of the Japanese attack, and, instead, the US was able to surprise the Japanese fleet. In the battle, all four of Japan's large aircraft carriers and a heavy cruiser were sunk, while the US lost one aircraft carrier and a destroyer. More than 300 Americans were killed, but the Japanese lost ten times as many. Midway would be the turning point in American fortunes in the Pacific War.

SABOTEURS

As Germany didn't openly attack the American homeland, what was U-boat *U-202* doing less than 200m (656ft) from the Long Island shore one morning in June 1942? The answer: it was part of a bizarre sabotage mission.

That day, *U-202* and another U-boat in Florida each dropped a team of four German agents at the American coast. The agents, who had all lived in America at some point before the war, were on missions to blow up power stations and factories. But, with only two months of intelligence training, their secret operation soon began to unravel.

The four agents from *U-202* made it to the beach in an inflatable raft, but within minutes they were discovered by coastguard John Cullen. When challenged, the leader of the saboteurs, Georg John Dasch, claimed that they were fishermen, before grabbing Cullen and stuffing $260 into his hand, hoping to buy Cullen's silence.

Outnumbered, Cullen left the men and went to inform his colleagues. In the meantime, the agents took the train to New York City, where they checked into a hotel. Six days later, and before attempting to sabotage anything, Dasch turned himself in to the authorities.

With Dasch's information, the FBI quickly rounded up the remaining agents across the country. None had yet attempted any sabotage. As Dasch and another agent, Ernst Peter Burger, had co-operated, they escaped the death penalty, receiving long prison sentences and being deported after the war. The remaining six would-be saboteurs were sent to the electric chair.

According to Hitler's architect, Albert Speer, the Führer was intoxicated by the idea of 'the downfall of New York in towers of flames', but with America so far from German-occupied Europe, this failed operation would be the only attempt of its kind.

ABOVE:
Coast Guardsman John Cullen (left) receiving the Legion of Merit for raising the alarm after encountering German spies on the Long Island shore.

The Mediterranean Theatre

American ground troops based in Europe first saw action in November 1942, when British and US forces broadened the Allied campaign in North Africa by landing in Morocco and Algeria. Six months later, the Allies had succeeded in pushing German forces out of North Africa, but it was already too late to prepare for a major invasion of German-occupied France that year, which was the priority. Instead, the Mediterranean was chosen as the point of assault, with the aim of knocking out Italy and approaching the German lines from the south.

Beginning in July 1943, Sicily was invaded with a major airborne and amphibious operation by US, British, Canadian, Free French, Australian and South African troops against Italian and German forces. Within six weeks, the island had been taken, allowing Allied shipping to resume in the Mediterranean. Also, in late July, a coup deposed Italian dictator Benito Mussolini, and the Italian government, though openly continuing the war, secretly began to approach the Allies about reaching a peace agreement.

In September, the Allies attacked the Italian mainland; within a month, the whole of southern Italy was in Allied hands – at which point their advance slowed. In January 1944, American-led Allied forces made an amphibious landing in Anzio, 46km (29 miles) south of Rome, with the intention of outflanking the German defensive line across Italy and occupying the capital. They were eventually successful in this, but it took them 136 days, with the Allies pinned down on the marshes of Anzio for much of the time. The battle cost the Allies 7000 lives, with 36,000 wounded or missing.

Two days after occupying Rome, the Italian campaign became of secondary importance – the Allied invasion of France had finally been launched.

BELOW: **Preparations for the Allied invasion of Europe. Tanks are boarded on to American landing craft at a naval base in Tunisia, before the assault on Sicily in July 1943.**

Bombing from Britain

From mid-1942, US bombers based in Britain launched raids across occupied Europe, targeting military positions, munitions factories, industrial sites, ports and railways in Germany, where the additional aim was to lower civilian morale, as well as in occupied France and the Netherlands. With America raiding by day and the British by night, the talk was of 'precision bombing', but it was estimated that only 20 per cent of bombs fell within 300m (1000ft) of their targets.

Most controversially, on the night of 13–14 February 1945, 722 British Lancaster bombers targeted the city of Dresden with high explosive bombs and incendiary devices. The following day, 527 American B-17 bombers took over the raid. The bombing and resulting firestorm destroyed about 60 per cent of the inner city, killing 25,000 people.

Seventy years later, the merits of the attack are still debated, with many arguing that the cultural city had no strategic value and was targeted when it was clear that Germany was going to lose the war. Defenders of the action, however, claim that it was a major rail transport and communication centre, with 110 factories and 50,000 workers contributing to the German war effort.

> 'Blacks could serve their country, but might not be served *in* their country.'

Not that life for bomber aircrews was without risk; quite the opposite. The 10-man crew on a B-17 'Flying Fortress' had a one-in-four chance of completing their tour of 25 missions before they could return to America – until the odds worsened in 1944, when a tour of duty was extended to 30 missions. By the end of the war, the United States Army Air Forces had lost almost 10,000 bomber aircraft, 8000 fighter aircraft and almost 80,000 personnel.

Operation Overlord

By the time it came to the Allied invasion of France in June 1944, America was producing 40 per cent of the world's armaments and an American, General Dwight Eisenhower, was leading the Allied armed forces. The US had entered the war late, but it was now the senior partner in investment, armament and manpower in the Anglo-American alliance.

Germany anticipated an Allied amphibious attack on occupied France, but thought that it would probably be in Pas de Calais – the nearest crossing point from Britain. Consequently, this area was particularly well defended. Instead, the Allies chose Normandy, further southwest and less well armed. However, as surprise was hugely important, bombing raids targeting transport links and supply columns were made not just in Normandy, but across France, so as not to give away the chosen location of the invasion.

D-Day

Just before midnight on 5 June, 1200 aircraft departed England to transport airborne divisions of US, British and Free French troops to their drop zones behind enemy lines in France. Naval bombardments began at 5.45 the following morning, with the first infantry landing craft reaching the five target beaches 45 minutes later. The beach landings were led by American, British and Canadian forces, with Polish, Norwegian, Free French and Dutch forces also involved. On that day, 6 June 1944, 132,000 Allied men were transported by sea to the beaches and a further 24,000 parachuted into Normandy or landed by glider.

SEGREGATION AND DISCRIMINATION

The war pulled the US out of the Depression, and the flow of black people in the South moving north for work resumed. Racial discrimination remained, however, and with the surge of migrants into Detroit, Michigan, competing for jobs and homes, race riots broke out there in the summer of 1943. Rioting raged for three days, leading to the deaths of 34 people, most of whom were black.

Discrimination hadn't ended in the armed forces, either. Blacks still served in segregated units and more often in non-combatant roles, such as trucking and construction. They were housed in poorer accommodation and were restricted from some bars and restaurants. They could serve their country, but might not be served *in* their country.

Once abroad, however, it was a different experience. In Britain, Italy and France there was no formal colour ban, so blacks were largely free to go where they pleased. But what then would life be like for them on their return to America? At the end of the war, as his ship passed the Statue of Liberty and docked in New York, one African-American soldier commented: 'Now we're niggers again.'

That may have been true in many cases, but the war years also loosened up social mobility by removing a large proportion of the young male population from the work force, allowing women and African-Americans to fill roles that had previously been blocked to them.

BELOW: Detroit factories employed Southern blacks in the war effort. But, with the city short of housing, race riots erupted.

RIGHT: The D-Day Landings, 6 June 1944. American soldiers are pulled ashore after their landing craft was sunk by enemy action off Utah Beach, Normandy, France.

The aim for the first day had been to advance 10–16km (6–10 miles) inland, four of the beachheads to link up, and a number of towns, including Caen, to be taken. None of these objectives was achieved and it would take two months to occupy Caen. Nevertheless, the beaches themselves were secured. Allied casualties on the first day were at least 10,000, with 4414 confirmed dead; the Germans lost 1000 men. But, although slowly at first, the Allied troops soon began pushing out from the beaches.

The Normandy landings remain the largest seaborne invasion in history, involving nearly 5000 landing and assault craft, 289 escort vessels and 277 minesweepers. Before Operation Overlord was completed, more than one million Allied troops would land in France.

From Normandy to Germany

In August 1944, around 50,000 German soldiers were cut off when the British and Americans managed to encircle them south of Caen in what has become known as the Falaise Pocket. From there, the Allies could approach Paris, completing the liberation of the French capital on 23 August. By September they were in Belgium; in October, the first German city, Aachen, fell.

But then in December came the German counter-offensive, pushing the Allied lines 100km (60 miles) back into Belgium. Referred to as the Battle of the Bulge for the way the Germans 'bulged' back into the Allied lines, the German advance through the Ardennes forest caught the Allies by surprise. Eventually, though, Allied heavy bombers were able to target German troops and supply lines,

The Holocaust

The all-black 761st Tank Battalion was among the American forces that liberated the Nazi concentration camp at Buchenwald, near Weimar in Germany in April 1945. For inmate Ben Bender, a 17-year-old Polish Jew, these were the first black faces he had ever seen. But there was another surprise for Bender: 'I could not understand why people wielding arms and steel would have tears in their eyes,' he said, when interviewed by the *New York Times* almost 50 years later. 'In Buchenwald people didn't cry. They moaned, like wounded animals.' Weeping at the sight of 20,000 emaciated prisoners, the soldiers helped where they could, although more than 2000 prisoners were too weak to be saved. Probably more than 42,000 people had already died at the camp from shootings, physical exhaustion from forced labour, and being used as human guinea pigs in medical experiments. Around another 13,500 prisoners died on forced evacuation marches from the camp in the days before the Allies arrived.

Buchenwald was just one of many camps. In all, perhaps 11 million people died in the Holocaust, including six million Jews – two-thirds of Europe's Jewish population. Other victims of Hitler's genocidal policies were communists, gypsies, ethnic Poles and other Slavs, Soviet citizens and Soviet POWs.

> 'In Buchenwald people didn't cry. They moaned, like wounded animals.'

weakening enemy fuel and ammunition supplies. From there, the Allies steadily pushed the exhausted Germans back into Germany.

BELOW: Slave labourers at the Buchenwald concentration camp, near Weimar, Germany, days after they were liberated by American soldiers in April 1945.

NATIVE AMERICANS

Although not permitted to vote in many states, the US government required all Native American men to register for military conscription. Many refused: the Seminole declared that they were still at war with the US, while the Iroquois objected because they didn't consider themselves to be American citizens. Still, one-third of all eligible Indian males and around 800 Indian women joined the armed forces to serve in the war.

In addition to their combat role, Native Americans proved particularly useful in secret communications. The US Marines established the Navajo code talker unit of around 400 men, where the bilingual soldiers devised a code in Navajo for use in radio communications – a code the Japanese never managed to crack. A similar approach was taken by Comanche and Choctaw soldiers.

RIGHT: Navajo-speaking soldiers making encrypted radio communications during the Pacific islands' campaign. The Japanese never managed to crack the code used by the Navajo.

The End in Europe

In Eastern Europe, Hitler and Soviet leader Josef Stalin had begun the war with a non-aggression pact, agreeing to divide Poland between them. Then, in 1941, Germany reneged on the deal and turned on the Soviet Union. Huge advances were made into Soviet territory, but after failing to capture the city of Stalingrad (now Volgograd) between August 1942 and February 1943, the German initiative in the East was lost, with large numbers of soldiers killed or captured. Then the Russians began to regain ground.

By early April 1945, the Allies were closing in on Germany from both sides. Fewer than two million German soldiers on the Eastern Front were fighting more than six million Soviet soldiers, while one million German soldiers in the West faced four million Western Allied soldiers. At the end of the month, as Soviet tanks were advancing through the streets of Berlin, Hitler committed suicide. Germany surrendered a few days later. The war in Europe was over.

The Later Stages in the Pacific

After the US victory at Midway in 1942, the American-led Allies began a drawn-out campaign of seizing Pacific islands, with the Japanese defending their conquests fiercely. It took six months for the Marines to capture Guadalcanal in the Solomon Islands, while high losses were suffered at Tarawa in Micronesia in 1943. The 4500-strong Japanese forces were well dug in and resisted the American amphibious landing. Within 76 hours, more than 1500 US soldiers had been killed, with almost all the Japanese soldiers fighting to the death, before the island was won. Of 1200 Korean labourers brought by the Japanese to Tarawa to construct the island's defences, only 129 survived.

ABOVE: For the first time in the war, Americans met serious Japanese opposition to an amphibious landing when US Marines came ashore on the beaches of Tarawa in 1943.

Raising the Flag at Iwo Jima

Closer to the Japanese home islands, Iwo Jima, a small volcanic island situated halfway between Tokyo and the Mariana Islands, was targeted in February 1945. Successive aerial bombardments since 1944 had not significantly affected the Japanese defences, which involved a massive network of hidden guns and bunkers. On 19 February, the Japanese waited until 30,000 US Marines had landed on the beaches, before opening fire, killing or wounding 2000 men before the end of the day. Four days of fighting later, the Marines reached the summit of Mount Suribachi, raising the Stars and Stripes flag there on 23 February. The photograph of this moment would become a symbol of American valour in the war.

It would be another month, however, before the island was finally secured. Again, casualties were very high, with Japanese losses in excess of 20,000 and only 1083 prisoners taken – the rest having fought to the death. The Marines lost 6800 men, with nearly 20,000 wounded. With such high losses, it remains a matter of debate among historians whether Iwo Jima was strategically worth the casualties sustained.

Kamikazes at Okinawa

The largest amphibious assault in the Pacific War came at Okinawa in April 1945. A large island only 550km (340 miles) from mainland Japan, Okinawa would, it was planned, be used as a base for later US air operations against the Japanese home islands. Before that, however, attacks on American naval vessels, many by suicidal Kamikaze pilots, caused 4900 American deaths and the loss of 38 ships, while inland 75,000 US soldiers were wounded or killed in the fighting. Before the island was finally captured, 94 per cent of 110,000 Japanese soldiers stationed there – along with many civilians – were killed defending it.

BELOW: In May 1945, the aircraft carrier USS *Bunker Hill* was attacked by two Kamikazes, causing a huge fire. Casualties exceeded 600, with 346 dead.

The Atomic Bomb

Despite huge Japanese military losses as the Americans neared Japan's home islands, and the firestorms caused by US bombing of the largely wooden houses of the enemy's cities, demands for an unconditional surrender were still being refused. There had been an immense cost in American lives in taking the Pacific islands, and it was now estimated that invading Japan itself could result in the deaths of at least another 40,000 Americans. On top of that there was concern that an invasion might provoke Japanese revenge attacks on Allied POWs.

While the war had been going on, the secret Manhattan Project had developed two usable atomic bombs. After weighing up all these considerations, President Harry S. Truman (having succeeded Roosevelt, who had died of a stroke that April) took the decision, with the consent of Britain, to drop an atomic bomb on the city of Hiroshima on 6 August. Although a major industrial city with a large military garrison, a bomb of that size inevitably also caused mainly civilian casualties.

When Japan still didn't surrender, a second bomb was dropped on Nagasaki, a major seaport, three days later. On the same day, the Soviet Union entered the Pacific War. Japan finally gave in, and a formal ceremony of surrender was performed on board USS *Missouri* in Tokyo Bay on 2 September. World War II was over.

At least 129,000 people were killed by the two atomic bombs, roughly half on the day each bomb fell. During the following months, many more died from the effects of burns and radiation sickness, exacerbated by malnutrition. The moral debate continues. Were the nuclear attacks on Hiroshima and Nagasaki justified in that they brought the war to a close? Or were they war crimes?

ABOVE: The end of World War II. The Japanese surrender delegation on board the USS *Missouri* in Tokyo Bay on 2 September 1945.

> 'At least 129,000 people were killed by the two atomic bombs.'

Counting the Cost

More than 16 million Americans served in the armed forces during the war, of whom 292,000 died in battle and 114,000 from other causes. Including civilians, German losses were between five and eight million, while Japanese losses were up to three million. Counting military and civilian deaths in all countries involved, more than 60 million people died in the war.

What had been achieved was the crushing of brutal Japanese imperialism in the Pacific, the removal of Italian fascism and the destruction of a genocidal German fascist regime that had conquered most of Europe.

The New Superpowers

America ended World War II as the greatest economic and military power in the world – the first superpower. The only nation with the potential to challenge it was the communist Soviet Union. United against the common foe of fascism, the US and the Soviet Union had been allies during the fighting, but even before the conflict ended the relationship between the two was breaking down into a war of a different kind.

OPPOSITE: The city of Nagasaki after the dropping of the atomic bomb on 9 August 1945. At least 35,000 people were killed and 60,000 others injured by the bomb, with more deaths following from the long-term effects of radiation.

8

THE EARLY COLD WAR

World War II had left Europe exhausted, and the wartime alliance between the Allies would quickly disintegrate. Internationally, American troops would see action opposing the expansion of communism, while at home the country would hunt down communists – both real and imagined.

In 1945, the Allies, led by the United States, the Soviet Union and Britain, decided the peace terms to end World War II. That October, the same three countries became the founder members of the United Nations. Yet, only three years later, President Truman would scribble to his Secretary of State, George Marshall: 'Will Russia move first? Who pulls the trigger? Then where do we go?' Much was changing in international relations – and very quickly.

Rather than a peaceful period of gradual reconstruction, by the summer of 1945 the victors were already haggling over the peace. Now that the old enemy of German fascism was out of the way, the vast differences between the capitalist democracies and Soviet communism re-emerged. The Soviet Union didn't retire to pre-war boundaries, but, instead, installed communist governments across Eastern Europe, thus reneging on a promise to allow free elections. It was as early as March 1946 that Winston Churchill uttered the words: 'from Stettin in the Baltic to Trieste in the Adriatic, an iron curtain has descended across the continent.'

OPPOSITE: Supporters of Senator Joseph McCarthy when he was facing censure charges in 1954. The name most associated with the anti-communist purges of the 1940s and 1950s, McCarthy – and his rabble-rousing methods – stirred the paranoia of Cold War America.

ABOVE: US military police in post-war Berlin. With the Soviet Union controlling East Berlin, the Americans, British and French each policed a zone in West Berlin.

Dividing Germany

The fate of Germany encapsulated the struggles between East and West. After the war, the country was to be shared by the Allies, with British, French and American forces occupying the West and the Soviet Union taking the East. But Berlin, the capital, was far in the east, so the city was divided like a mini version of the whole nation, with British, French and American zones in the western part of the city, and the Russian sector in the eastern part. That settled the borders for the time being, but how was the country to be reconstructed? And what kind of economic system or government would it have? That was undecided.

Supporting Greece

Previously isolationist, the two World Wars had proved to America the interdependency of nations. Wary of how far Stalin hoped to expand Soviet influence by diplomacy or coercion, the US now felt that supporting independence in Europe was in the national interest in the longer run.

When Britain, in economic crisis, was unable to support anti-communist forces in Greece in 1947, Truman presented his case to Congress: 'Totalitarian regimes imposed upon free people, by direct and indirect aggression, undermine the foundations of international peace and hence the security of the United States...'. The speech, which became known as the Truman Doctrine, depicted the world on the brink of falling either towards freedom or totalitarianism – by which it was understood he meant communism. Persuaded, Congress agreed for aid to be sent to Greece.

The Marshall Plan

Across war-torn Europe, US Secretary of State George Marshall witnessed the poverty and slow recovery of the continent and concluded that the area was ripe to fall prey to communism. To avoid such an eventuality, Marshall proposed an aid programme – the Marshall Plan – to revive 'a working economy in the world so as to permit the emergence of political and economic conditions in which free institutions can exist'.

As this would involve opening up Soviet satellite states to free-market economics, Stalin soon pulled out of the discussions, but from 1948 to 1952, the US provided $13 billion of aid to Western Europe. In the same period, the Soviet Union drained roughly the same amount from Eastern Europe.

Such was the anxiety regarding the Soviet Union that, in March 1948, Truman even asked Congress to reintroduce peacetime conscription, arguing that since the end of World War II, 'the Soviet Union and its agents have destroyed the independence and democratic character of a whole series of nations in eastern and central Europe'. The only other occasion peacetime conscription had been introduced was in 1940 – and the country had gone to war little more than a year later.

ABOVE: The first consignment of American Marshall Aid Plan sugar arrives in London in February 1949.

The Berlin Blockade

Three years after the war's end, Germany was still dependent on Allied supplies and had been reduced to a barter economy. In June 1948, the US, Britain and France introduced a new currency – the Deutschmark – into their German zones, which included West Berlin. Quickly, goods began appearing in West German shops again, but how did this make the East look? Stalin's response was to blockade the roads to West Berlin, cutting off supplies to that part of the city.

Already commentators were describing the broader situation between East and West as a 'Cold War' – a war of nerves. Now those nerves would be tested. The West did not aggravate the situation militarily, but the Americans and British flew in aid, with, at its peak, aircraft landing every 30 seconds to supply the two million people of West Berlin.

The Soviets could have escalated the situation and shot down the planes, but they didn't. The airlift lasted until May the following year, when Stalin lifted the blockade. As historian David Reynolds writes: 'His bluff had been called and he had no stomach for war.' A bloody situation had been averted.

> 'The two World Wars had proved to America the interdependency of nations.'

ABOVE: Children in West Berlin watch as an American plane brings in supplies to the blockaded city in 1948. Over an 11-month period, the US, Britain and other Western Allies flew more than 200,000 flights to supply Berlin.

Following the blockade, the Truman administration argued for the creation of the North Atlantic Treaty (later to become NATO), under which the US, Canada and Western European countries promised loyalty to each other should one come under attack. This only reinforced the iron curtain, but the situation was already escalating further east when, in the same year, the Soviet Union began testing atomic bombs. Meanwhile China – the world's most populous country – had come under communist control.

The Korean War

Occupied by Japan during World War II, Korea had, like Germany, been carved up by the victors. Soviet forces had taken over northern Korea and American troops the south. The 38th Parallel, where the two armies met, became the dividing line between two political systems – the Soviets backing the communist North, America supporting the South.

Then, in June 1950, North Korea invaded the South. This took the US by surprise. But America's response would surprise Stalin, too. Because the US hadn't resisted the communist takeover of China, Stalin had approved North Korea's plans to control the whole of Korea, guessing, it would seem, that America would not get involved. But, remembering where unchecked aggression of 1930s' dictatorships had led, Truman felt that, 'if South Korea was allowed to fall Communist, leaders would be emboldened to override nations closer to our own.'

> 'In June 1950, North Korea took the US by surprise and invaded South Korea.'

LAS VEGAS

'The gangsters who run the places are all urbane and charming,' observed the English writer and actor Noël Coward in Las Vegas in 1955. 'They are curious products of a most curious, adolescent country.'

America was still, in European eyes, a young nation, and Las Vegas was a new town in a young state – Nevada only having entered the Union during the Civil War. Keen to attract outsiders, in the 1930s the Nevada authorities legalized gambling and prostitution, and offered quick divorces. Then, in 1941, mobster Meyer Lansky had sent Ben 'Bugsy' Siegel to Nevada to run the Trans America Wire service – which was essential for bookmakers across the country to learn horse racing results. Siegel soon made it part of his agreement with the bookmakers that any who wanted his wire service had to give him a share of their profits. He was also, journalists Sally Denton and Roger Morris argue in their book *The Money and the Power*, still profiting from a wartime drug trade coming into the US via Mexico.

Siegel's ambition was to build an upmarket casino in Las Vegas, which at the time was a small, unremarkable desert town. He succeeded – though he wouldn't live to enjoy the success. In December 1946, he opened the Flamingo Hotel & Casino, but already mobsters were unhappy about the sums they had invested in his lavish project. Its budget had risen from $1 million to $6 million, with rumours circulating that Siegel, or his girlfriend Virginia Hill, had been skimming money off the construction costs. Although by the following summer the Flamingo was already showing a profit, it was too late to save Siegel. He was shot dead at his home in Los Angeles. No one was ever tried for his murder.

ABOVE: The 'Rat Pack' – Frank Sinatra, Dean Martin, Sammy Davis Jr, Peter Lawford and Joey Bishop – outside Las Vegas's Sands Hotel in 1962.

Las Vegas, however, lived on. Others casinos, often backed by Mormon bankers, followed the Flamingo's success. During the 1950s, the city's population tripled to more than 65,000 and there were enough casino jobs to employ 17,000 people. Starry names, such as Ella Fitzgerald, Judy Garland and Frank Sinatra, performed there.

On the surface it all seemed legal, but the Kefauver Committee of 1950–51 – a Senate investigation into interstate crime – was well aware of the city's links to organized crime. Authors Denton and Morris claim that Meyer Lansky, still laundering drug money through Vegas, was behind most of the casinos on the Vegas Strip, and that $3 million was being skimmed for every $1 million reported in the casinos – the undeclared income finding its way into Swiss bank accounts.

For all its gaudy charm, by the end of the decade, Las Vegas was employing three times as many police as any other city of its size, and Nevada had the highest crime and suicide rates in America.

'Unprepared for the Chinese attack, the UN soldiers were overrun and fled.'

With the Soviet Union boycotting the United Nations at that time, Truman was able to win UN support for US-led troops to be committed to South Korea. In September, General Douglas MacArthur landed behind enemy lines at the port of Inchon. Soon Seoul, the southern capital, was back in Allied hands. Emboldened, MacArthur pushed into North Korea, capturing the capital Pyongyang and ignoring warnings from China not to advance any nearer their border.

The result was that on 25 November 1950, the UN soldiers were overrun by thousands of Chinese soldiers. Unprepared, the UN soldiers fled and the front line was pushed back south again, past the 38th Parallel. For a time, Seoul was in Chinese hands. When MacArthur openly proposed invading China he was dismissed from the whole conflict. Instead, the war dragged on into a stalemate until a ceasefire was agreed in 1953. The borders were returned to where they had been at the start – the 38th Parallel. In total, the US participation had involved 5.7 million men and women, with 34,000 American soldiers killed in battle.

The Red Scare

During the war, US Army code-breakers had intercepted cables between Moscow and the Soviet embassy in Washington, and found that 349 Americans had been in secret communication with Soviet agents. Among others, the evidence

BELOW: Ethel and Julius Rosenberg in a prison van in March 1951 after being found guilty of spying for the Soviet Union. Two years later they were sent to the electric chair.

OPPOSITE: Convinced that strikes at movie studios were part of a communist plot in Hollywood, J. Parnell Thomas, Chair of the House Committee on Un-American Activities (HUAC), began targeting the film-making industry in 1947.

incriminated scientist Klaus Fuchs, who had passed details of the American atomic test to the Soviet Union, thus allowing them to develop their own bomb. He eventually admitted his guilt, was imprisoned and later emigrated to East Germany. Then there was Julius Rosenberg, who had been fired from the US Army when it was discovered that he had been a member of the Communist Party. The evidence revealed that Rosenberg was the leader of a Soviet spy ring, and that he and his wife, Ethel, had also passed information about the atomic bomb to the Soviet Union. The couple were tried and executed in the electric chair in June 1953.

> 'McCarthy warned of "a final all-out battle between Communistic atheism and Christianity."'

Considering that these high-profile cases occurred at the same time as a rise in East–West tensions and labour unrest during the 1940s – three million workers were on strike in early 1946 – it was perhaps unsurprising that the belief took hold that there were communist plots afoot in America. Truman gave the FBI, under J. Edgar Hoover, licence to investigate federal employees, although the president soon baulked when it was found that Hoover's FBI was 'dabbling in sex life scandals and plain blackmail when they should be catching criminals.'

In public life, the chairman of the House of Representatives' House Committee on Un-American Activities (HUAC), J. Parnell Thomas, was convinced by 1947 that strikes at movie studios were being inspired by communism and that films were being used to spread communist propaganda. HUAC targeted Hollywood, issuing subpoenas to actors and film-makers to be quizzed about their political affiliations and those of others in their community.

The following year, the Communist Party leadership was found guilty of trying to overthrow the government, although it had taken no steps to achieve this beyond circulating books and pamphlets advocating such behaviour. By 1951, however, many states had banned the operation of the Communist Party and had placed restrictions on its members, including, in some cases, the removal of welfare benefits. Most states also introduced loyalty oaths for public employees, requiring them to swear that they did not support any subversive causes. Major industries were targeted, too, and radical unions, such as the United Electrical Workers. University professors and teaching unions also came under suspicion. As a consequence, a wave of paranoia swept through the education system, with schools and colleges racing to purge their text books of anything that might be considered politically suspect.

Senator McCarthy

In 1950, Republican Senator Joe McCarthy of Wisconsin escalated the 'reds under the beds' scare, warning in one of many apocalyptical speeches of 'a final all-out battle between Communistic atheism and Christianity'. Just as communist governments were oppressing Catholics in Poland, Czechoslovakia and Hungary, the anti-communist purges in America generated the fervour of religious persecution. Often described as witch-hunts, once you were under suspicion for communist sympathies, it was very hard to prove your innocence. One method was to become an informer, naming colleagues or former friends, as a way of shifting the blame and throwing attention elsewhere. In a political climate pitched as capitalism vs. communism, good vs. evil, the simplistic rabble-rousing of McCarthyism was able to flourish.

OPPOSITE: **Critics of Senator McCarthy accused him of demagoguery, baseless defamation and mudslinging, while he claimed that 'McCarthyism is Americanism with its sleeves rolled'. By 1954, he had lost political and popular support and was censured by the Senate.**

The Blacklist

People working in the film, radio and television industry who had been accused of communist sympathies – however inaccurately – quickly found themselves blacklisted. The writer Dorothy Parker had had a series of Hollywood commissions throughout the 1940s, but her work for the studios dried up in 1950 when her name appeared in the *Red Channels* pamphlet listing 151 people of questionable loyalty to America. In all, it is estimated that more than 300 people were blacklisted in Hollywood and 1500 in television and radio.

In 1955, folk singer Pete Seeger refused before HUAC to name personal and political associations on the grounds that this would violate his First Amendment rights to free speech. Indicted for Contempt of Congress, he had, for some years, to notify federal authorities when he planned to leave the Southern District of New York.

American culture had benefited in the 1930s from new immigrants who had fled Nazi Germany, such as conductor Otto Klemperer, film-maker Billy Wilder and actor Peter Lorre. But the persecution during America's anti-communist years generated traffic in the opposite direction. Klemperer's left-wing views led to his American passport not being renewed, and he moved to West Germany in 1954. Blacklisted American film directors Joseph Losey and Jules Dassin left America for good, establishing new careers in Europe.

McCarthy's Fall

Like the Salem witch trials of the 1690s, the mounting hysteria whipped up by Senator McCarthy only stopped when the inquisitors overreached themselves by targeting the establishment. With Salem the magistrates ceased being credulous when accusations were made against a senior churchman; similarly, when McCarthy suggested that there were communists in the US Army, the military was well able to fight back.

BELOW: **For refusing to answer questions before the House Committee on Un-American Activities on the grounds that it would violate his First Amendment right to free speech, musician Peter Seeger was indicted for Contempt of Congress in 1955.**

TRAMPING ON CHAPLIN

Despite compiling a file 2000 pages long, the FBI never found any evidence that Charlie Chaplin was a communist, but he had defended the civil liberties of communists and during World War II had been outspoken that the US should help the Soviet Union. For this, he attracted powerful enemies.

When 22-year-old would-be actress Joan Barry filed a paternity suit against Chaplin, the federal authorities escalated the case, indicting the star in 1944 under the Mann Act – a seldom-used statute dusted down when they wanted to harass someone – which held that it was a federal crime to transport a woman across a state line for immoral purposes. Although blood tests proved that Chaplin was not the father of Joan Barry's child, he *had* paid for her rail fare to New York, where he had met her. During his trial, the prosecution attacked Chaplin as a 'master mechanic in the art of seduction'. Despite the scientific evidence, he lost the paternity case and was forced to pay child support. That was a blow to the comedian's name, although the financial cost wouldn't hurt him too much.

Like many Hollywood figures, however, Chaplin wasn't American. Although the London-born comic had lived in America for 40 years, making his name there, he had always retained his British passport. This would now be used against him. While he was abroad in 1953, his opponents saw their opportunity and his re-entry permit was rescinded. A Justice Department spokesman cited the clause that foreigners might be barred on grounds of 'morals, health or insanity, or for advocating Communism or associating with Communists or pro-Communist organizations'.

Bitter at his treatment, Chaplin did not appeal the decision and settled in Switzerland, only visiting America again in 1972 to receive an honorary Oscar.

ABOVE: Charlie Chaplin (foreground, second from left) and Joan Barry in court during Barry's paternity suit against the Hollywood star in December 1944. Despite blood tests proving that he wasn't the father of her child, Chaplin lost the case.

With growing ill feeling among the public and politicians towards McCarthy, in 1954 he was censured by the Senate. By then an alcoholic, he was largely ignored politically, dying three years later. Although McCarthy fell from favour, the spirit of the time, of guilt by suspicion, lasted throughout the 1950s and, in some cases, into the 1970s, before burning out.

> 'Bonnie and Clyde's story of outsiders resonated with Depression-era readers.'

Covert Operations

While on the one hand the US was developing ever-larger long-range nuclear weapons, on the other it was beginning to explore secretive work that did not require a nuclear arsenal or even troops on the ground. Formed in 1947, the Central Intelligence Agency (CIA) helped, in 1953, to topple the Mossadegh government in Iran, which had threatened Western access to its oil supplies. The following year, the CIA trained a 500-strong 'Liberation Army' in Guatemala to overthrow the democratically elected socialist government of Jacobo Arbenz, whose reform programmes challenged the interests of America's United Fruit Company. Landing in the American ambassador's plane, exiled Colonel Carlos Castillo Armas then seized power. His rule may have suited the interests of the United Fruit Company, but Armas imprisoned thousands of political opponents, ended secret ballots and disenfranchised three-quarters of the electorate. After three years in charge, he was assassinated.

Neither Mossadegh's or Arbenz's had been communist governments, but during the Cold War the fight would be broadened to include countries that it was feared might fall prey to communism, as well as those that were anti-Western.

BELOW: Laika became the first animal to go into orbit when she was launched in the Soviet Sputnik 2 in November 1958. In 2002, it was admitted that she had died just a few hours into the mission.

The Space Race

With only seven per cent of the world's population, America, in 1950, accounted for half of its manufacturing production. But, in October 1957, it suffered a severe shock to its self-confidence when the Soviet Union beat the US into space with the launch of the first satellite, Sputnik 1. The following month, in Sputnik 2, Laika became the first dog in space. In response, Eisenhower immediately established NASA (National Aeronautics and Space Agency), while the 1958 National Defense Education Act ensured federal support for the teaching of maths and science in schools. The 1960s would see the results of America's efforts to catch up in space.

The War of Nerves

Although America had become involved in Korea, it had not stepped in when French-Indochina fell to communist rule in 1954, nor, despite condemning the action, when Soviet forces invaded Hungary after the 1956 uprising. That would have risked direct confrontation with Moscow, and no one wanted that. The Cold War would, however, last for the next 30 years with different levels of intensity.

The following decade would see open fighting and near nuclear war between the countries of the East and those of the West, but there was mounting tension at home, too – that between black and white.

KILLING SPREES

Young lovers on the run, stealing cars and shooting victims before a bloody denouement with the law – that was Bonnie Parker and Clyde Barrow in the early 1930s, right? Well, it could have been, but in the 1950s it was also 19-year-old Charles Starkweather and his 14-year-old girlfriend, Caril Ann Fugate. Between November 1957 and January 1958, Starkweather killed 11 people in Nebraska and Wyoming, beginning with a service station attendant who had refused to give him credit, before he turned on Fugate's mother and stepfather, and even her two-year-old half-sister. Then, when Fugate joined Starkweather, the couple went on a killing spree, shooting people as they stole money and cars. When they were caught, Starkweather was sent to the electric chair, while Fugate, who has always maintained her innocence, served 17 years of a life sentence.

Strangely, for such a sordid story, Starkweather and Fugate captured the popular imagination in a romantic way. The 1973 film *Badlands* is loosely inspired by their story, while the two are the subject of Bruce Springsteen's 1982 song 'Nebraska'. Similarly, Bonnie and Clyde, who robbed grocery stores and killed 13 people before being gunned down by police in Louisiana in 1934, have been celebrated in song and on film, most prominently in a 1967 movie starring Faye Dunaway and Warren Beatty.

Benefiting from attractive photographs reproduced in newspapers, Bonnie and Clyde's story resonated with Depression-era readers. Here, it seemed, was a couple fighting back against an uncaring system, even if the people they were robbing were hardly doing much better than they were. They were the ultimate outsiders.

But perhaps there is another element to the appeal of these crime couples. Is it that violence, guns, and riding off into the wilderness are part of the myth of America? Rather than a cowboy with a horse, it becomes a thief with a car, alone against the world – except perhaps for a lover caught up in a *folie à deux*.

Just as the myth of the violent-but-just cowboy in an unjust land is attractive, so the murderous pair are recast as desperate individuals fighting against an unfair system. The idea carries something of America's frontier spirit with it into the modern age.

RIGHT: Young, in love and stylish, outlaws Bonnie Parker and Clyde Barrow captured the popular imagination in the early 1930s.

As was shown repeatedly across the 1950s and 1960s, desegregation – whether of schools or elsewhere in society – was not solely a race issue. Like so much of the history of America in the previous century, it illustrated conflict – not only between the authority of the federal government and that of individual states, but also between attitudes in the north and south.

Before the Civil Rights Movement

The Jim Crow segregation laws that had been introduced by the Southern states at the beginning of the twentieth century – which decreed separate lunch counters and drinking fountains for black and whites, as well as ruling that blacks had to board buses by the rear door and give up their seat to a white person if the bus became crowded – were still in place after World War II. Blacks were also often denied voting rights in the south, where state laws made it difficult for them to register. In some places it wasn't simply a case of sending off a form: for a black person, voting often meant visiting the registration office in the few, possibly inconvenient, hours when it was open each month, and then having to answer obscure questions. In Alabama one such question was: 'If the President does not wish to sign a bill, how many days is he allowed in which to return it to Congress for reconsideration?' Unsurprisingly, in Alabama and Mississippi in the early 1960s, less than 10 per cent of the black population of voting age was registered.

BELOW: Desegregating schools in the South. The first black pupils at Little Rock Central High School, Arkansas, leaving the school under escort from paratroopers in 1957.

Small Steps

Since the 1930s there had been improvements across the country as a whole for African-Americans. For instance, in 1932, the Supreme Court ruled that black defendants on trial for life must have adequate legal presentation; in 1946, the Committee on Civil Rights recommended legislation against discrimination in jobs and voting, as well as a federal anti-lynching law; and two years later the armed forces were desegregated. In 1947, Jackie Robinson became the first African-American to play in a major league baseball team, opening the door for others to follow.

The population was changing, too. While in 1910, 90 per cent of blacks lived in the south, by the 1960s, half lived in the north; overall, the African-American population was now more urban than rural. The poor, however, remained disproportionately non-white, and the rising expectations of blacks intensified resentment against racial subjugation in the south, as well as discrimination in the north. 'Race,' writes historian David Reynolds, 'remained America's Achilles heel, the worm in its rosy apple of prosperity.'

School Days

In 1896, the Supreme Court had permitted the segregation of pupils into black and white schools under the decree that facilities be 'separate but equal'. But with equality being left to individual states to ensure, black schools in the south had become distinctly unequal. In 1954, following the efforts of the National Association for the Advancement of Colored People (NAACP), led by black lawyer Thurgood Marshall, the Supreme Court heard a case regarding segregation in Kansas's schools. It ruled that even if schools were equal, segregation on race 'generates a feeling of inferiority' in the pupils, and concluded that 'separate educational facilities are inherently unequal'. To many, this sounded like a new birth of the freedom that had been promised after the Civil War. To some segregationists, however, it was 'socialist doctrine', representing how the federal government had, in the words of Judge Tom Brady of Mississippi, 'usurped the sacred privilege and right of respective states of this union to educate its youth'. In his argument, it wasn't a matter or race, but political authority.

Just as equality in segregated schools had been left to the individual states to enforce, so now it would be up to the Southern political

LEFT: In 1947, Jackie Robinson joined the Brooklyn Dodgers, becoming the first African-American to play in a major league baseball team.

> 'To many, desegregating schools sounded like the new birth of the freedom that had been promised after the Civil War.'

elite to see that schools were desegregated. The Supreme Court may have made its ruling, but politicians weren't going to hurry it along if they didn't have to. Even President Eisenhower admitted privately that he thought the Supreme Court's decision 'set back progress in the South at least 15 years' and that to force desegregation was 'just plain nuts'. But, while the politicians were dragging their feet, black Americans were taking a stand.

Back of the Bus

On Thursday 1 December 1955, Rosa Parks, a 42-year-old seamstress in Montgomery, Alabama, ignored a driver's order to give up her bus seat to a white person. Consequently, Parks, who was also secretary of the Montgomery chapter of the NAACP, was arrested and charged under Montgomery's segregation laws. She later explained her action as a way of finding out 'what rights I had as a human being and a citizen'.

When Parks was bailed the following evening by the president of Montgomery's NAACP, it was decided to use her case to protest against segregation. On the day of her trial, a bus boycott among African-Americans was observed across the city.

That same day, the Montgomery Improvement Association was formed, electing as its leader 26-year-old Martin Luther King Jr. Highly educated, with a PhD from Boston University, King had been raised in Georgia before becoming a minister in Montgomery. From his first speech, he called for non-violent protest against oppression. 'In our protests there will be no cross burnings,' he said, in reference to the Ku Klux Klan, 'no white person will be taken from his home by a hooded Negro mob and brutally murdered.' King reminded the crowd that the law – federal law, at least – was already on their side: 'If we are wrong, the Supreme Court of this nation is wrong. If we are wrong, the Constitution of the United States is wrong.' A non-violent protest, the bus boycott – which had originally been planned for a single day – continued. Over time, the bus company and local businesses began to feel the pinch.

Not that in the following weeks there wasn't violence *against* blacks. There was, and it included the shattering of the front of King's house by a bomb. Nevertheless, a case against segregated buses made its way through the courts. The following November, the Supreme Court declared Montgomery's segregated buses unconstitutional. Peaceful protest and legal doggedness had worked. In all, the bus boycott had lasted more than a year, but by Christmas 1956, Montgomery had ended segregation on its transport system. Encouraged, African-Americans in other southern cities began bus boycotts.

ABOVE: Rosa Parks has her fingerprints taken after being arrested for refusing to give up her seat to a white passenger on a bus in Birmingham, Alabama, in December 1955.

The Little Rock Nine

The events at Central High School in Little Rock, Arkansas, came nine months after the desegregation of Montgomery's buses. Despite an order from the Federal District Court to desegregate the schools, the governor of that state, Orval Faubus, had blocked integration, arguing that if he did, 'blood would run in the streets', and that he was therefore acting to preserve the peace. So when the nine black teenagers arrived for their first day at the school on 4 September, Faubus sent the National Guard to block their path. A crowd of more than 400 white men and women gathered, some shouting: 'Go home, niggers.' Giving up, the teenagers went home.

> 'While the politicians were dragging their feet, black Americans were taking a stand.'

Race, though, was not the only issue here; class played a role too. In Little Rock, there were other high schools, some in wealthier areas, but it was only Central High, which catered for mainly working-class families, that had been selected for desegregation. Amis Guthridge, spokesman of the anti-desegregation Capital Citizens' Council, whipped up resentment, telling poor whites that the rich were making sure 'the only race-mixing that is going to be done is in the districts where the so-called rednecks live.' His point was that poor whites had most to fear economically and socially from black social mobility.

Governor Faubus's act in blocking integration was one of defiance against the Supreme Court. When he wouldn't back down, President Eisenhower went over his head, sent in the paratroopers and federalized Arkansas' 10,000-strong National Guard.

The black pupils went to school, but their troubles were not over. Often racially abused by other pupils, one was suspended after she tipped food over a pupil who had been taunting her, only to be later expelled. The others, however, managed to complete the school year.

The following year it was decided to close all four of Little Rock's public schools in order to avoid a repeat of the situation. It would take a Supreme Court decision to reopen them.

BELOW: 'Race mixing is communism' and 'Stop the Race Mixing March of the Anti-Christ' read placards held by protestors against school desegregation outside the capitol building in Little Rock, Arkansas, in 1959.

Non-violent Protests

Further black protest came in the form of sit-ins staged across the south in 1960–61. Taking their lead from Mahatma Gandhi's non-violent action, black groups such as the Congress on Racial Equality (CORE) and Martin Luther King's Southern Christian Leadership Conference (SCLC) were well organized, with young members, both black and white, preparing for protests by role-playing what they would do and say when provoked.

Globally, they were encouraged, too – in 1960 alone, 16 African countries gained their independence from European nations. 'They were getting their freedom,' said John Lewis, one of the founders of the Student Non-Violent Coordinating Committee (SNCC), 'and we still didn't have ours in what we believed was a free country.'

Freedom Rides

Again, federal law would prove to be at odds with state practices. In 1960, the Supreme Court ruled that segregation on interstate buses and trains was unconstitutional. This, however, was not being enforced – the new administration of President John F. Kennedy, who had been elected by a very small margin in 1960, being unwilling to risk alienating Southern Democrats opposed to desegregation.

BELOW: College students at a cafe sit-in, in Little Rock, Arkansas, in January 1962. The Civil Rights Movement was characterized by non-violent protest, such as sit-ins and marches.

ABOVE: Passengers, including Freedom Riders sponsored by the Congress of Racial Equality (CORE), escape their Greyhound bus after it has been set on fire by whites protesting against the desegregation of interstate buses in May 1961.

Activists such as James Farmer of CORE realized that, in order to win, they had to make it more dangerous for the federal government *not* to enforce federal law than to enforce it. To achieve this, they would, in a non-violent way, provoke violence, thus embarrassing the government into taking action. This helped broaden the issue beyond local legislation and state politics. Beginning in May 1961, Freedom Rides involved pairs of volunteers – one white, one black – who would board interstate buses, with the black volunteer refusing to move from a seat at the front and the white volunteer sitting at the back. In addition, in waiting rooms, the black volunteers would try to use the whites-only facilities. As anticipated, some of the volunteers were beaten up and jailed, and several buses were even firebombed. Although President Kennedy tried to calm the situation, violence against Freedom Riders continued. But within five months of the Freedom Rides beginning, the Interstate Commerce Commission announced that all buses and terminals must display signs announcing that all seating was desegregated. Direct action had won.

Violence, however, would continue. The Ku Klux Klan was reborn and other white vigilante groups were established. In 1962, the prospect of a black student being admitted to the University of Mississippi sparked a campus riot that had to be suppressed by federal troops, with Mississippi's National Guard being brought under federal control. In June 1963, black civil rights activist Medgar Evers was assassinated in Jackson, Mississippi, while in Birmingham, Alabama, four children were killed in the bombing of a black church.

> 'The Ku Klux Klan was reborn and other white vigilante groups were established.'

To those who criticized direct action, Martin Luther King responded with these words in 1963: 'We have waited for more than 340 years for our constitutional and God-given rights. The nations of Asia and Africa are moving with jet-like speed toward the goal of political independence, and we still creep at horse-and-buggy pace toward the gaining of a cup of coffee at a lunch counter.'

Marches and sit-ins kept the issue in the headlines. In August 1963, King's march on Washington culminated in his 'I have a dream' speech delivered on the steps of the Lincoln Memorial to a crowd of around 250,000 people. Following this, Kennedy proposed a new civil rights bill. The bill hadn't got far before Kennedy was assassinated in November, but his successor, Lyndon B. Johnson, pushed it through, even telling Congress that it would be a fitting way to honour JFK's memory. The Civil Rights Act, signed by Johnson in July 1964, made illegal all forms of segregation and discrimination.

OPPOSITE: A hundred years after Lincoln's Emancipation Proclamation, 'the life of the Negro is still sadly crippled by the manacles of segregation and the chains of discrimination' – Martin Luther King Jr delivering his 'I have a dream' speech in Washington, D.C. in August 1963.

Freedom Summer

The obstructive voting regulations against blacks, however, remained in place, so volunteers, both black and white, including many student activists, set out to increase voter registration. Protesting in Selma, Alabama, in January 1965, King was jailed, along with many teachers and their schoolchildren; when, two months later, protesters tried to take their case to the state capital in Montgomery, state troopers barred their way, before mounted police attacked.

Two weeks later, King led a large crowd on the 80km (50-mile) march from Selma to Montgomery. When Alabama's governor George Wallace – who had declared in his inaugural address two years earlier 'segregation now, segregation tomorrow, segregation forever' – refused to provide protection for the marchers, President Johnson overruled him by federalizing the National Guard and sending in the US Army.

ABOVE: In Selma, Alabama, in March 1965, police attack civil rights activists attempting to march to Montgomery to protest against race discrimination in voter registration.

The following week, Johnson asked Congress for a voting rights act by which the federal government would be able to eliminate all local and state obstacles to voting for blacks. The act was signed that August; within three years, black registration to vote had reached 60 per cent of potential voters in Mississippi and Alabama.

Ratified in the Fourteenth Amendment in 1868, full citizenship had been left to the liberty of the states to enforce. Now, 97 years later, the freedom of those states *not to enforce* had been overridden by the federal government.

The Watts Riots

In August 1965, Watts, a black area in Los Angeles, erupted into racial violence. Beginning with a minor event – after white police arrested a black man for drunk driving – the situation escalated into riots. After six days of burning and looting, 34 black people were dead. Among some of those responsible for the rioting, there was some sense of satisfaction. Not only had they kicked back at the L.A. police, whom they regarded as racist, they had also drawn attention to the causes of their unrest.

While there was no segregation in Los Angeles or elsewhere outside the South, there was still discrimination. Blacks were more likely to be unemployed or in lower-level work, while they often paid more for housing than whites. Where in its earlier years the Civil Rights movement had been most active in the South, in the mid-1960s racial conflict intensified in other cities in other states, police violence against the black community often being blamed for provoking riots. Protesting in 1966 against Chicago's discrimination of its one million blacks in the housing market, Martin Luther King was shocked at the reception they received in middle-class white suburbs – with Nazi flags, bottles being lobbed and taunts of 'young monkeys' or 'white trash' being spat at Civil Rights supporters. 'I have never seen,' said King, 'even in Mississippi and Alabama, mobs as hostile and hate-filled as I've seen in Chicago.'

> 'After six days of burning and looting, 34 black people were dead.'

BELOW: Police search African-American youths in the Los Angeles district of Watts in March 1966, during the second race riot in eight months. While there was no segregation in Los Angeles, there was still discrimination.

MISSISSIPPI BURNING

In Longdale, Mississippi, in late May, 1964, two civil rights activists – James Chaney, a 21-year-old black Mississippian, and Michael Schwerner, a 24-year-old white New Yorker – spoke at Mount Zion Methodist Church, raising the idea of opening a freedom school to help the congregation pass the literacy requirements to register to vote.

Learning of the freedom school idea, members of the Mississippi White Knights, a Ku Klux Klan splinter group, hatched a plan to rid the area of the two activists. First, as a way of luring Chaney and Schwerner back to Longdale, 24 armed Klansmen burnt down Mount Zion Church. This worked; on 21 June, Schwerner and Chaney, joined by Andrew Goodman, a 20-year-old white New Yorker, returned to the town to see what had happened.

ABOVE: The murdered civil rights activists (left to right) Andrew Goodman, James Chaney and Michael Schwerner.

Driving out of Longdale that evening, the three were followed by 26-year-old Deputy Sheriff and White Knights member, Cecil R. Price, who stopped them before escorting them to a secluded junction. There, another car of seven Klansmen joined Price. Chaney was beaten and shot three times, while Schwerner and Goodman were each shot once in the heart. The bodies were buried in an earth dam. From the red clay later found in Goodman's lungs, it appeared that he had been buried alive.

When the three men were reported missing, the FBI launched a major manhunt. The activists' bodies were found several weeks later on the strength of a tip by an FBI informant, later revealed to be a local highway patrolman. In the ensuing FBI investigation, a number of suspects were identified, with James Jordan and another conspirator confessing their roles. But Mississippi officials refused to prosecute for murder – a state crime. The 18 men whom the FBI had identified were charged with conspiring to deprive the activists of their civil rights – the only way they could be tried under federal government authority.

After legal wrangling, the trial began in Meridian, Mississippi, in October 1967. Seven of the men were found guilty, including Price, with sentences ranging from three to 10 years. Having become a major prosecution witness, James Jordan, who had been one of the conspirators to shoot the victims, was tried separately, receiving a four-year sentence.

But the convictions weren't over. With the jury reaching a deadlock over the case against Edgar Ray Killen, a preacher, whom, it is believed, planned and directed the killings ,but who had not carried out the shootings, the judge decided not to retry him. Only in June 2005, 40 years after the killings, was he retried, with a jury convicting him on three counts of manslaughter. Interviewed in prison in December 2014, Killen said that he remained a segregationist and did not believe in racial equality.

OPPOSITE: By the later 1960s, the civil rights movement was fragmenting. While providing helpful community social programmes, the Black Panthers were a revolutionary organization, calling not for integration, but black separatism – and they were not opposed to violence.

There were further riots in Detroit and Newark in 1967. Some commentators pointed to agitators or communist manipulation as the cause, but an investigation by the Presidential Commission found poverty, unemployment and improper police practices to be factors. Blacks made up about 10 per cent of the American population, but constituted almost one-third of those living below the poverty line.

In the spring of 1968, violence erupted in more than 100 cities. This had a very precise trigger: on 4 April, while standing on a hotel balcony in Memphis, Tennessee, Martin Luther King was shot dead by white petty criminal James Earl Ray.

Black Power

By the time of Martin Luther King's death, his non-violent protests and ideas of integration had lost some ground to new black movements. Activist Stokely Carmichael was now calling for more direct confrontation. On release after his 27th arrest in June 1966, he addressed a crowd of 3000 people in Mississippi: 'We been saying "freedom" for six years and we ain't got nothin'. What we gonna start saying now is Black Power!'

This wasn't the first time the term 'Black Power' had been heard, but it now began to take hold, and it marked a turning point in the Civil Rights movement.

> 'In the spring of 1968, violence erupted in more than 100 cities.'

While Carmichael never resorted to violence, at times his rhetoric seemed likely to provoke it. 'When you talk of Black Power, you talk of building a movement that will smash everything that Western civilization has created,' he said. Having worked closely with white activists in groups such as the Student Non-Violent Co-ordinating Committee, many black activists now became increasingly extremist and combative.

More extreme, the Black Panther movement was formed that October in San Francisco. Theirs was a revolutionary manifesto, when, at the height of the Vietnam War they sought common cause with Vietnamese communists. Further, calling not for integration but for black separatism, they were prepared to use guns to try to achieve their goals. Although the movement did some worthwhile social work, it also became tainted and bloodied by drug trafficking, bank robberies, rape and murder. By the end of the decade the Black Panthers – and their armed wing, the Black Liberation Army – had been destroyed by the police and FBI.

The separatist black Muslim movement Nation of Islam had built support in urban ghettos from the 1950s, before raising its profile to a national level through the oratory skills of its leader, Malcolm X. Born Malcolm Little, he had changed his surname to symbolize the African family name of the slave ancestor that he would never know. For a time, Malcolm X was considered a firebrand, until, gradually moving to a more racially tolerant position, he became alienated from the sectarian views of the leadership of the Nation of Islam. He was assassinated by three of its members in 1965.

Perhaps the best-known supporter of the Nation of Islam was Muhammad Ali. His name, too, tells a story of African-American history. Born Cassius Clay, he was named after his father Cassius Marcellus Clay Sr, who, in turn, had been named after a white nineteenth-century slave abolitionist and politician. In 1964, having just become World Heavyweight Champion, Clay joined the

STONEWALL RIOTS

The Civil Rights movement prompted other groups to push for similar rights. With homosexual acts still criminalized in all states (other than Illinois in 1962), few establishments welcomed openly gay people. The Stonewall Inn in Greenwich Village, New York, became popular among some of the city's most marginalized residents, with its customers including drag queens, transgender people and male prostitutes. Police raids on gay bars were common, but, during one at the Stonewall in June 1969, the customers fought back, the bar went up in flames, and over the next few days there were riots in the neighbourhood. The following month, the Gay Liberation Front was formed, and, during the next year, other gay rights groups were established, with the first Gay Pride march marking the anniversary of the Stonewall Riots. From the 1970s, states began to decriminalize homosexual acts, with the Supreme Court invalidating all remaining laws against homosexuality in 2003.

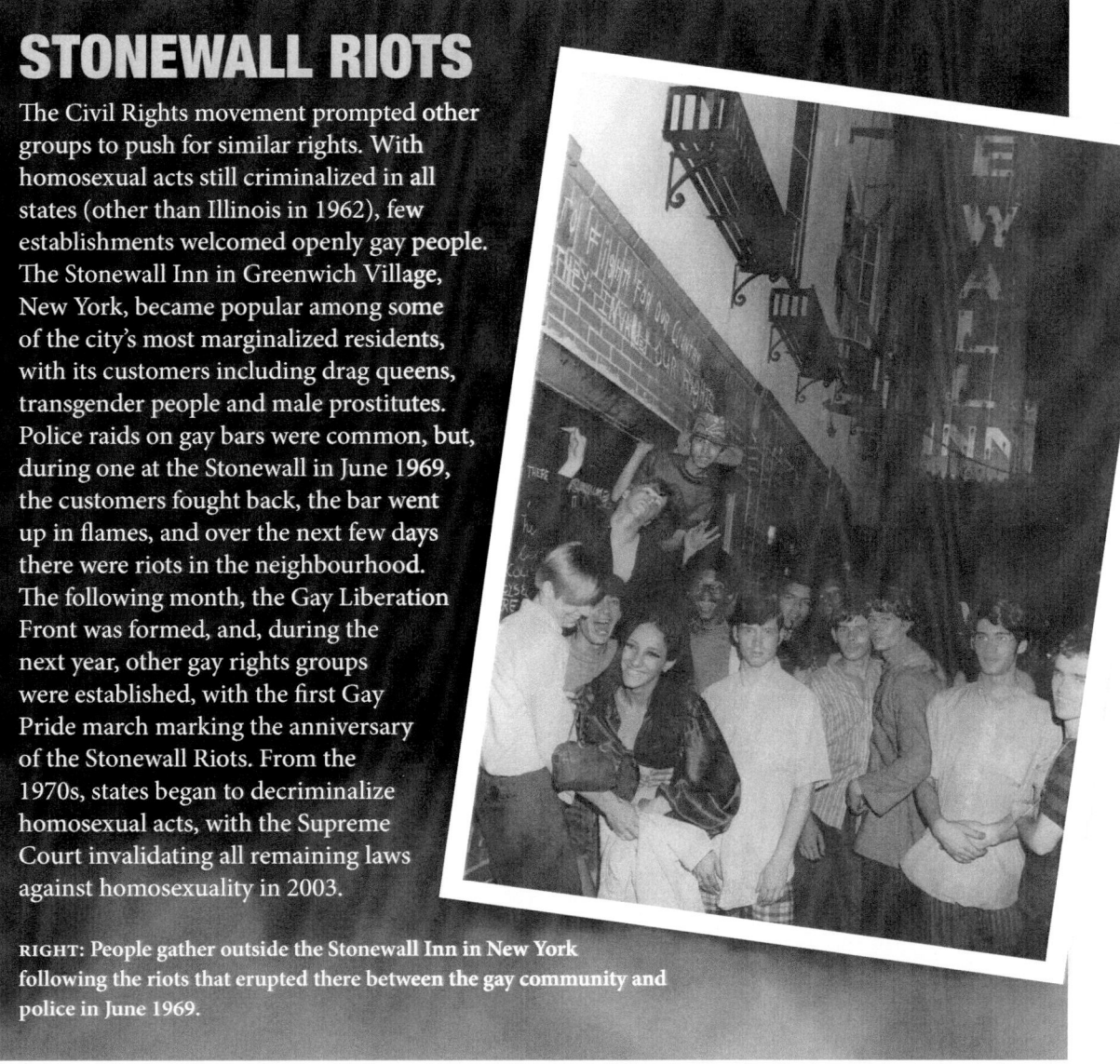

RIGHT: People gather outside the Stonewall Inn in New York following the riots that erupted there between the gay community and police in June 1969.

Nation of Islam, changing his name to Cassius X and then, later, Muhammad Ali. 'His transition from being a white clone into a symbol of black pride and then of radical separatism was a parable of sixties' America,' writes historian David Reynolds. Although in later years Ali would step back from his early calls for separatism and become something of a beacon for peaceful relations between the races, he remained a Muslim until his death in 2016.

Sign of the Times

By the mid-1960s, the Civil Rights movement had achieved immense change in making segregation and discrimination illegal, while stirring other rights movements. But there had also been associated mob violence, murders and assassinations. America, however, was already involved in a foreign war, and more assassinations were to come in what would be a tumultuous decade.

OPPOSITE: Boxer Muhammad Ali speaking to the Press outside the United Nations building in New York in March 1964, with, wearing glasses, the Nation of Islam's Malcolm X.

10

THE 1960s

During a turbulent decade, America would, on discovering Russian missile bases in Cuba, draw near to the brink of war with the Soviet Union, before becoming ever more deeply embroiled in a costly, increasingly unpopular and – for the first time – televized war fighting communism in Vietnam.

IN 1959, THE dictatorship of US-backed Fulgencio Batista in Cuba was overthrown by revolutionary forces led by Fidel Castro. Although Castro was not originally a Marxist, his land reforms threatened American commercial interests on the island, and he would go on to link himself with, and take aid from, the Soviet Union. Within a few years, America's greatest Cold War enemy not only had an ally less than 160km (100 miles) from Florida, but was building military bases on Cuba, too. The US had to wonder: would other, larger, Latin American countries now fall to communism?

Consequently in January 1961, the US broke off diplomatic relations with Cuba, and the CIA began drawing up plans to depose the new leader by way of an invasion of the island by anti-Castro exiles. Newly elected President John F. Kennedy was, however, unwilling to risk America being regarded as an imperialist power, and stripped the mission of any overt US involvement. Without air support, the operation was crippled; when it was launched in April, all 1400 Cuban exiles were captured or killed on the beaches of Cuba's Bay of Pigs.

OPPOSITE: The funeral of President John F. Kennedy on 25 November 1963. His widow Jackie Kennedy leads their children down the White House steps, while following on the left is JFK's brother, Attorney General Robert F. Kennedy, who himself would be assassinated five years later.

ABOVE: A group of Cuban soldiers after routing the invasion by exiles at the Bay of Pigs in 1961. Stripped of any overt US-backing in the form of air support, the invasion had been a fiasco.

A week earlier, the US had suffered another embarrassment when the Soviet Union had dented America's pride once again, when it became the first nation to put a man in space. In response, Kennedy announced that America would put a man on the Moon before the end of the decade.

Emboldened by success in space and the US failure at the Bay of Pigs, as well as America's lack of reaction when Soviet-controlled East Germany had built a wall across Berlin to stop East Germans leaving for the West, Soviet Premier Nikita Khrushchev chose to strengthen his position in the Caribbean.

During the summer of 1962, the CIA noted the build-up of Soviet troops and equipment in Cuba, but it was not until 16 October that spy planes spotted evidence of Soviet medium-range nuclear missile bases on the island. Kennedy was advised by his joint chiefs of staff to launch a full military invasion of Cuba, but the president chose a more cautious path, announcing a blockade of the island.

Initially, Soviet ships en route to Cuba showed no signs of recognizing the blockade, and when a Russian submarine was seen supporting them, a US destroyer moved into position to engage the vessels. Was a world war about to break out? The world held its breath. Then, the Soviet ships stopped… and turned back. 'We're eyeball to eyeball,' said Secretary of State Dean Rush, 'and I think the other guy just blinked.'

An immediate conflagration had been averted, but there were still Soviet missiles in Cuba directed at the United States. Anxiously, the world watched and waited. As the US began making plans for air strikes and a possible invasion, on 27 October, only 11 days after the missiles had been spotted, an American U-2 spy plane was shot down over Cuba, killing its pilot.

Were nuclear missiles about to be launched? Who would be the first to blink this time? Again it was Khrushchev, who had a much smaller nuclear arsenal. Proposing that he and Kennedy show 'statesmanlike wisdom', the Soviet leader withdrew his missiles on the agreement that the US wouldn't invade Cuba. Khrushchev also asked that America remove its nuclear missiles from Turkey, which Kennedy refused to do publicly – while secretly acquiescing.

The Cuban missile crisis was as close as the superpowers came to nuclear war. The following summer, they made a step towards détente, signing a treaty banning nuclear tests in the atmosphere. US conflict with communist regimes would, however, continue, but not directly against the Soviet Union. Instead, America would fight both overtly and covertly, and most bloodily in southeast Asia.

> 'Were nuclear missiles about to be launched? Who would be the first to blink this time?'

BELOW: Kennedy addresses the nation during the Cuban Missile Crisis in 1962, stating that America would 'regard any nuclear missile launched from Cuba against any nation in the western hemisphere as an attack by the Soviet Union on the United States'.

Vietnam and the Domino Theory

Like Germany after World War II and Korea in 1950, Vietnam was in 1956 divided into two parts: a communist North and a capitalist South. The country had been part of the French colony of Indochina since the late nineteenth century, when, in the 1940s, a nationalist movement, the Viet Minh, led by Ho Chi Minh, began to emerge. From the early 1950s, the Viet Minh had received support from the new communist government in China, and, through insurrections in the north of Vietnam, had eroded France's desire to keep its colony. After the defeat of their garrison at Dien Bien Phu in 1954, the French gave up, and, as the French withdrew, Vietnam was partitioned, albeit initially on a 'temporary' basis, at the Geneva Conference of 1956. President Eisenhower and others, however, were worried that if the whole of Vietnam fell into communist hands, the rest of southeast Asia would follow, like 'a row of dominoes'. That would then pose a threat to Australasia.

RIGHT: Buddhist monk Thich Quang Duc sets himself on fire in Saigon in June 1963, in protest at the persecution of Buddhists by the US-backed South Vietnamese government. In the following months, five more Buddhist monks would kill themselves in the same way.

Elections were supposed to be held in Vietnam in 1956 to decide on a new government across a unified country. But, fearing that Ho Chi Minh's communists might win, Eisenhower blocked them, backing instead a separate South Vietnam state, and propping it up with $1 billion of economic aid and military assistance. Its leader, Ngo Dinh Diem, was anti-communist, anti-French and a Catholic in a largely Buddhist country, and in a rule that harked back to colonial ways, he prevented land reforms, and relied on the landed elite and his relatives to maintain power.

By the end of the 1950s, a communist guerrilla movement in the South backed by North Vietnam and called the Viet Cong (Vietnamese Communists) had been formed. In response, in late 1961, President Kennedy increased American aid and 'military advisers' to help bolster the South. When Kennedy came into office in 1961, there were 2000 American troops in Vietnam; by the end of 1963, there were 16,000. This escalating trend would continue throughout the decade.

What had largely been a covert war became front-page news when attacks on Buddhists by Diem provoked large protests. Photographs of monks sitting in flames as, having poured petrol over their gowns, they set fire to themselves, went around the world. Reluctantly, Kennedy accepted the advice of aides that the US should, for the sake of stability in South Vietnam, support a military coup against Diem. On 1 November 1963, the generals toppled Diem, later shooting him and his brother.

Kennedy ordered a review of his options in Vietnam, including the possibility of US withdrawal, but he never read the report. Before the end of the month he, too, was dead.

JFK's Assassination

Riding in a motorcade in Dallas, Texas, on 22 November 1963, President Kennedy was shot, dying on the way to hospital. But more than half a century later, who – and on whose orders – delivered the fatal shot, remains a question still pondered by many. The Warren Commission investigation into the shooting reported in September 1964 that three rifle shots were fired by a lone gunman from the Texas School Book Depository building as the motorcade passed. That lone gunman was 24-year-old Lee Harvey Oswald, a former US Marines marksman who had defected to the Soviet Union in the late 1950s, before returning to Texas. He had begun working at the book depository the previous month.

With a witness description of a sniper firing from the building, Oswald was soon challenged on a street by a policeman. Pulling out a revolver, Oswald shot the policeman dead, before fleeing into a cinema, where he was arrested. Two days later, Oswald

BELOW: The assassination of John F. Kennedy in Dallas, Texas, on 22 November 1963. In the back of the car, Jackie Kennedy leans over the wounded president before the fatal, final shot hits.

was being led through Dallas Police Headquarters when Jack Ruby, a local nightclub operator, stepped out of the crowd and shot him. Within two hours, Oswald himself was dead, while Ruby would die in prison four years later awaiting retrial over his murder charge.

Although the Warren Commission found that both Oswald (and Ruby) had been acting alone, other witnesses said that the second and third shots – the third being the fatal one to Kennedy's head – didn't come from the book depository. Was there a conspiracy? Certainly for many people it was too shocking to accept that one unstable young man with a rifle could kill the president.

Scepticism about the assassination among the general public and even on Capitol Hill was still strong enough that in 1976 a House Select Committee on Assassinations (HSCA) was established. It concluded that JFK was probably assassinated as part of a conspiracy. It didn't suggest who the conspirators might be, though it ruled out many suspects, such as the governments of the Soviet Union and Cuba, as well as the Mafia, FBI, CIA and Secret Service.

Would any part of the US security services seriously have wanted Kennedy dead? There was the suggestion that he was regarded by some right-wing zealots as having gone soft on communism as he had promised not to invade Cuba, had looked as if he might withdraw from Vietnam, and had sympathized with the Civil Rights movement, which some regarded as communist subversion. The HSCA also reported that the security services had withheld information from the Warren Commission.

Was there a sinister reason for this or was it just secretive agencies being true to their nature, and giving away as little as possible? Or was the fatal shot a terrible error that the Secret Service then hushed up? One theory suggests that in the commotion after Oswald's first shot, a Secret Service agent in the car behind the president's accidentally fired his weapon, killing JFK.

Conspiracy, cock-up or the efforts of a lone, deranged gunman, Kennedy's assassination stunned the world. The presidency, though, had to continue. Two hours after the shooting, Vice-President Lyndon B. Johnson, who had been in the motorcade that day, was sworn in as president on Air Force One as the plane prepared to leave Dallas.

ABOVE: Two hours after the Kennedy assassination, Vice-President Lyndon B. Johnson is sworn in as president on board Air Force One. Jackie Kennedy stands beside him.

> 'It concluded that JFK was probably assassinated as part of a conspiracy.'

Viet Cong Gains

The coup against Diem had not improved the situation in South Vietnam. Instead, it had led to instability, with six governments coming and going in the following 18 months. Meanwhile, the Viet Cong gained effective control of half of the South, with North Vietnamese Army units pressing southwards. It was becoming ever more difficult, and, unlike in the Korean War, America – though supported by the South Vietnamese Army, South Korea, Australia and New Zealand – didn't have the peace-keeping banner of a United Nations flag to help maintain popular support.

Advisers to President Johnson ranged from a few 'doves' who advocated cutting their losses and pulling out of Vietnam, to a majority of 'hawks', who felt that they could not allow South Vietnam to fail because America had already invested so much in the conflict.

It was decided to escalate efforts to save the South. Following the killing of eight Americans at the US base at Pleiku in February 1965, bombing against North Vietnam began and the number of US troops in Vietnam increased vastly. Johnson, for his part, tried to dodge his exposure to any potential political and public disapproval by not seeking full Congressional support, instead relying on a resolution from August 1964 that authorized him to take 'all necessary measures' against armed attack on US forces. Nor did he ask Congress to increase taxes to fund the war, instead increasing government borrowing.

The Guerrilla Advantage

By the end of 1967, nearly half a million US troops were in Vietnam and 16,000 had died. The bombing of North Vietnam caused great damage, but had little effect on the course of the war, as factories were simply rebuilt in the countryside, and supply lines established through the jungle and Cambodia to support the Viet Cong in the South. As James Thomson of the National Security Council remarked, the North Vietnamese knew very well that 'some day we're going

RIGHT: US aircraft bomb a military target in North Vietnam in June 1966. Although the bombing of North Vietnam caused immense damage, it had little long-term effect on the war, as factories were simply rebuilt in the countryside.

to go home'. It was a classic guerrilla war situation: the Viet Cong, backed by the North Vietnamese Army (NVA), could win by holding out; America could only win by achieving total victory.

Yes, America had tanks, helicopters and aeroplanes, but these all cost it the element of surprise. Between 1966 and 1968, the CIA noted that less than one per cent of nearly two million Allied small unit operations resulted in enemy contact. They were losing many casualties to an enemy they often couldn't find. In contrast, in the same period, three-quarters of the battles were fought at the Viet Cong's choosing of time and place.

One method to flush out the enemy was to drop defoliating chemicals, such as Agent Orange, to destroy forests and fields. Between 1962 and 1971, the US sprayed 76 million litres (20 million gallons) of defoliants on Vietnam, Laos and parts of Cambodia. The severity of the long-term health and ecological consequences of this are still being hotly debated.

Furthermore, the Viet Cong were being supplied by North Vietnam, but North Vietnam was itself being supplied by China and the Soviet Union. America, however, wasn't going to bomb *those* supply lines, as that would antagonize the communist heavyweights.

The Tet Offensive

On 30 January 1968, during a temporary truce for Vietnam's New Year holiday of Tet, the NVA and the Viet Cong launched major assaults on cities and towns all over the South. It was an immense shock for the US, and a further blow against support for the war when it was reported on American television news each evening.

Although in terms of propaganda the Tet Offensive was a victory for the Viet Cong, it turned into a military defeat. Within a few weeks, the US had responded, killing or wounding most of the Viet Cong leadership. From then on, America's main enemy was the NVA, but with both sides digging in, the war was reaching a stalemate.

In March, Johnson addressed the nation. Saying that bombing would cease and that peace negotiations were being opened, he indicated how unpopular the war had made him by announcing that he would not be standing for a second term.

> 'By the end of 1967, nearly half a million US troops were in Vietnam and 16,000 had died.'

BELOW: Saigon under attack from the Viet Cong and North Vietnamese Army during the 1968 Tet Offensive. Having caught the US forces completely by surprise, the Tet Offensive was a great propaganda victory for the communists.

My Lai Massacre

In the efforts to regain dominance after the Tet Offensive, US military intelligence suspected that the My Lai settlements in Quảng Ngãi Province were harbouring members of the Viet Cong. A search-and-destroy mission was planned, with the orders from Colonel Oran K. Henderson, the 11th Infantry Brigade commander, being to 'go in there aggressively, close with the enemy and wipe them out for good'. In turn, Captain Ernest Medina told his troops that the genuine villagers would have left for market, so any remaining people would be Viet Cong members or their supporters, who should be shot. Opinions differ on Medina's exact orders, but some, including platoon leaders, later claimed that they were told to kill 'suspects', including women and children.

On 16 March, around 100 soldiers, led by Captain Medina, landed in helicopters at My Lai. With Medina's command post remaining outside the villages, the 1st Platoon, led by Second Lieutenant William Calley Jr, entered the hamlet of Tu Cung. Although they met no resistance from villagers, the troops soon began firing indiscriminately at them. 'They were shooting women and children…,' remembered Private Michael Bernhardt, who refused to shoot anyone. A number of women and girls were gang-raped. The 2nd Platoon also killed more than 70 people, while seven of its men were wounded by mines and booby traps.

Flying overhead, helicopter pilot Hugh Thompson Jr landed and intervened, telling American soldiers that if they shot any more villagers he would shoot them in return. He rescued at least 12 villagers and saw them on to helicopters, before reporting the incident, which led to the operation being called off.

ABOVE: The massacre by a US Army platoon of between 347 and 504 unarmed Vietnamese men, women and children in the My Lai settlements in 1968 was one of the darkest episodes of the war for America.

'I don't remember seeing one military-age male in the entire place, dead or alive,' Private Bernhardt would later say, but Lieutenant Calley reported a body count of 90 Viet Cong, with no civilians dead. Fighting a guerrilla war, body count rather than territorial gain was valued by the US military, and some officers were willing to accept civilian dead as Viet Cong to boost their body count numbers. As the Viet Cong was a guerrilla army drawn from civilians, the distinction between the two was, at times, blurred. Despite Thompson's report it was decided that there was no basis for an investigation.

A year passed before Ronald L. Ridenhour, a door gunner who had not been at My Lai but had heard about the massacre from some of those present, compiled statements from witnesses. Returning home after completing his tour of duty, he sent the evidence to 30 members of Congress. Three took up his plea to look into the incident. With word spreading, that November – 18 months after the massacre – journalist Seymour Hersh's story of My Lai was published through the Associated Press wire service.

Trials began the following November, at which Lieutenant Calley claimed that he was following orders from Captain Medina. Medina, in turn, denied giving the order to kill civilians and was acquitted. Convicted for the premeditated

LEFT: Besieged and bombarded for five months in 1968, the Marines at Khe Sanh were finally rescued and the combat base abandoned.

THE SIEGE OF KHE SANH

An important outpost in the northwestern mountains of South Vietnam, the Khe Sanh Combat Base was just 23km (14 miles) south of the Demilitarized Zone that separated North and South Vietnam and 11km (7 miles) from the border with Laos.

By early 1968, North Vietnamese troops had succeeded in encircling the base, cutting it off by land and pounding it daily with artillery. What followed was one of the longest, bloodiest battles in the war. For five months, supplies and reinforcements were flown in to the base, while a massive American aerial bombardment was launched, dropping more than 100,000 tons of bombs on the surrounding area.

While the effectiveness and ethics of high-altitude B-52 bombers dropping 65-ton bombs on patches of jungle was debatable, psychologically they were crucial. 'When the Marines see the piles of smoke rising across the valley,' wrote English journalist David Leitch, reporting for the *Sunday Times* from inside Khe Sanh in February 1968, 'they feel that someone is remembering them.'

But bombs were not the only weapon. To keep the North Vietnamese Army at bay, in the first four weeks of the siege, 60,000 tons of the incendiary weapon napalm were dropped on the area surrounding the base, setting the jungle on fire.

The siege ended when a relief operation broke through to the Marines. But with the base finally liberated, the new American commander in Vietnam, General Creighton Abrams, decided to evacuate Khe Sanh for good, deeming it too risky to maintain such a vulnerable position. With the Americans gone, on 9 July, the North Vietnamese flag was raised at the base.

In all, almost 3000 US and South Vietnamese soldiers were killed in the siege and relief operation, with more than 9000 wounded, while the NVA saw more than 2500 killed in action. It was the first US combat base to be abandoned due to enemy pressure.

THE ASSASSINATION OF ROBERT F. KENNEDY

Having been Attorney General while his brother John F. Kennedy was president, by the summer of 1968 Robert F. Kennedy was a senator running as a Democrat candidate in the primaries for the presidential election. Following an address to his campaign supporters at the Ambassador Hotel, Los Angeles, on 5 June, Kennedy was being led out through the kitchen when he was shot by 24-year-old Sirhan Sirhan. The following day, Kennedy died from his wounds.

Sirhan, a Jordanian citizen from a Palestinian Christian family, had moved to America when he was 12. In recent months, he had become fixated on assassinating Kennedy after the senator pledged to send fighter jets to support the state of Israel. Easily apprehended after the shooting, Sirhan was sentenced to death, but this was commuted to life when California abolished the death penalty in 1972.

Coming just two months after Martin Luther King's assassination, Johnson called for tougher gun laws, but he had said the same after JFK's death to no effect. His presidency would now virtually be bookended by the assassinations of two Kennedy brothers.

murder of 22 civilians, Calley's life sentence was reduced to 20 years on appeal; he eventually served three and a half years under house arrest. Charges were brought against 12 other men, but none was found guilty, though five were court-martialled and others demoted. In contrast, 30 years after My Lai, Hugh Thompson and his fellow helicopter crewmen were awarded the Soldier's Medal for their actions in saving Vietnamese lives that day.

To some extent, My Lai can be seen as a crisis of discipline and morale among the forces in a controversial war that was costing many American lives while showing no signs of long-term victory. It may have been the bloodiest massacre in the conflict – the US estimate is 347 dead, the Vietnamese figure is 504, with ages ranging from one to 80 – but other soldiers later reported that there had been 'a My Lai each month for over a year' during 1968–1969.

> 'His presidency would now virtually be bookended by the assassinations of two Kennedy brothers.'

Flashpoint in Chicago

Before Lyndon Johnson left office, the Vietnam War would provoke scenes of violence in America. Following anti-war college campus demonstrations and sit-ins, physical encounters with the police became more common, as did active draft resistance and the destruction of draft cards. And when anti-war protesters converged outside the Democratic Nation Convention in Chicago that August, the mayor sent out 12,000 armed police, supported by the Illinois National Guard to confront them. Caught by TV news cameras were scenes of armed forces clubbing not the marginalized or suppressed, as might have happened earlier in the Civil Rights movement, but white, middle-class, well-educated Americans. The violence divided the nation. Abe Ribicoff, Democrat Senator for Connecticut, deplored the 'Gestapo tactics' of the police, but Hubert Humphrey, who would become the

ABOVE: Protesters surround a police car at the Democratic Party convention in Chicago in August 1968. An increasingly unpopular conflict at home, the war in Vietnam provoked many mass demonstrations across the United States.

Democrat candidate in the election, dismissed the demonstrators as people who 'feel that all they have to do is riot and they'll get their way'.

The clashes in Chicago did not discourage protests. The following year, millions across America – united across age, race and wealth – demonstrated against the war in the Vietnam Moratorium.

The Manson Murders

When followers joined Charles Manson's so-called Family, they may have thought they had found the guru to give meaning to their lives. In fact, they had entered what would turn into a murderous cult. In 1968, Charles Manson, having spent more than half his life in and out of young offenders' institutions and prisons, had recently managed to tap into the Californian hippie scene. The slight, good-looking 34-year-old's ambition was to become a singer-songwriter, and one of his songs even appeared as a Beach Boys B-side after he had temporarily befriended one of the group. His real talent, however, turned out to be the manipulation

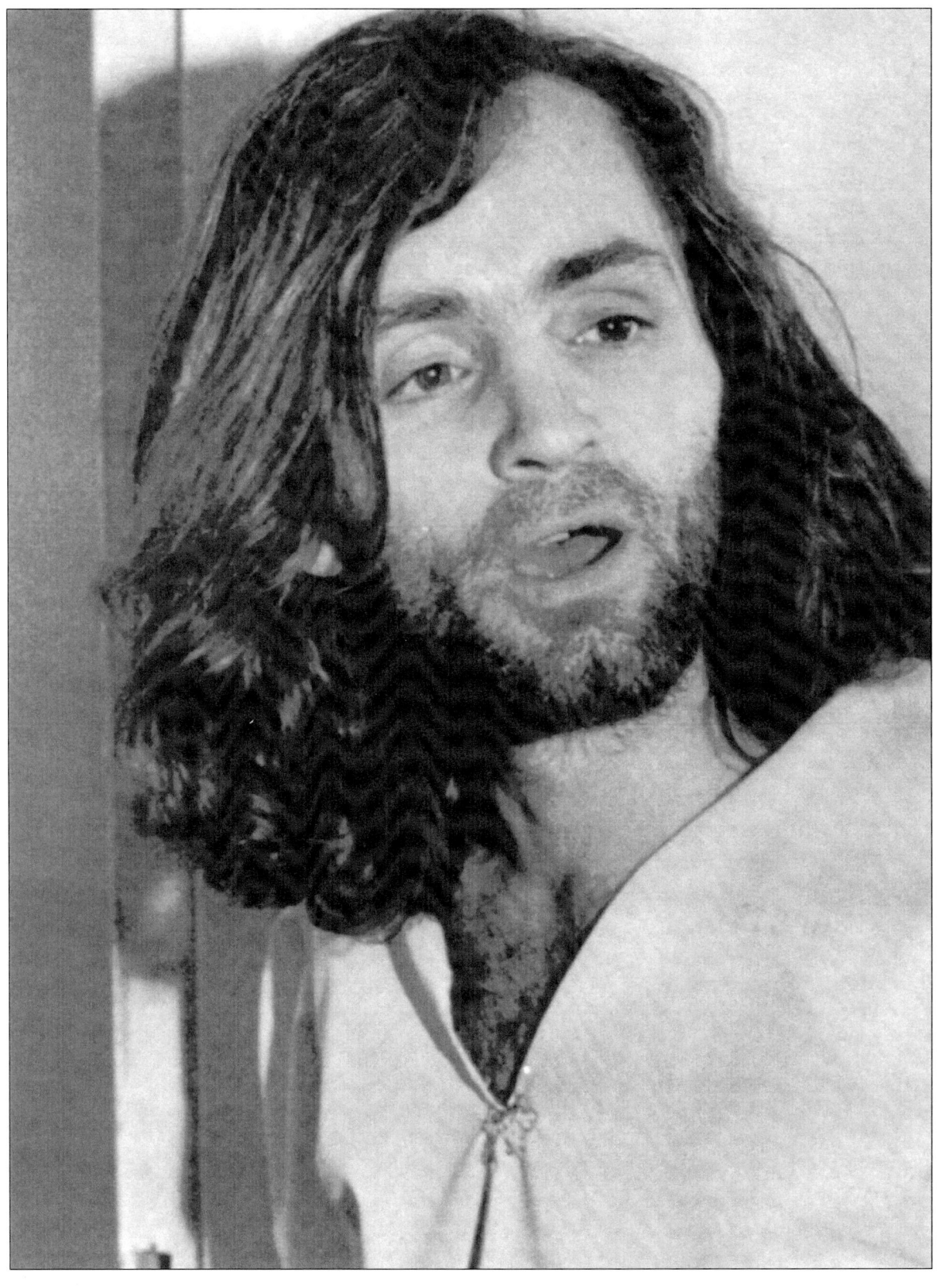

of unstable young minds, and soon he was collecting druggie dropouts in San Francisco and Los Angeles.

Prophesying a black–white race war based on his insane interpretation of the Book of Revelation and a nonsensical reading of the Beatles' 1968 song 'Helter Skelter', Manson had a dark charisma so mesmerizing that at its height his Family had 35 members.

Such was his control of the Family that he didn't even need to lead them into carnage. Instead, he sent others to do his bidding. It was Family member Tex Watson who broke into film director Roman Polanski's house in Benedict Canyon, Los Angeles, on 8 August 1969. Polanski was away, but his wife, model and actress Sharon Tate, was at home with three friends. Watson was accompanied by Susan Atkins and Patricia Krenwinkel. Outside, Linda Kasabian was their driver, and Manson remained at the Family's ranch. What followed were fatal stabbings and shootings of a heavily pregnant Tate and her friends Abigail Folger, Voytek Frykowski and celebrity hairdresser Jay Sebring. Each was stabbed multiple times, while a passer-by, Steven Parent, was shot dead.

It was a crime that shocked and frightened not only Hollywood, but the entire United States and beyond. In a decade that had seen much racial violence, war and brutal altercations at demonstrations, the frenzy that Manson had generated seemed to be utterly without motive. The house where Polanski and Sharon Tate were living was known to Manson, as it had formerly been occupied by Terry Melcher, the record producer son of singer Doris Day and friend of the Beach Boys. But there seems to be no reason why Tate and her friends were targeted, or why the following day Manson and 10 of his family murdered a supermarket executive, Leno LaBianca, and his wife Rosemary, a dress shop co-owner. The LaBiancas were completely unknown to Manson. With two further deaths of people in Manson's sphere, a total of nine murders were committed by the Family over a five-week period.

Even when Manson and the other suspects were arrested, his sinister hold over the Family continued. Those on trial often acted in chilling unity in the courtroom, while other members of the cult uninvolved in the killings failed to disband despite their leader's absence.

With Linda Kasabian – who had not participated in the killings themselves – acting as a prosecution witness, Manson and the rest received death sentences that were later commuted to life. All it had taken for some dropouts to become mass murderers was to fall under the spell of Charles Manson.

ABOVE: Manson Family members Susan Atkins, Patricia Krenwinkel and Leslie Van Houten arriving in court in June 1970. Van Houten wasn't involved in the killings at Sharon Tate's house, but admitted her part in murdering Leno and Rosemary LaBianca.

OPPOSITE: Charles Manson in court in June 1970. The following month he carved an X into his forehead. Susan Atkins, Patricia Krenwinkel and Leslie Van Houten soon copied him.

ABOVE: Audience members look on as Hells Angels beat a fan with pool cues at the Rolling Stones' Altamont Free Concert in California in December 1969. By the end of the one-day festival, four people were dead.

Deaths at Altamont

Four months after the Manson murders, the world of 1960s' pop music would be sullied by a violent death. Having drawn criticism on their 1969 US tour for charging high ticket prices, the Rolling Stones announced that the tour's final concert on 6 December 1969 would be free. But the concert, held after a last-minute change of venue at the Altamont Speedway in San Joaquin County, California, was ill-prepared, with a low stage leaving the bands vulnerable to the audience rushing them.

Having providing security for other bands, a group of Hells Angels was asked to keep the stage clear of crowd members. In return, although some dispute this, it is said that they were paid $500 in beer – which they could drink throughout the day-long festival.

During the course of the day, the mood at the concert was fractious, with some of the 300,000-strong crowd fighting each other, as well as the Hells Angels, and even throwing bottles at the performers. The behaviour of the Hells Angels, some now drunk, also deteriorated. While performing, Marty Balin of Jefferson Airplane was knocked unconscious by an Angel.

The violence reached its peak when, during the Rolling Stones' set, 18-year-old Meredith Hunter, high on amphetamines, tried to climb on stage. Following a scuffle with Hells Angels, he was pushed back into the crowd, before re-emerging with a revolver. Seeing this, Hells Angel Alan Passaro pulled out a knife, stabbing Hunter twice and killing him. On the stage, the Rolling Stones were aware of the commotion, but not its severity, and played on.

Pleading self-defence, Passaro was acquitted of murder, but Hunter's death was not the only fatality at the festival. Two people were killed in a hit-and-run, and another drowned in a drainage ditch. In addition, there were numerous thefts. In contrast with the 'peace and love' atmosphere at the Woodstock Festival in New York State four months earlier, Altamont was a sour end to a decade that had seen such a burst of creativity in rock and roll.

Nixon in the White House

By the time Republican Richard Nixon entered the White House in January 1969, the US presence was at its height in Vietnam, with 543,000 military personnel in the country. Although Nixon was determined to end the war, the heaviest bombing came in his first few months, and peace talks were still in deadlock when Ho Chi Minh died that September.

There was, however, some positive news for America: having been beaten into space by the Soviet Union and having suffered a disaster when a fire during a test at Cape Kennedy caused the deaths of three astronauts, in July 1969 the Apollo 11 mission fulfilled Kennedy's pledge to put a man on the Moon before the end of the decade.

The 1960s ended with 200 Americans still dying each week in Vietnam, while the US looked for a way to withdraw from the conflict without losing face. Meanwhile, at home, anti-war protests were becoming more radical and violent. If the decade drew to a close with a public sense of disenchantment with the government, things would become even worse over the next few years.

> 'The 1960s ended with 200 Americans still dying each week in Vietnam.'

LEFT: The inauguration of President Richard Nixon in January 1969. Nixon was determined to end the war in Vietnam, but it would take longer than he hoped and he would no longer be in office when the end finally came.

11

DISCONTENT AND REVIVAL

In the 1970s, Richard Nixon succeeded in finally disentangling America from Vietnam, but his underhand methods of government would lead to his downfall – while also revealing a sinister culture of espionage within the United States.

F OR HIS OWN protection, President Nixon was ushered, in May 1970, from the White House to his retreat at Camp David, 100km (62 miles) outside Washington, D.C. America wasn't under attack from a foreign power, but from some of its own people, as a crowd of 100,000 protesters amassed in the capital, some smashing windows and dragging parked cars to use as road blocks.

They had been provoked by the shooting of students by the Ohio National Guard at Kent State University earlier that month. The students, reacting to news that the war in Vietnam was being expanded to target Viet Cong forces in Cambodia, had been demonstrating for four days and had set fire to the college's officer training corps building. Although some students were still throwing stones, the main demonstration was largely dispersing, when at least 29 of the 77 guardsmen fired on the crowd. In all, four students were killed – two of whom had been walking between classes and were uninvolved in the demonstration. Another nine were injured.

OPPOSITE: A demonstrator at the University of California, Berkeley, throws a tear gas canister at police in May 1970. Anti-Vietnam War and related protests intensified across America after the US invasion of Cambodia in April 1970.

RIGHT: Protesting students at Kent State University in Ohio in May 1970 flee after tear gas is fired by the National Guard. After four days of demonstrations, National Guardsman opened fire on the protesters, killing four students and injuring nine others.

BELOW: Five days after the Kent State shootings, 100,000 people gathered in Washington, D.C. in protest. On seeing the carnage and the military presence, Charles Colson, counsel to Richard Nixon, remarked: 'This is a nation at war with itself.'

It remains unclear why the guardsmen fired when no order had been given. Some of them later claimed that they had been fired upon, although this has never been established, and the crowd posed little physical threat – the closest person hit by the guardsmen's bullets was 22m (71ft) away. A President's Commission found the guardsmen's actions unjustified and eight were indicted by a grand jury. The charges, however, were dismissed on the grounds that they were too weak to warrant a trial.

Other protests were sparked by the shootings. Four days later, 11 people at the University of New Mexico were attacked by the National Guard armed with bayonets; the next week, police and state highway patrolmen killed two students and wounded nine others at the all-black Jackson State University in Mississippi. In all, 450 colleges across America closed following both violent and non-violent protests.

'This is not the greatest free democracy in the world,' remarked Charles Colson, counsel to Richard Nixon, on seeing the 82nd Airborne Division brought in to Washington to restore order. 'This is a nation at war with itself.'

Attica Prison Riot

In September the following year, 2200 prisoners at Attica Correctional Facility in New York State rioted, taking 42 staff hostage. The prison chapel was burned down and guards were beaten, with one thrown out of a window. He later died from his injuries.

Railing against overcrowding and the brutality of the prison guards, the prisoners drew up a list of 27 demands. Although New York Correction Commissioner Russell Oswald agreed to improve conditions for the prisoners, negotiations broke down over the rioters' call for an amnesty from prosecution for their rioting. Four days of talks had ended in deadlock when tear gas was dropped into the prison, before New York State Police troopers fired into the smoke, killing 25 inmates and 10 hostages.

With an investigation launched into the handling of the siege, the New York State Special Commission reported that, with the exception of Indian massacres in the late nineteenth century, the State Police assault 'was the bloodiest one-day encounter between Americans since the Civil War'.

> **'Four days of talks had ended in deadlock when tear gas was dropped into the prison.'**

BELOW: Attica State Prison shortly after New York State Police troopers ended the four-day riot and siege in 1971. When the uprising was over, 43 people were dead, including 10 prison officers and civilian staff, and 33 inmates.

ABOVE: President Richard Nixon and Chinese Premier Zhou Enlai normalize relations between the two countries in February 1972. Or, as Nixon said privately: 'We're doing the China thing to screw the Russians and help us in Vietnam.'

Nixon in China

Determined to extricate America from the war in Vietnam without losing face, Nixon calculated that a thaw in relations with China would help detach it from North Vietnam and make US negotiations with Hanoi easier. It would also, he hoped, exploit a recent split between China and the Soviet Union. Following a secret mission by national security adviser Henry Kissinger to Beijing in 1971, Nixon flew to China the following February to begin normalizing relations between the two countries.

His calculation proved correct. The Soviet Union, fearing being isolated if China and America became too close, softened its stance towards the US, and that summer the president went to Moscow to agree a deal on arms control. Nixon's achievement was welcomed as a step towards ending the Cold War, but he had only managed this success by bypassing Congress, bureaucracy and the media. Such methods would prove to be the president's undoing.

> 'The climate of secrecy and paranoia that Nixon had cultivated was to blame.'

In Vietnam, US troop numbers had already been reduced, but periodic heavy bombing continued during negotiations. Then, in January 1973, Nixon announced that a ceasefire to end the war had been agreed. American forces would pull out and POWs were to be returned, with South Vietnam guaranteed the right to determine its own political future. That was a guarantee only in theory: Nixon had failed to mention that North Vietnamese troops had been allowed to remain in the South.

The Chilean Coup

How long do state visits last? A few days? Perhaps a week. In late 1971, Cuban Prime Minister Fidel Castro made a state visit to Chile that lasted a month. Castro was the guest of Marxist President Salvador Allende, who, since his election the previous year, had begun nationalizing industries, including US-owned copper mines. Fearing a government like that of Cuba emerging in South America, the Nixon administration had already authorized $10 million for the CIA to support opposition to Allende. In addition, America hampered Allende's economic development plans by persuading the World Bank to cease any loans to Chile. Then, on 11 September 1973, the Chilean military attacked the government, with fighter jets firing into the presidential palace. Refusing to surrender, Allende shot himself.

Washington promptly recognized the new military junta led by the commander in chief of Chile's armed forces, General Augusto Pinochet Ugarte. Pinochet's free-market politics may have suited American commercial interests, but his brutal regime involved the kidnapping and murder of more than 3000 political opponents, including two Americans.

It would not be until 1990 that, after much pressure, Pinochet would relinquish power. Later arrested for human rights violations, he died while awaiting trial in 2006.

Watergate

In the 1968 election, Nixon had only just scraped into the White House, but in 1972 he won a landslide victory. Yet, within two years he would be forced to resign.

Although it would have seemed ridiculous to suggest so at the time, Nixon's presidency began to unravel on the night of 17 June 1972, when five men were arrested breaking into, and attempting to bug, the Democratic National Committee in the Watergate apartment complex in Washington.

One of the men was said to be a former CIA employee, and an investigation led by *Washington Post* reporters Bob Woodward and Carl Bernstein, and aided by secret tips from the FBI's Associate Director Mark Felt, managed to link the burglars to payments from the Committee to Re-elect the President. Nixon denied any White House involvement in the burglary – and, to be fair, he probably didn't know about it in advance. But the climate of secrecy and paranoia that he had cultivated was to blame. He had sanctioned break-ins and wire-taps of opponents, and the arrested burglars did have ties to the White House, as well as to an underworld of CIA agents and anti-Castro Cuban activists.

Personally, Nixon had set up a special intelligence operation of 'plumbers'

ABOVE: General Augusto Pinochet flanked by heads of the Chilean Navy and Air Force after his successful military coup in Chile in 1973. The CIA had secretly spent millions of dollars helping Pinochet into power.

to plug government leaks, such as the Pentagon Papers, which revealed that American bombing in southeast Asia under President Johnson had reached into Laos and Cambodia. Similarly, Nixon's dirty tricks targeted Democrat candidates running in 1972. To give one example, they destabilized Democrat Senator Edmund Muskie's efforts by forging a letter to a New Hampshire newspaper, claiming that Muskie had made disparaging remarks about French-Canadians. With stronger contenders displaced, ultimately the Democrat party fielded George McGovern, one of its weaker candidates, and Nixon won a firm victory.

ABOVE: White House counsel John Dean had organized the cover-up following the Watergate break-in. But, with the investigation claiming ever more senior White House figures, in April 1973 he agreed to testify before the Senate committee.

More broadly, Nixon's methods were characteristic of the time. In response to anti-war protests, the secret services and law enforcement agencies had, since the mid-1960s and without legal authority, bugged and kept leftist movements under electronic surveillance. Specifically, the FBI's Counter Intelligence Program, COINTELPRO, was established to target civil rights organizations.

The End for Nixon

While Nixon was providing hush money to keep the Watergate burglars and their associates quiet, a Democrat-dominated Senate established a committee to investigate the whole matter. The more questions that were asked, the higher the trail led – right up the White House. Under questioning, one aide revealed that Nixon taped his White House conversations. Although earlier presidents had recorded some of their conversations, Nixon had taped more than 3000 hours. After some obstructions, the president was forced to hand over the tapes, evidence from which allowed a case for impeachment to begin.

With the release of a transcript that revealed Nixon attempting to stop the FBI's investigation into Watergate, his fate was sealed. Republican support in Congress fell away and, with impeachment looming, Nixon resigned on 9 August 1974. He is the only American president to have done so.

Watergate had brought Nixon down, but the affair was a testament to American democracy. Nixon's shady dealings had surfaced and justice had prevailed. Furthermore, a number of his White House staff served prison terms. Between 1974 and 1976, Presidential and Congressional committees investigated the misdeeds of the intelligence community, exposing the FBI's COINTELPRO and fuelling a broader suspicion among the American people of the federal government and law enforcement.

OPPOSITE: With his family beside him, Richard Nixon resigns in August 1974. Perhaps beginning to understand the nature of his downfall, Nixon bade farewell to his White House staff with the words: 'Those who hate you don't win unless you hate them, and then you destroy yourself.'

The End in Vietnam

Nixon had been able in 1973 to withdraw US ground troops, while continuing the bombing campaign to support an independent South Vietnam. But the South was a fragile, corrupt state where, two years later, inflation was at 65 per cent and soldiers were deserting the army. In March 1975, the North Vietnamese Army suddenly pushed through the South and the following month all of Vietnam and Cambodia fell to communists. In the final days, a mob gathered at the US embassy in Saigon as people tried to catch the final places on the helicopters that were airlifting Americans and refugees to warships in the South China Sea. On 30 April, the last US helicopter left, just hours before NVA tanks bulldozed the gates of the presidential palace. Thus ended America's 15-year involvement in Vietnam.

Financially, and in terms of casualties, the war had been a hugely costly failure for America. It had claimed 58,000 American lives and an estimated two million

THE JONESTOWN MASSACRE

Leo Ryan's final days began in November 1978 when, as chairman of a congressional subcommittee with jurisdiction over US citizens living abroad, he flew to Guyana in Latin America to investigate Jim Jones's Peoples Temple cult.

Having claimed holy powers from an early age, Jones had set up the Peoples Temple in Indianapolis in 1956. Emphasizing racial integrity, in its early years the church's mix of Christianity and socialism did some good work in the community, such as organizing soup kitchens. Nine years later, the Temple moved to California.

But Jones was a con man: he used spies to steal information that he could use to foster his claim to be clairvoyant, and stooges would fake being wheelchair-bound before he 'healed' them. He was also excellent at controlling people and at raising money. By 1975 the Temple's assets were estimated to be $10 million. Of course, members had to offer up everything they had to Jones – their possessions, their children and their bodies. When accusations began to surface of the misappropriation of funds, Jones sought a new home for the Temple, and bought remote land in the Guyanese jungle. In May 1977, 1000 members of the Temple left California for their new life in Jonestown, Guyana.

Described as an agricultural commune, Jonestown was, from the reports of those who escaped, more like a concentration camp, where members worked 11-hour shifts in the fields, camped in unsanitary conditions, were fed inadequate rations and suffered a number of ailments. If they didn't work hard enough, they were subjected to public beatings by armed guards. Meanwhile, to keep the people suppressed and maintain Jones's claims that he was now God, telephone calls were forbidden, mail was censored, and passports and money confiscated.

Leo Ryan was joined on his trip to Guyana by concerned relatives of cult members and some journalists. Reaching Jonestown in two small aircraft, Ryan's group spent two days talking to Temple members, before preparing to fly out with 14 members who wanted to leave the cult. The first departing aircraft was already taxiing down the runway when one of the supposed defectors on board, Larry Layton, opened fire on the passengers. With that, other members who had escorted the visiting party back to the planes began shooting, killing Ryan, three journalists and a defecting Temple member, while wounding others. Survivors fled into the fields as other passengers managed to subdue Layton and radio for help.

Vietnamese. In addition, the US had dropped a greater tonnage of bombs on Vietnam than it had on Germany, Italy and Japan combined during World War II, causing not just destruction, but long-term ecological damage. Since 2000, US Congress has allocated more than $84 million in operations to decontaminate Vietnamese land from the effects of Agent Orange and other chemical weapons.

After Vietnam, there were consequences on Capitol Hill, too. Following Johnson's and Nixon's waging of a war without ever making a formal declaration, in November 1973 the War Powers Act was passed. This prevented a president using US troops in combat for more than 60 days without congressional approval.

> 'The war had claimed 58,000 American lives and an estimated two million Vietnamese.'

When the Guyanese Army cut through the jungle into Jonestown the following day, they found 909 dead bodies, 260 of them children. The few who had hidden in the fields had survived, but almost all the Peoples Temple members had either drunk, or been injected with, cyanide, while Jones himself had died of a gunshot wound to the head.

Like a Pied Piper, Jones had led his followers into the wilderness. When his cult was threatened, Jones himself, it is assumed, brought about its destruction. Until the 11 September attacks in 2001, the Jonestown mass suicide was the largest single loss of American civilian life in a deliberate act.

ABOVE: There were 909 victims in the Jonestown massacre in Guyana, November 1978. Members of Jim Jones's Peoples Temple cult had either drunk or been injected with cyanide.

ABOVE: President Ronald Reagan announcing the Strategic Defense Initiative (SDI) in 1983. Commonly known as the 'Star Wars' project, this system, would, if it worked, intercept enemy nuclear missiles and destroy them.

The New Cold War

'Peace does not come from weakness or retreat. It comes from the restoration of American military superiority,' declared Ronald Reagan in 1976, when he was challenging President Gerald Ford as the Republican candidate. Reagan didn't win that time, and Democrat Jimmy Carter replaced Ford in the White House. However, when Reagan did become president in 1981, his tone was markedly belligerent in contrast to that of Ford or Carter. Denouncing the Soviet Union as 'the evil empire', in 1983 he announced the Strategic Defense Initiative (SDI). Commonly known as the 'Star Wars' project, this system, would, if it worked, intercept enemy nuclear missiles and destroy them.

Anti-communist Reagan was in fact strongly opposed to nuclear weapons. And with a new, relatively young, reforming Soviet leader, Mikhail Gorbachev, now in office, Reagan and his Soviet counterpart began a series of summits in Europe to discuss arms reductions, culminating, in December 1987, in a treaty on intermediate-range nuclear weapons. It was the first time that the superpowers had ever reduced their arsenals.

Space Shuttle Disasters

Beginning operational flights in 1982, NASA's five Space Shuttles flew 135 missions before being retired almost 30 years later. In that time, they suffered two disasters. In January 1986, Space Shuttle *Challenger* fell apart 76 seconds into a flight, leading to the deaths of its seven crew members. Not designed to be

ASSASSINS

Less than three months into his presidency, Ronald Reagan was the victim of an assassination attempt. On 30 March 1981, 25-year-old John Hinckley Jr was among the crowd outside the Hilton Hotel in Washington as Reagan left after addressing a conference. Just 4.6m (15ft) from the president, Hinckley was able to fire six times at him, although only the final bullet hit Reagan. The president suffered a punctured lung, but, rushed to hospital, the 70-year-old recovered well after surgery. Of the other shots, Secret Service agent Tim McCarthy was hit as he shielded the president, while police officer Thomas Delahanty and White House Press Secretary James Brady were also wounded. All survived the shooting, though Delahanty had to retire from the police and Brady was left partially paralysed. Brady later successfully campaigned for stricter gun controls, with the Brady Act of 1993 making federal background checks on firearm purchases a requirement. Hinckley, meanwhile, having been found not guilty by reason of insanity, was detained under institutional psychiatric care until his release in 2016.

On 8 December the previous year, Mark Chapman had shot dead former Beatle John Lennon outside the songwriter's apartment building in New York City. Chapman's legal team first put forward a plea of insanity, but, in June 1981, Chapman changed his mind and, saying that his actions had been the will of God, pleaded guilty. Convicted for second-degree murder, he was sentenced from 20 years to life, and, as of 2016, has been denied parole nine times.

ABOVE: Police and Secret Service agents surge to disarm John Hinckley Jr after his assassination attempt on Ronald Reagan in Washington, D.C. in 1981.

used in such cold temperatures, a seal had failed on a rocket booster, causing an explosive fuel leak. Investigating the disaster, a commission found that NASA's organizational structure had led to warnings from engineers being ignored.

Seventeen years later, in February 2003, Space Shuttle *Columbia* disintegrated as it re-entered the Earth's atmosphere. Again, all seven crew died. This time, a suitcase-sized piece of foam insulation had broken off a rocket booster during the launch, puncturing a 15–25cm (6–10in) hole in the orbiter's wing. Although this didn't affect the mission in space, when the orbiter returned to Earth, hot gases penetrated the wing, causing the spacecraft to become unstable and slowly break apart.

Suspended for more than two years, when the Space Shuttle program relaunched, all subsequent missions, with one exception, were flown to the International Space Station, so that the crew could use it as a haven if similar damage to the orbiter prevented safe re-entry.

Covert Operations

Even as Reagan and Gorbachev were discussing the reduction in the numbers of their nuclear weapons, the Reagan administration was spending massively on arms, with the Defense Department's budget almost doubling between 1980 and 1985.

With the exception of CIA aid in opposing Cuban forces fighting in Angola in 1975–76, President Ford and Carter's governments had been restrained in their involvement abroad. Reagan reversed this. The US now became active in a new Cold War battlefield – in its so-called backyard of Central America and the Caribbean. The 1983 military coup in Grenada provided the opportunity for a US military assault and occupation. Meanwhile, in Nicaragua, the CIA created and armed the anti-communist 'Contra' rebel force, which succeeded in hampering the efforts of the country's socialist Sandinista government.

In November 1986, Reagan's administration was tainted by the revelation that the US had sold weapons to Iran, by then under the rule of fundamentalist Islamic clerics. Illegal under US law, the sale had been part of a much-denied deal to win the release of American hostages held in Lebanon. Furthermore, of the money received, $30 million had been diverted by National Security Council member Oliver North to fund the Contras in Nicaragua, after Congress had cut off official funds for the rebels because of their appalling human rights record.

At first the president denied trading arms for hostages, before an investigation forced him to address the nation, admitting that that was exactly what he had done. Although weakened, Reagan's administration continued. A number of government and CIA staff were convicted of withholding evidence, though most were pardoned by Reagan's successor, President George H.W. Bush, in 1992.

The End of the Cold War

By the late 1980s, the economic burdens in the Soviet bloc had become unsustainable, while Gorbachev's liberalizing policies were encouraging a 'freedom of choice' among Warsaw Pact member states. When free elections in Poland and Hungary elected non-communist governments in 1989, the Soviet premier, unlike his predecessors, did not send in tanks to bring the countries back into line, but said that he would respect their decisions. Soon, mass protests swelled in East Germany against its hard-line communist government. When other Warsaw Pact countries opened their borders to the West, East Germany, already near bankruptcy, was left isolated. Nor did Gorbachev step in to save it. When East Germany lifted restrictions on travel on 9 November, East Berliners flocked across the Berlin Wall, and, over the following weeks, tore it down.

After 40 years, the Iron Curtain had been lifted. The American forces based in Western Europe had not gone into battle or fired their missiles. Having faced near war over the Cuban Missile Crisis, and fought proxy wars in Korea and Vietnam, America could watch as the Cold War ended peacefully.

Within two years, though, interest would find a new focus of worry – in the Middle East, with American troops fighting in Iraq, the first of a number of conflicts in the region.

OPPOSITE: The Space Shuttle *Challenger* falling apart less than two minutes after launching in January 1986. A seal had failed on one of the rocket boosters, causing an explosive fuel leak. All seven astronauts on board were killed.

12

THE SOLE SUPERPOWER

With the Soviet Union breaking up after the end of the Cold War, the US was left as the sole superpower. But with America becoming the target of Islamist terrorism and with instability in the Middle East, war and bloody conflict was not over for the United States.

IN THE 1980s, Iraq waged an eight-year war against Iran, only for it to end in stalemate, leaving a massive debt and mounting domestic discontent for its dictator Saddam Hussein. His remedy was to attack another neighbour. This time it was the small emirate of Kuwait, the invasion of which increased his regional influence, gave him a victory to enjoy at last, and doubled his nation's oil reserves. He now controlled 20 per cent of the world's oil.

However, this proved to be another miscalculation on Saddam's part. Although Iraq had received intelligence and equipment from the US, the United Kingdom, NATO and other Arab states that were worried by the Islamic revolutionaries in Iran, invading Kuwait was regarded very differently. Kuwait, unlike Iran, was a small state on friendly terms with Western powers; within hours, the UN Security Council had condemned Iraq.

Although some in Washington, such as the chairman of the joints chiefs of staff, Colin Powell, hoped that sanctions would persuade Saddam to withdraw

OPPOSITE: The National September 11 Memorial in New York City. The September 11 attacks in 2001 killed 2996 people and injured more than 6000 others. A new age of suicidal terrorism had reached the West.

from Kuwait, President George H.W. Bush was keen to take military action, telling a conference: 'We're dealing with Hitler revisited, a totalitarianism and a brutality that is naked and unprecedented in modern times.'

Saddam's human rights abuses were indeed terrible. Human Rights Watch later estimated that 250,000 people had been murdered or had 'disappeared' during Saddam's brutal dictatorship, while, among many other offences, the gassing of Kurds in the north of Iraq in 1988 had resulted in the deaths of at least 50,000 people. There was also the issue of Saddam's weapons of mass destruction (WMD). Chemical weapons had been used against Iran during the Iran–Iraq War, while biological weapons were being tested. Was Saddam planning to use these more widely?

With a UN Security Council resolution secured, giving Saddam an ultimatum to withdraw from Kuwait by 15 January 1991, a US-led force of an international alliance was established. It included French and British forces, along with support from Saudi Arabia, Egypt and – despite being no friend of America but close to Iran – Syria.

Following intensive bombing against Iraq's air defence and command systems in Iraq and Kuwait, ground operations – with 540,000 American troops and 250,000 from the other Allies – were launched from Saudi Arabia on 24 February. Within 100 hours, Kuwait had been retaken. An estimated 35,000–80,000 Iraqi troops were killed, with 240 coalition soldiers lost. Almost a quarter of the American losses, and more than half of the British deaths, were a result of 'friendly fire' – a feature of modern warfare where long-range artillery and aircraft attack distant targets that they can't see.

Bush stopped the assault once Kuwait was liberated, despite criticism that he should have pressed on, invaded Iraq and toppled Saddam. Writing seven years later, Bush defended his reasons for not invading Iraq, arguing that the international coalition would have immediately collapsed, and 'the United States could conceivably still be an occupying power in a bitterly hostile land'. He was right – as his son would find out a decade later.

> 'The gassing of Kurds in the north of Iraq in 1988 had resulted in the deaths of at least 50,000 people.'

The Battle of Mogadishu

As part of a United Nations' operation to provide humanitarian aid and stabilize Somalia after it had fragmented into civil war in the early 1990s, the US Marines were sent to the country in 1992. The following October, a combination of various US special forces began a mission to capture leaders of the Habr Gidr clan in Somalia's capital, Mogadishu. With 19 aircraft, 12 vehicles and 160 men, the operation was planned to take no more than an hour. In fact, the mission not only failed to capture its targets, but lasted for 15 hours after two Black Hawk helicopters were shot down, leaving the survivors isolated. As a fierce urban battle broke out, an immense combined task force of American, Malaysian and Pakistani ground troops, along with armoured vehicles and helicopters, was sent in to rescue the stranded soldiers.

In all, 18 US soldiers were killed and another 73 were wounded, with Malaysia and Pakistan also suffering a fatality each. The losses on the opposing side were immense, with the UN estimating that between 300 and 500 Somali fighters had been killed.

The Battle of Mogadishu not only resulted in America scaling back its involvement in Somalia, but also cast a shadow over US foreign policy. Although President Bill Clinton's commitment of air power to the NATO bombing of Serb positions in 1999 during the Bosnian civil war did finally end a conflict that the UN and European Union had failed to resolve, America had not intervened in the Rwandan genocide in 1994.

The Los Angeles Riots

When 25-year-old African-American Rodney King was spotted speeding through the San Fernando Valley in the early hours of 3 March 1991, California Highway Patrol pursued him. King, who had been drinking, attempted to outrun them.

LEFT: A US soldier on patrol as part of a United Nations' force in Mogadishu, Somalia, in 1993. The failed US mission to capture Somali warlords that October was the bloodiest battle American troops had been involved in since the Vietnam War.

ABOVE: A looted shop set on fire during the Los Angeles Riots in April 1992. The riots erupted following the acquittal of four police officers who had been charged with – and had been filmed – assaulting African-American Rodney King.

When finally cornered by the Los Angeles Police, King and his two passengers climbed out of the car. However, when King, who was unarmed, did not comply with the LAPD's requests to lie on the ground and instead attempted to flee, a vicious beating from the cops ensued, with King being hit 56 times. Caught on videotape by a local resident, the footage of the beating was later broadcast on a Los Angeles TV station, before building into a nationwide story of police brutality against an unarmed black man.

The four officers were charged with assault and using excessive force, but when they were acquitted at a trial the following April, parts of Los Angeles, centred around the African-American South Central area, erupted into six days of rioting. Apart from looting and arson, the violence, which was racially mixed, often targeted Hispanic and Korean communities. The Rodney King trial may have been the flashpoint, but, more broadly, the rioting was attributed to the frustrations of poverty suffered during the early 1990s recession.

As rioting spread across the city, a curfew and the deployment of a federalized California Army National Guard eventually brought the situation under control, though by that time 55 people had been killed (10 by law enforcement agencies or the National Guard) and more than 2000 injured.

The following year, federal charges of civil rights violations were brought against the police officers who had beaten Rodney King, with two being found guilty and sentenced to 32 months in prison.

Oklahoma City Bombing

Two years to the day after the end of the siege at Waco, 26-year-old Timothy McVeigh detonated a car bomb in front of a federal building in Oklahoma City, killing 168 people, including 19 children, and injuring more than 600 others.

McVeigh had served in the US infantry during the First Gulf War, but, on leaving the army, had drifted, becoming increasingly alienated, touring gun shows and developing a loathing of what he regarded as an increasingly socialist government. Deciding to target a federal building, McVeigh and his co-conspirator Terry Nichols built a 2300kg (5000lb) bomb, which they mounted on the back of truck. Lighting a two-minute fuse, McVeigh left the truck outside Oklahoma City's Alfred P. Murrah Federal Building.

HURRICANE KATRINA

The costliest natural disaster in the history of the United States, Hurricane Katrina caused severe destruction along the Gulf coast from Florida to Texas in August 2005. At least 1245 people were killed in the storm and the ensuing floods. Much of the damage and loss of life occurred in New Orleans, where, with levees breached in 50 places, 80 per cent of the city was left under water. The third most intense tropical cyclone to hit America, Katrina displaced more than one million people, causing the largest diaspora in US history.

While the Coast Guard, which had rescued 35,000 people, was recognized with an official entry in the Congressional Record, there was criticism of the broader response to the disaster, leading to the resignation of the Federal Emergency Management Agency director and the New Orleans Police Department superintendent. Investigations later found the US Army Corps of Engineers responsible for building inadequate flood defences in New Orleans.

When tracked down, McVeigh claimed that his bombing was in revenge for the government's actions at Waco. Found guilty, among other charges, of using a weapon of mass destruction, he was executed by lethal injection in June 2001. Terry Nichols received a life sentence.

The War on Terror

In the twentieth century, airline crews had been trained to stay calm and comply with hijackers' requests in order to see the plane landed safely at whichever airport the hijackers chose. The events of 11 September 2001 changed all that. Within 75 minutes, four American airliners on domestic flights from airports on the eastern seaboard were hijacked by terrorists and were crashed. The first two, 17 minutes apart, flew into the Twin Towers of the World Trade Center in New York, while the third hit the Pentagon Building outside Washington. Learning of these suicidal attacks, the passengers and flight attendants on the fourth plane realized that complying with hijackers would see them all killed. With the hijackers flying the plane towards Washington, D.C., the passengers and flight attendants decided to fight back and attempted to storm the cockpit. In the struggle, the plane was brought down, crashing over Pennsylvania farmland and killing all on board.

The deadliest terrorist actions ever in America, the September 11 attacks killed 2996 people and injured more than 6000 others. Suspicion immediately fell on al-Qaeda, a network of radical Islamic fundamentalist cells co-founded by Saudi national Osama bin Laden. Originally allied with US-backed anti-communist forces, al-Qaeda had formed to counter the Soviet occupation in Afghanistan. At the time of the September 11 attacks, its members were still being sheltered by Afghanistan's Islamic fundamentalist Taliban regime. Over the years, however, al-Qaeda had evolved to view the United States, with its forces in Saudi Arabia and its backing of conservative Middle Eastern states, as one of its enemies.

> 'President George W. Bush addressed Congress, using the term "war on terror" for the first time'.

On 20 September, President George W. Bush addressed Congress, using the term 'war on terror' for the first time. This, he stated, would begin with al-Qaeda, but 'will not end until every terrorist group of global reach has been found, stopped and defeated'. By Christmas 2001, the US, supported by British troops and Afghanistan's Northern Alliance, had removed the Taliban from power in Afghanistan. However, they had not captured Bin Laden, and the Taliban would eventually regroup. American forces, joined by those from 42 other NATO nations, would remain in Afghanistan.

Weapons of Mass Destruction

In 1991, the first President Bush had likened Saddam to Hitler, and in 2002 his son described an 'axis of evil', naming Iraq, Iran and North Korea as three countries 'arming to threaten the peace of the world. By seeking weapons of mass destruction, these regimes pose a grave and growing danger'.

Regarding the September 11 attacks, there was no real evidence of Iraq sponsoring al-Qaeda, but George W. Bush was swept up in the idea of toppling Saddam. After Iraqi forces were defeated in Kuwait in 1991, there had been hopes in Washington that Shi'a Islam and Kurdish uprisings in Iraq would remove Saddam's minority Sunni Islam government, but the dictator had put them down viciously. Meanwhile, UN inspectors had been thwarted during the 1990s in their efforts to verify fully whether or not Iraq had developed any further weapons of mass destruction. Following a policy of containment, in 1998, America and Britain had bombed Iraqi military installations. However, apart from an intelligence claim that weapons of mass destruction were being developed, by February 2003 none had been found.

As war approached, efforts were still being made to persuade Saddam to be fully transparent about the weapons, but, not expecting to be invaded, he continued to play with and confuse the inspectors. The UK had wanted a UN resolution backing the use of force, but, when the Security Council disagreed and that became impossible to achieve, the United States, supported by Britain, Spain and Poland, invaded Iraq in March 2003.

Within three weeks, Baghdad had fallen and by the end of the year Saddam had been captured. Occupation had been swift, with American casualties limited to 139. But after much searching, no weapons of mass destruction were ever discovered. For reasons of his personal hubris before the wider Arab world, Saddam had been bluffing. What kind of peace would follow? Having neglected much in the way of planning what a post-Saddam Iraq would look like, a power

OPPOSITE: The South Tower (left) of the World Trade Center in New York seconds after a United Airlines 767 was flown into the building on the morning of 11 September 2001. A quarter of an hour earlier, an American Airlines 767 had been flown into the North Tower (right).

vacuum developed after the dissolution of the country's largely Sunni Muslim army and the dismissal of government officials. Soon Sunni- and Iranian-backed Shi'a insurgent factions were battling each other and the occupying forces for dominance.

With a new constitution in 2005, parliamentary elections were held. After a trial, Saddam was found guilty of crimes against humanity and hanged the following year. Despite efforts to wind down US involvement, however, an increase in sectarian violence led to more troops being deployed to Iraq in 2007. This was largely successful; two years later, the US handed security responsibilities to Iraqi forces. At the end of 2011, President Barack Obama withdrew American troops from Iraq.

There had been 4804 deaths among 22 coalition military personnel, 4486 of these being American. John Hopkins University estimated that the number of Iraqi deaths by 2011, both directly from violent action and indirectly through the breakdown of infrastructures, was 461,000. However, American involvement in Iraq was not yet over.

Finding Bin Laden

At the time of the September 11 attacks, Osama bin Laden was believed to be living in Afghanistan. He would subsequently evade capture for many years, his whereabouts unknown. Almost a decade later, he was located living in a secure compound in the town of Abbottabad in Pakistan, about 160km (100 miles) from the Afghan border. On 2 May 2011, US Navy SEALs on two Black Hawk helicopters began an operation to kill him. Landing in the grounds of Bin Laden's compound, the SEALs fought their way through his house before finding the al-Qaeda leader. He and four members of his household were shot dead. Bin Laden's body was removed by US forces and given a Muslim burial at sea.

Islamic State

As President Obama was attempting to reduce US presence in Iraq, unrest across the Middle East drew America and other countries into greater involvement in the region. In 2011, US air strikes as part of a NATO coalition force supported the toppling of dictator Colonel Gaddafi in Libya. Following the withdrawal of US troops in Iraq, the level of violence rose once again as militant

ABOVE: President Barack Obama and Secretary of State Hillary Clinton, along with members of the national security team, receive an update on the Navy SEALs mission to assassinate Osama bin Laden in May 2011.

ENHANCED INTERROGATION

Within months of the invasion of Iraq in 2003, Amnesty International began reporting cases of human rights abuses involving torture and sexual humiliation carried out by US military police on Iraqi prisoners, most notoriously at Abu Ghraib Prison. The violations – sometimes proudly photographed – included physical and sexual abuse, rape and murder. In defending their actions against charges of torture, sleep deprivation and hooding, most of the abusers claimed that they were following orders and policy directions on interrogation methods. In addition to court martials and demotions, 11 American soldiers received prison sentences for the abuses, the longest being 10 years.

Some of the US policy about interrogation methods might not always have been clear, however. Shortly after the September 11 attacks, Vice-President Dick Cheney had stated that in this new time of suicidal attacks, the government 'needed to work through, sort of, the dark side' in combating the terrorists.

Although used on a limited basis by the CIA during the 1990s, it is believed that the practice of extraordinary rendition – of shackling and transporting terrorism suspects from one foreign state to another for interrogation – was expanded massively with the inception of the 'war on terror'. It has been alleged that hundreds of flights carried suspects across Europe and the Middle East to secret prisons, where they were tortured and held for months.

Some suspects were taken to the US base at Guantánamo Bay in Cuba, where, beyond the jurisdiction of the territorial United States, a detention camp was established in 2002 that could hold prisoners without trial. More than 770 prisoners from more than 50 countries have been held at the camp, the highest proportion being Afghan, followed by Saudi, Yemeni, Pakistani, and other Asian, Middle Eastern and European nationalities. President Obama repeatedly stated his desire to close Guantánamo. By 2022, the number of prisoners held at the camp had been reduced to 35, some being transferred to prisons in their home countries and some released. But with the US government considering the remaining prisoners too dangerous to release, while at the same time lacking sufficient admissible evidence to bring them to trial, the 35 prisoners held at Guantánamo remain in limbo.

groups fought, with Sunni groups attacking the country's Shi'a population and the Shia-led government.

In 2014, the fundamentalist Sunni Islam jihadist group Islamic State merged with its counterpart in the civil war in Syria to take control of towns in western and northern Iraq, including Fallujah and Mosul. Notorious for its beheadings of prisoners, public floggings, kidnappings and ethnic cleansing, Islamic State's advance prompted an increase in US military aid to the Iraqi government forces, with air attacks on Islamic State-held territory, as well as humanitarian aid drops. In 2015–16, with American and other coalition forces acting as advisers on the ground, the Iraq army succeeded in regaining ground taken by Islamic State jihadists. By 2019, Islamic State had lost its last significant territory in the Middle East.

Similarly, in Afghanistan, although security was transferred to Afghan forces, the US and NATO withdrawal slowed in 2015 as al-Qaeda tried to regroup in the area. With Islamic State becoming a presence there, too, US and other NATO

ABOVE: The 45th president of the United States, Donald Trump is the first never to have held public office or to have served in the military. Even before he entered the White House, Trump had made history.

forces remained in the country. In February 2020, the US government and the Taliban signed an agreement, backed by the UN Security Council, to bring peace to Afghanistan. The Afghan government, however, having been unable to agree their own terms with the Taliban, were left out of this monumental international discussion. The agreement stated that the US would withdraw its military forces by the summer of the following year if the Taliban pledged to stop al-Qaeda operating in Taliban-controlled areas and if it entered talks with the Afghan government.

Once the US withdrawal began, followed by other NATO forces who didn't have the might to remain without America, Taliban attacks on Afghan government-held positions surged. In the final month, August 2021, the situation deteriorated rapidly. The Afghan government collapsed and the Taliban retook Kabul. With echoes of the Fall of Saigon in 1975, people struggled to make their way to western embassies to find passage out of the country. At worst, some clung fatally to the fuselage of planes departing Kabul. The West was pulling out, but where did that leave the Afghan people?

With the international withdrawal, which included most humanitarian and financial support, the economy collapsed and within a year many people were facing famine. The country was more peaceful, though the Taliban in parts came under attack from remaining elements of Islamic State and also from the Republican insurgency. Women were removed from holding positions of public office and, as had been the case when the Taliban had controlled the country 20 years earlier, girls were banned from education after primary school. 'The abandonment of Afghanistan and its people,' former British Prime Minister Tony Blair wrote, 'is tragic, dangerous, unnecessary, not in their interests and not in ours.'

Reality TV Presidency

'He has neither the temperament nor the judgement to be president.' These were the words of Republican Mitt Romney in March 2016, spoken, not about a Democrat opponent, but about Donald Trump, his own party's candidate in the 2016 presidential election. Like a contestant on reality TV – the genre that had turned the billionaire property developer into a star – Trump drew huge attention by saying much that was outrageous, and to many, offensive. His aggressive election speeches grabbed headlines with his slurs – stating that many Mexican immigrants were rapists and drug mules, and repeatedly claiming that his opponent, Hillary Clinton, was 'crooked'.

He enraged many, but Trump's 'Make America great again' populist campaign resonated with others, crucially white, blue collar workers in the 'rust belt' states, where families were still struggling after the 2008 financial crash. With parts of the electorate disenchanted with Establishment politics as embodied by the Clintons, outsider Trump represented change. Ultimately, Clinton won the popular vote by three million votes, but Trump defeated her in the Electoral College.

During the four turbulent years that followed, Trump – the first president with no experience of government office or the military – remained the outsider even while in the White House. He regularly dismissed news media as 'the enemy of the people' reporting 'fake news', while he himself made many false or misleading statements – the *Washington Post* calculated an average of more than 20 a day. He often deflected attention from the news agenda by stoking conspiracy theories, even retweeting messages from supporters of the QAnon movement, who believed that a cabal of cannibalistic paedophiles operating a global child sex trafficking ring were conspiring against his presidency. In demanding federal funding to build a wall between the US and Mexico, which the Senate blocked, he caused the longest government shutdown (at 35 days) in US history. He also denied citizens from several Muslim-majority countries entry into the US.

'He has neither the temperament nor the judgement to be president.'

The Covid-19 Pandemic

When the Covid-19 virus reached America in the spring of 2020, Trump didn't initially wear a face mask when social distancing wasn't possible, despite the advice from the Centre for Disease Control (CDC), and he praised those in Democrat states who violated stay-at-home orders. By December 2022, more than one million people had died in the US from Covid-19, with 333 deaths per 100,000 people – a figure slightly higher than the UK, which had been slow to respond to Covid-19, and much higher than the death rates in Canada and Mexico. That said, the US was very successful in developing a vaccine, but had to contend with Covid sceptics, many who no longer trusted mainstream media but selected their truth from unverified sources on social media. While Covid scepticism was a global phenomenon, its characteristic US hue has been a distrust of big government, leading to beliefs that the virus and/or the

BELOW: With the Covid-19 lockdown threatening livelihoods and some people regarding it as an unjust infringement on civil liberties, protestors flout social distancing rules at a 'Reopen Pennsylvania' demonstration in Harrisburg, Pennsylvania, on 20 April 2020.

vaccines were a government/big pharma conspiracy, and that lockdowns, social distancing and mask-wearing were unjustifiable infringements of civil liberties. Nevertheless, by December 2022, 69 per cent of the US population was fully vaccinated. Those still dying of Covid-19 were almost all unvaccinated.

Impeachment and Insurrection

In 2019, Trump was impeached for the abuse of power and obstruction of Congress after he tried to put pressure on Ukraine to investigate Democrat candidate Joe Biden. Trump was acquitted, but his presidency reached its nadir on 6 January 2021, when, refusing to accept that he had lost the 2020 election, he whipped up supporters to disrupt efforts by Congress to count the Electoral College votes, which would formalize Biden's victory. Repeating false claims of election irregularities, Trump called his supporters to action: 'If you don't fight like hell, you're not going to have a country anymore.' Following a rally, more than 2000 supporters stormed the Capitol in Washington D.C. Trump initially resisted sending in the National Guard, but later in the day did tell his supporters to 'go home in peace'.

> 'Two days later, the President was permanently suspended from Twitter "due to the risk of further incitement of violence".'

Two days later, the President was permanently suspended from Twitter 'due to the risk of further incitement of violence' and the following week the House of Representatives impeached him for incitement of insurrection, making Trump the only president to be impeached twice. When a significant enough majority wasn't achieved in the vote to convict, he was acquitted. But the shadow of criminal proceedings would hang over the former president. In 2022, a criminal investigation was opened after it was learned that Trump had violated the Presidential Records Act in taking a number of top secret documents with him when he left office. Furthermore, that December, the US House Select Committee on the January 6 Attack recommended criminal charges against Trump for obstructing an official proceeding, conspiracy to defraud the US, and inciting or assisting an insurrection.

Roe vs Wade again

'When you're a star,' Donald Trump bragged in 2005, women 'let you do anything. Grab 'em by the pussy. You can do anything.' After a video clip of Trump saying these words resurfaced during his election campaign in 2016, he apologized, but over the years at least 25 sexual misconduct allegations had been made against him, allegations that he has denied.

In response to Trump's electioneering rhetoric and policies, the Women's March in Washington D.C. was planned for the day after his January 2017 inauguration. Ultimately, the march drew more than 470,000 people, with more than three million participating in marches nationwide. It would be the largest single day protest in US history.

One area that shifted more socially conservative under Trump was reproductive rights. In the Roe vs Wade case in 1973, the Supreme Court had ruled that, following a person's right to privacy as part of the Fourteenth Amendment, a woman had the right to have an abortion. This overruled many existing federal and state laws. While abortion rights – a woman's right to choose versus the rights of the unborn child – remained a highly contested subject in the US, it was not until 2022 that a significant change happened in the law. That summer, the Supreme Court overruled, by 5 to 4, the verdict of Roe vs Wade, arguing, among other points, that the Constitution made no reference to abortion in the first place and that overruling the 1973 verdict would 'return the issue of abortion to the people's elected representatives'. That is, it would become a state matter. Within months, 13 states, largely in the South, had made abortion illegal.

Although he had left office, Trump played a role in this. In 2020, he had controversially managed to appoint the conservative Amy Coney Barrett, succeeding the liberal Ruth Bader Ginsburg, to the Supreme Court, less than six weeks before the election, which Trump went on to lose. When Barack Obama had earlier nominated a more liberal judge to the Supreme Court during *his* final year in office, the Senate had blocked it, stating that the next Supreme Court justice should be chosen by the next president. In fact, Trump was the first president since the 1930s to appoint three supreme court judges during a single term in office. With Coney Barrett's appointment, the balance of the Supreme Court had tipped in a socially conservative direction and Roe vs Wade was overruled.

Black Lives Matter

In May 2020, George Floyd, an unarmed African-African, was killed during his arrest after being suspected of passing a counterfeit $20 bill at a shop in Minneapolis, Minnesota. Although Floyd was already handcuffed, police officer Derek Chauvin knelt on his neck and back for nine minutes, ultimately leading to Floyd's asphyxiation. Chauvin was later convicted of Floyd's murder.

As news of Floyd's death spread – his final minutes were filmed by a bystander – protests erupted across the US and the globe in support of the Black Lives Matter movement, which had been begun in 2014 following earlier cases of police brutality. Despite Covid-19 lockdowns, in the largest demonstrations

BELOW: 6 January 2021, Washington, D.C. Following a rally at which Donald Trump had repeated his claim that the election had been 'stolen by emboldened radical-left Democrats', a mob of more than 2000 stormed the Capitol Building in an effort to disrupt Congress from formalizing the victory of Joe Biden.

in US history, an estimated 15 million to 26 million people protested across the country against police racism. Curfews were imposed in more than 200 cities and although most protests were peaceful, there were cases of rioting and looting, along with 14,000 arrests and 19 deaths. A number of monuments celebrating figures now associated with racial injustice, such as a statue of Confederate general J. E. B. Stuart in Richmond, Virginia, and a statue of Christopher Columbus in Saint Paul, Minnesota, were defaced or toppled, prompting a wider examination of the history of racial injustice in the US and beyond.

Despite the headlines, some argue that killings such as Floyd's do not reflect systematic racial violence among the police. And when Harvard economist Roland G. Fryer Jr – a 'Southern black boy', as he describes himself – examined data across a number of US cities, he found no evidence of racial discrimination in police shootings, though he did find that black men and women were far more likely to suffer non-lethal violence from police. Perhaps Fryer's study wasn't wide enough, he admitted, though other studies found the same pattern of evidence.

At liberty with guns

Whether or not the police of all races are likely to shoot black people, there is a broader issue of gun crime among civilians in the USA, which perhaps says more about continued segregation decades after the Civil Rights Movement and poverty. In Chicago in 2014, for instance, where the black and white populations are roughly equal in number, 2460 black people were shot, lethally or non-lethally, compared with 78 white people.

Regularly the US public is shocked by mass shootings, such as that at Sandy Hook Elementary School in Newtown, Connecticut, in 2012. But responses vary from those who ask for stricter gun laws to those who call for more people to be armed so that they can fire back – though an FBI study found that in 160 incidents from 2000 to 2013, on only one occasion did armed members of the public stop a shooter.

Mass attacks, however, as shocking and extreme as they are, are not typical of most shootings. Because, on average, 35 people in America are shot every day, seven of them children. Usually the victims are poor and not white, unlike most of those killed and injured in mass school or college shootings. The USA has the world's highest per capita gun ownership. There are more gun-related deaths in proportion to the population in the US than in Mexico. 'What happened to life, liberty and the pursuit of happiness?' outsiders might ask.

Glory, Hallelujah

It might seem a grim topic on which to end a history of America, but these shootings and the debates around them reach to the core of what the United States is. As many pro-gun advocates argue, it is written in the Second Amendment, adopted in 1791, that 'the right of the people to keep and bear

BELOW: A Black Lives Matter Juneteenth demonstration in Los Angeles in 2020. Juneteenth is a federal holiday held every 19 June to mark the anniversary of the emancipation of slaves in Texas on 19 June 1865.

arms shall not be infringed'. Others counter that the Amendment says the arms are for 'a well-regulated militia being necessary to the security of a free state'; that is, an organized military force, not armed individuals. And others point out that even if the Second Amendment had meant individuals, it was written and agreed more than 200 years ago, in a world of slavery, in which there were no votes for women and when arms meant carrying a musket, not a submachine gun.

Beyond the different interpretations of the Second Amendment, is there in the US's relationship with firearms, a residue of the idea of the homesteader defending their property with a rifle? The frontier may have gone, but, for better or worse, the rugged life of the West has become, for many at least, part of the national identity.

And in the world of industry and commerce, where the US has been so successful, firearms prove their mettle. In lobbying for gun rights, the National Rifle Association may champion civil liberties, but the very might of the NRA's campaigning, funded in part by gun manufacturers, is indicative of a very American characteristic – that of unfettered big business.

Meanwhile, from state courts to the Supreme Court, laws on gun control are periodically tightened and relaxed, challenged and amended. For those people who have their bills defeated, it may seem an injustice, but this is American liberty at work, the liberty to lobby for these laws and to change them.

Emotionally and legally, America's gun laws embody ideas central to the identity of the United States – that neither individuals, nor states can be unduly limited by an overreaching federal government. That was key to the Founding Fathers belief laid down in the Tenth Amendment in the Bill of Rights.

> **'The history of America has been bloody, but that doesn't mean that it has always been shameful.'**

If enough Americans wanted to amend the Second Amendment, they could. Prohibition was introduced by one amendment in 1919, and repealed by another in 1933. That such strong, opposing views are held about gun laws is evidence of the success of the United States as a democracy, with a government, as Abraham Lincoln said at the Gettysburg Address, 'of the people, by the people, for the people'.

The history of America has been bloody, but that doesn't mean that it has always been shameful. It was bloody conflict that threw off the shackles of British rule in the Revolutionary War; it was armed conflict that held the Union together and ended slavery in the Civil War; and it was by going to war that fascism was defeated in World War II. Furthermore, the non-violent Freedom Riders of the Civil Rights Movement knew that they were courting violence in the fight against segregation and discrimination.

The USA may be criticized for its persecution of its native people or for its imperialism, but these accusations can be levelled at many other countries, too, particularly the more powerful ones. Perhaps it is preferable to consider the valour of the volunteers and conscripts who have served the USA, from Iraq and Afghanistan to Vietnam and Korea, from the world wars to the Civil War and back to the Revolutionary War. Better to remember the bravery of the Civil Rights activists, of the soldiers raising the flag at Iwo Jima, of the young men landing on the beaches of Normandy at D-Day, and to honour those who fell at Shiloh, Yorktown, Saratoga, and in many other conflicts.

BIBLIOGRAPHY

Berlin, Ira. *Many Thousand Gone: The First Two Centuries of Slavery in North America*. Massachusetts: Belknap Press, 2000.
Brown, Dee. *The American West*. New York: Simon & Schuster, 1994.
Brion Davis, David. *Inhuman Bondage: The Rise and Fall of Slavery in the New World*. New York: Oxford University Press, 2006.
Bryson, Bill. *Made in America*. London: Secker & Warburg, 1994.
Denton, Sally and Morris, Roger. *The Money and the Power: The Making of Las Vegas and its Hold on America, 1947-2000*. New York: Alfred A Knopf, 2001.
Ekirch, A. Roger. *Bound for America: The Transportation of British Convicts to the Colonies, 1718-1775*. New York: Oxford University Press, 1987.
Friedrich, Otto. *City of Nets: A Portrait of Hollywood in the 1940s*. London: Headline, 1987.
Grenier, John. *The First Way of War: American War Making on the Frontier, 1607-1814*. New York: Cambridge University Press, 2005.
Jenkins, Philip. *A History of the United States*. (Fourth Edition) London: Palgrave, 2012.
McNab, Chris. *Native American Warriors 1500-1890CE*. London: Amber, 2010.
McPherson, James M. *Battle Cry of Freedom: The Civil War Era*. (New Edition) London: Penguin, 1990.
Milner, Clyde A; O'Conner, Carol A.; Sandweiss, Martha A. (eds) *The Oxford History of the American West*. New York: Oxford University Press, 1996.
Nolan, Frederick. *The Wild West: History, Myth and the Making of America*. London: Arcturus, 2003.
O'Brien, Greg. *A Chronology of Native Americans*. London: Amber, 2011.
Reynolds, David. *America: Empire of Liberty*. London: Penguin, 2009.
Savage Jr, William W. (ed) *Cowboy Life: Reconstructing an America Myth*. Boulder: University Press of Colorado, 1975.
Storr, Anthony. *Feet of Clay: A Study of Gurus*. London: Harper Collins, 1996.
Walwin, James. *A Short History of Slavery*. London: Penguin, 2007.
Wood, Betty. *The Origins of American Slavery*. New York: Hill & Wang, 1998.
Wood, Gordon S. *The American Revolution: A History*. London: Weidenfeld & Nicolson, 2003.

INDEX

References to illustrations are in *italics*

Abenaki 26
abortion rights 216–217
Adams, John 43
Afghanistan 210, 211, 212, 216
African Americans
  and Civil Rights Act 90, 91, 165
  civil rights movement 156–71
  in the Civil War 80–1, 81, 84, 85–6, 89–90
  Great Migration 110
  Ku Klux Klan 90–1, 110–11, 163, 167
  lynchings 110–11, *111*
  and police shootings 216
  race riots 110, 133, 166, *166*, 168
  segregation 92, 109, 110, 133, 157–63, 165
  and sharecropping 92
  voting rights of 91, 158, 165
  in World War I 109, *109*
  in World War II 133, 136
  see also slavery/slaves
al-Qaeda 211–214
Alamo 64–5
Allende, Salvador 195
Altamont Free Concert 188, 188–9
America, origin of name 15, 43
Amherst, Jeffrey 14
Anderson, Robert 75–6
anti-war protests 184–5, *185*, *190*, 191–2, *192*
Antietam, Battle of 80
Appomattox 86
Arbenz, Jacobo 154
Arbuckle, Roscoe 'Fatty' 118, 118–19
arms dealing 203
assassinations 86–7, 104, *178*, 178–9, 184, 201
Atkins, Susan 187, *187*

Atlanta, Georgia 63, 85
atomic bomb *140*, 141
Attica Prison riot 193, *193*

banks 120, 123
Barry, Joan 153
Bataan, Philippines 128, *128*
Bender, Ben 136
Berlin, Germany 138, 144, *144*, 145, *146*
Berlin, Ira 23
Bernhardt, Michael 182
Bernstein, Carl 195
Biden, J., President 216
Bill of Rights 48, *48*
bin Laden, Osama 210, 212
Bioff, Willie 122
Black Elk 99
Black Lives Matter 217–18
Black Panthers 168, *169*
Black Power 168

Bonnie and Clyde 155, *155*
Bonus Marchers 120
Booth, John Wilkes 86, 87
Boston Tea Party 38–9, *39*
Brady, James 201
Brady, Tom 159
Brandywine *44*
Bridge Gulch Massacre 69
Britain
    America declares war on *58*, 58–9
    and Civil War 80
    convicts from 30–2, *32*
    early English settlers 19–26
    and Europe's war in America 32–5
    and France 33–5, 38, 45, 58, 59
    and Native Americans 14, 20, 22, 24, 27–8, *29*, 50–1, 59
    and Revolutionary War 36–51
    Seven Years' War (1756–63) *32–3*, 33, 35, 37
    and slavery 22–4
    World War I 107–8
    World War II 125, 130–2, 134–5, 144
Brown, John 73, *74*, 75
Browne, George 122
Buddhist monks 176–7, 178
buffalo 96–7, *97*
Buffalo Bill 101, *102–3*
Bull Run Creek 77
Bunker Hill *40–1*, 41, 44
Bunker Hill, USS 139
Burr, Aaron 56
bus boycotts 160
Bush, George H.W. 203, 206, 207
Bush, George W. 210

Calley, William 182, 184
Capitol Hill 59
Capone, Al 113
Carmichael, Stokely 168
Carnegie, Andrew 85, 95
Castro, Fidel 173, 195
Central America 203
Challenger (space shuttle) 200–1, *202*
Chaney, James 167
Chaplin, Charlie 153, *153*
Chapman, Mark 201
Charleston, South Carolina 45, 75–6, *76–7*
Cheney, Dick 213
Cherokee 8, 59, 61, 87
Chicago 96, 113, 122, 166, 184–5, *185*
Chile 195
China 65, 127, 148, 194, *194*
Christian missionaries 18
CIA 154, 173, 174, 195, 203
Civil Rights Act 90, 91, 165

civil rights movement 156–71
    see also African Americans; slavery/slaves
Civil War 70–87
Clark, William 54–6, *55*
Clinton, Bill 207
Clinton, Hillary *212*
Cobb, Howell 85–6
cold war 142–55, 200, 203
colonisation 104–5
Colson, Charles 192
Columbia (space shuttle) 201
Columbus, Christopher 10, 12, *13*, 15
Comanche 96, 100
communism
    in Central America 203
    cold war 142–55, 200, 203
    Communist Party 151
    decline of 203
    and entertainment industry 152, 153
    House Committee on Un-American Activities *149*, 151, 152
    and Korean War 146, 148
    and Marshall Plan 144–5
    and McCarthy, Joseph *142*, *150*, 151–2, 154
    spies 148, *148*, 151
    Truman Doctrine 144
    see also Soviet Union/Russia; Vietnam War
concentration camps 136, *136*
Congress on Racial Equality (CORE) 162, 163
Constitution 47, 47–8
Continental Army 41, 43–6
Continental Congress 40, 43
convicts 30–2, *32*
Coral Sea, Battle of 129
Cornwallis, Charles 45–6
cotton production 50, 62
Counter Intelligence Program (COINTELPRO) 197
Covid-19 pandemic 215–6
Coward, Noël 147
cowboys 8–9, 100–1, *102–3*
Craft, Ellen and William 71–2, *72*
Crockett, Davy 64
Cuba 104, 105, 173–5, *174*, 195, 213
Cullen, John 130, *130*
Custer, George 98

D-Day 132, 134, *134–5*
Dane, Karl 117, *117*
Dasch, George John 130
Davis, Jefferson 81
de Oñate, Juan 17
de Soto, Hernando 15–17, *16–17*

Declaration of Independence *42*, 43
Delano, Columbus 97
Delmont, Bambia Maude 118–19
Denton, Sally 147
desegregation 157–63
disease 12, 14, 46
Donner Party 68
Douglas, Stephen A. 73
Douglass, Frederick 81, 85, 89
Dresden, Germany 132
duelling 56
Dust Bowl 120, 123
Dustan, Hannah 26

Earp, Wyatt 101, *101*
earthquakes 115, *115*
Eighteenth Amendment 113
Eisenhower, President 160, 161, 175, 178
Ekirch, A. Roger 32
Ellwood Oil Field 126
Emancipation Proclamation *80*, 80–1
England *see* Britain
Erie Ring 95
Everett, Edward 82

Fallen Timbers, Ohio 57
Faubus, Orval 161
FBI 151, 167, 195, 197
Fillmore, Millard 71–2
First Amendment 48
Fitts, Buron 119
Florida, and the Spanish 15–18, 25
food from America 12
Forrest, Nathan Bedford 84, *88*
Fort Carillon 33–4
Fort Duquesne 33, 34
Fort Mystic 27
Fort Pillow 84, *84*
Fort Sumter 75–6, *76–7*
Fourteenth Amendment 90, 92, 165
France
    and black soldiers in WWI 109
    and Britain 33–5, 38, 45, 58, 59
    early settlers 14, 18–19, 20, 53–4
    and Europe's war in America 33–5
    and Native Americans 14, 18–19, 28, *28*
    Revolutionary War 45
    Seven Years' War *32–3*, 33, 35, 37
    and Vietnam 175
    World War II *124*, 132, 134–5, *134–5*
Franklin, Benjamin 100
Freedom Rides 162–3, *163*
freedom school 167
Frelinghuysen, Theodore 61

French and Indian War *32-3*, 33-4, 35, 37
Fuchs, Klaus 151
Fugate, Caril Ann 155
Fugitive Slave Law 69, 71-2

Garfield, James A. 104
Gay Liberation Front 171
Germany
  end of cold war 203
  World War I 107-8
  World War II 130-2, 135-8, 144, 145
Geronimo *97*, 99
Gettysburg Address 82, *82*, 219
Gettysburg, Battle of 82, 93
gold, finding 15-17, 20, *66-7*, 68-9
Goodman, Anthony 167
Gorbachev, Mikhail 200, 203
Grant, Ulysses S. 77, 85
Great Depression *106*, 120, 123
Great Migration 110
Greece 144
Grenada 203
Grenier, John 26
Guantánamo Bay 213
Guatemala 154
gun control 48, 201, 218
Guthridge, Amis 161
Guy, Cy 91

Hamilton, Alexander 56
Hastings, Lansford W. 68
Henderson, Oran K. 182
Hinckley, John 201
Hiroshima, Japan 141
Hollywood 117-19, 122, 151, 152, 153
Holocaust 136
homosexuality 171
Hoover, Herbert 120
House Committee on Un-American Activities *149*, 151, 152
Humphrey, Hubert 184-5
Hunley, CSS 83
Hunter, Meredith 188-9
Hurricane Katrina 209
Hussein, Sadam 205-7, 210-12

immigration 96, 112
Indian Removal Act 1830 59, 61
interrogation methods 213
Intolerable Acts 1774 39
Iran 203, 205, 206
Iraq 205-7, 210-213
ironclads 83
Iroquois 18-19, 28, 33, *51*, 137
Islam 169, 171, 210-13, 212-14
Islamic State 212-14

Italy, WWII 131
Iwo Jima *6*, 138

Jackson, Andrew 61
Japan, World War II 126-9, 138-41
Jefferson, Thomas 43, 47, 53, 54, 57, 58, 62, 64
Jenkins, Philip 91, 95, 101, 127
Jewish people 136
Jim Crow laws 92, 158
Johnson, Ben 91
Johnson, Henry 109
Johnson, Lyndon B. 165, 179, *179*, 180, 181
Jonestown Massacre 198-9
Jordan, James 167

Kansas-Nebraska Act 1853 73
Kasabian, Linda 187
Kennedy, Jackie *172*, 179
Kennedy, John F. 162, 165, *172*, 173-5, *175*, *178*, 178-9
Kennedy, Robert F. 184
Kent State University 191-2
Khe Sanh 183, *183*
Khrushchev, Nikita 174, 175
Killen, Edgar Ray 167
King, Martin Luther *156*, 160, *164*, 165, 166, 168
King, Rodney 207-8
Klemperer, Otto 152
Korean War 146, 148
Krenwinkel, Patricia 187, *187*
Ku Klux Klan 90-1, 110-11, 163, 167
Kuwait 205-7

La Salle, René-Robert Cavelier, Sieur de 20, *20*
Lansky, Meyer 147
Las Vegas 147
Layton, Larry 198
League of Nations 110
Lee, Richard Henry 43
Lee, Robert E. 76, 77, 80, 82, 85, 86
Leitch, David 183
Lennon, John 201
Lewis, John 162
Lewis, Meriwether 54-6, *55*
Lexington 41
Lincoln, Abraham 75, 76, 80-1, 82, 84, 85, 86-7
Little Big Horn 98
Little Rock School, Arkansas 157, *158*, 161
Lochner case 96
Longdale, Mississippi 167
Los Angeles 115-19, 166, *166*, 207-8

Louisiana 20, 53-6, 91
Luciano, Charles 'Lucky' 114
Lusitania, HMS 107-8, *108*
lynchings 110-11, *111*

MacArthur, Douglas 148
Madison, James 47, 59
Maine, USS 104, *104*
Malcolm X 168, *170*
Manassas, Battle of 77
Manson, Charles 185-7, *186*
manufacturing boom 95-6
maps *9*, *19*, *35*, *54*
Maranzano, Salvatore 114
Marshall Plan 144-5
Masseria, Joe 114
McCarthy, Joseph *142*, *150*, 151-2, 154
McKinley, William 104
McPherson, James M. 82
McVeigh, Timothy 208-209
Meade, George 82
Medina, Ernest 182
Mediterranean Theatre (WWII) 130-1, *131*
Mee, Charles L. 47
Mexico 64-5, 108
MGM 119
Midway, battle of 129, *129*
Mississippi river 20
Mississippi White Knights 167
Missouri Compromise 64, 73
mobsters 113-14, 122, 147
Mogadishu, Somalia *206-7*, 207
Mohegans 27, 28
Monitor, USS 83
Montgomery Improvement Association 160
Montgomery, Robert 122
Morris, Roger 147
Muhammad Ali 168, *170*, 171
Mulholland, William 116-17
Murray, John (Earl of Dunmore) 44
mutinies 46, *46*
My Lai Massacre 182, *182*, 184

NAACP (National Association for the Advancement of Colored People) *110*, 159, 160
Nagasaki, Japan *140*, 141
Narragansetts 27-8
NASA 154, 200-3
Natchez 28, *28*
Nation of Islam 168, 171
National Rifle Association 218
Native Americans
  assimilation of 59
  and buffalo 96-7, *97*

and Christianity 18
and the Civil War 87
and disease 14, *14*
and the English 14, 20, 22, 24, 27–8, *29*, 50–1, 59
and Europe's war in America 33
and the French 14, 18–19, 28, *28*
gold rush 69
Indian Removal Act 1830 59, 61
kidnapped settlers 100
numbers of 12, 61
and Revolutionary War 50–1, *51*
scalping 26
and the Spanish 15–18, *16–17*
and US expansion *8*, 57–8, 59, 61, 96–9
in World War I 109
in World War II 137
Navajo 96, 137
Neutrality Acts 123, 125
New Deal 123
New Mexico, early settlers 18, 65
New Orleans 54, 59, 211, *211*
New York 85, *85*, 95, 114, 130, 193
Nicaragua 203
Nixon, Richard 189, *189*, 191, 194, *194*, 195–7, *196*
North, Oliver 203
nuclear weapons 141, 154, 174–5, 200

Obama, Barack 212, 217
Ohio Valley 33, 38, 57
Okinawa 139
Oklahoma 100
Oklahoma City 208–209
Operation Overlord 132, 134–5, *134–5*
Ortiz, Juan 15
Oswald, Lee Harvey 178–9
Owens Lake and Valley, California 116–17

Pacific campaign (WWII) 128–9, 138–41
Paine, Thomas 43, *49*, 50
Palmer, Mitchell 112, *112*
Panama Canal 105, *105*
Parker, Cynthia Ann 100, *100*
Parker, Dorothy 152
Parks, Rosa 160, *160*
Passaro, Alan 189
Pearl Harbor *127*, 127–8
Pequot War 27, *27*
Petersburg 85
Philadelphia 45, 50, 51
Philippines 104, 128
Pilgrim Fathers 24–5, *25*
Pinochet, Gen Augusto 195, *195*

Plessy, Homer 92
Polk, James K. 65
Pontiac's Rebellion 28, *29*
poverty 95, *95*
Powhatan 20
Price, Cecil R. 167
prison riots 193
Prohibition 113–14
Pueblo 18
Puritans 24–5

Quebec 18, *34*, 34–5, 38

race riots 110, 133, 166, *166*, 168, 207–8, *208*
Rappe, Virginia 118–19
Reagan, Ronald 200, *200*, 201, 203
Remington, Frederic 101
Revolutionary War 36–51
Reynolds, David 92, 96, 145, 159, 171
Richmond, Virginia 86, *90–1*
Ridenhour, Ronald L. 182
Robinson, Jackie 159, *159*
Rockefeller, John D. 94, 95
Roe v Wade 216–217
Rolling Stones 188–9
Roosevelt, Franklin D. 123, *123*, 125
Roosevelt, Theodore 105
Rosenberg, Ethel and Julius *148*, 151
Ross, John 59, *60*, 61, 87
Ruby, Jack 179
Rush, Dean 175
Ryan, Leo 198

Salem witch trials 30–1, *31*
San Francisco 115, *115*
Sandy Hook school 218
Saratoga 45
Savage, William W. 100
scalping 26
Schenck, Joe 122
schools, segregation in 157–61
Schwerner, Michael 167
Scott, Dred 73, *73*
Second Amendment 48, 218–19
Seeger, Pete 152, *152*
segregation 92, 109, 110, 133, 157–63, 165
Selma 165, *165*
Seminole 61, 137
September 11 attacks *204*, 210–12
Seven Years' War *32–3*, 33, 35, 37
sharecropping 92
Sherman, William 85
Shiloh, Battle of 77, *78–9*
Shipp, Thomas 111, *111*
Siegel, Ben 'Bugsy' 147

Sirhan Sirhan 184
sit-ins 162, *162*
Sitting Bull 98, 99
slavery/slaves
　abolition of 61–2, 72–5, 86, *90–1*
　and Civil War 71–3, *80–1*, 81, 85–6
　and Constitution 48
　in District of Columbia 76
　early years of 22–5, *23*, *50*, 61–2, *63*, 64
　Emancipation Proclamation *80*, 80–1
　escaping 71–2
　Fugitive Slave Law 69, 71–2
　Missouri Compromise 64, 73
　post freedom 89–90
　rebellions 62
　and Revolutionary War 44, 46, 50
　slave trade 24, *24*, 62
smallpox 14, 46
Smith, Abram 111, *111*
Somalia *206–7*, 207
Sons of Liberty 38
South Carolina, slavery 23, 25
Soviet Union/Russia
　arms control deal 194, 200
　Bolsheviks 112
　cold war 142–55, 200, 203
　and Cuba 173–5
　space race 154, 174
　World War II 137–8
　see also communism
space race 154, 174, 189
space shuttles 200–3, *202*
Spain 15–18, *16–17*, 53–4, 104
spies 130, 148, *148*, 151
St Clair, Arthur 57
St Francis Dam *116*, 117
St Valentine's Day Massacre 113, *113*
Stalin, Josef 137, 144, 145, 146
Stamp Act 1765 38
Star Wars project 200
Starkweather, Charles 155
Stonewall riots 171
Stono rebellion 25
strikes 96
student demonstrations *162*, 162, 165, *190*, 191–2, *192*
Student Non-Violent Coordinating Committee (SNCC) 162, 168
Supreme Court 61, 73, 91, 92, 96, 159–60, 162

Taliban 210, 212–13
Tarawa 138, *138*
Tate, Sharon 187
taxation 37–8
Tecumseh 58, 59

Tenth Amendment 48, 218
Tet Offensive 181, *181*
Texas, early settlers 64–5, 96
Thirteenth Amendment 86
Thomas, J. Parnell *149*, 151
Thompson, Hugh 182, 184
Thomson, James 180–1
Tillman, Ben 105
tobacco 12, 21, *22*
Truman, Harry S. 141, 143, 144, 145, 146, 148, 151
Trump, Donald 214–17, *214*
Turner, Nat 62
Tweed Ring 95

U-boats 130

Valdinoci, Carlo 112
Van Houten, Leslie *187*
Vanderbilt, Cornelius 95
Vesey, Denmark 62, *62*
Vespucci, Amerigo 15, *15*
veterans 93, 121

Vietnam War 175–8, *176–7*, 180–4, *180–1*, 189, 194, 198–9
  anti-war protests 184–5, *185*, 190, 191–2, *192*
Virginia 19–23, 76

Waco siege 208–9
Waldseemüller, Martin 15
Wall Street Crash 119–20
Wallace, George 165
Wampanoag 24, 27–8
war on terror 209–14
War Powers Act 1973 199
Warren Commission 178, 179
Washington DC 51, *58*, 59, 76
Washington, George 32–3, *36*, 44, 45, 46, *47*, 48
Washington, Jessie 111
water supplies 115–17
Watergate 195–7
Watie, Stand 87, *87*
Watts riots 166, *166*
Weapons of Mass Destruction 210

White League 91
Wilson, Woodrow 107, 108, 110
Winthrop, John 24
witchcraft 30–1
Wolfe, General James 34
women's rights 216–17
Wood, Gordon S. 45, 46, 51
Woodward, Bob 195
World War I 107–9
World War II 6, 123–41
Wounded Knee massacre 98–9, *99*
Wyoming Valley, Massacre of *51*

Yorktown *45*, 45–6

PICTURE CREDITS

Alamy: 16/17 (World History Archive), 18 (Jason O Watson/historical-markers inc), 19 (The Protected Art Archive), 31 (Chronicle), 35 (Niday Picture Library), 36 (Stocktrek Images), 51t (Universal Images Group), 57 (Niday Picture Library), 62t (Glasshouse Images), 62b (Andy Murphy), 72t (Mary Evans Picture Library), 74 (Painting), 85 (Artokoloro Quint Lox), 88 (Niday Picture Library), 101 (NSF), 108 & 111 (World History Archive), 113 (Pictorial Press), 120 (Heritage Images), 155 (Pictorial Press), 161 (Vintageusa1), 182 (World History Archive), 218 (IOS/Espa-Images)

Alamy/Everett Collection: 12, 32, 59, 146, 150, 160, 164, 166, 169, 186, 194

Alamy/Granger Collection: 8, 14, 15, 20, 32/33, 46, 52, 55, 90/91, 92, 100, 133, 158

Alamy/North Wind Picture Archive: 21, 22, 23, 24, 27, 28, 29, 47, 51b, 54, 56, 68, 69

Amber Books: 84

Art-Tech: 34

Cody Images: 137, 166/167, 183

Dreamstime: 204 (Jgorzynik)

Getty Images: 50 (Universal Images Group), 98/99 (De Agostini), 117 (Moviepix), 145 (Hulton), 147 (Michael Ochs Archive), 153 (Hulton), 154 (Universal Images Group), 156 (Flip Schulke Archives), 159 (Hulton), 171 (Fed W McDarrah), 174 (Hulton), 175 (Keystone-France), 185 (Hulton), 188 (Bill Owers/20th Century Fox), 189 (Henry Groskinsky/Life), 192b (Hulton), 195 (Horacio Villalobos), 196 (Hulton), 197 (Gjon Mili/Life), 199 (Frank Johnston/The Washington Post), 201 (Mike Evers/AFP), 206 (Peter Turnley), 208 (Ted Soqui), 211 (Spencer Platt), 214 (Jim Watson), 215 (Nicholas Kamm/AFP), 217 (Tayfun Coskun/Anadolu Agency)

Getty Images/Archive Photos: 26, 64, 72b, 91, 110, 121, 128, 144, 162, 163, 167, 172

Getty Images/Bettmann: 58, 95, 116, 118, 122, 130, 142, 152, 165, 170, 187, 190, 192t, 193, 200

Library of Congress: 10, 13, 25, 39–45 all, 48, 60, 63, 66/67, 70, 73, 78–83 all, 93, 94, 97, 102/103, 105, 106 (Dorothea Lange), 109, 112, 114/115, 123, 126 (Dorothea Lange), 148, 149, 179

NASA: 202

U.S. Department of Defense: 6, 76/77, 86, 104, 124, 127, 129, 131, 134/135, 136, 138–141 all, 180, 181, 209

White House: 212 (Peter Souza)